Managerial Skills for Executive Action

Douglas C. Basil

American Management Association, Inc.

About the Author

DOUGLAS C. BASIL is professor of management at the Graduate School of Business Administration, University of Southern California in Los Angeles. He holds a bachelor's degree from the University of British Columbia, a postgraduate diploma in business administration from the London School of Economics, and a doctorate from Northwestern University.

Dr. Basil has had extensive consulting experience with such firms as Remington Rand, Univac, Quaker Oats, Union Carbide, TransconLines, and Pepsi-Cola. He has given lectures and conducted executive development programs in Australia, Colombia and other South American countries, Belgium, France, the United Kingdom, and **South Africa. Two of his most recent books were published in Rio de Janeiro and Buenos Aires.**

Dr. Basil has utilized his extensive industrial experience to bring an organizational reality both to this book and to his classroom teaching of graduate students and mature executives.

© American Management Association, Inc., 1970.
All rights reserved. Printed in the United States of America.

This book may not be reproduced in whole or in part without the express permission of the Association.

International standard book number: 0-8144-5210-8
Library of Congress catalog card number: 76-116693

First printing

Preface

THE EMPHASIS on managerial skills in this book reflects the author's basic philosophy that the effective practice of management requires the judicious application of a set of managerial skills rather than the utilization of abstract principles. Short case histories, illustrating the application of managerial skills in the realistic world of business, are presented throughout in order to provide concrete examples of the difficulties involved in the successful utilization of these skills.

The sophisticated and experienced manager knows that he can never find a definitive solution to managerial problems. Rather, he substitutes problems of lesser magnitude for those of greater magnitude. A classic example is the promotion of one of three essentially equal subordinate managers to solve a managerial problem involving the need for greater direction or specialization of an activity. Although the promotion will solve the problem of direction, it creates new problems of communication, of coordination, and of decision making, as well as potential interpersonal problems relating to status. These problems may not be as significant as that of direction or specialization, but they are still created by the solution of the original problem.

The accent in these pages is on the pragmatic application of managerial skills. The book is designed to help the practicing manager sharpen his managerial skills and therefore presents the nuances of such skills rather than basic concepts. The book does not pretend to be a theoretical construct on management; rather, it is a prescriptive and diagnostic approach to managerial decision making.

Contents

1

An Overview
of Managerial Skills

A MANAGER must develop a set of new skills to complement his set of technical skills. These are primarily interpersonal or leadership and managerial skills, complemented by conceptual skills.

The manager utilizes a complete set of skills to coordinate or manage the resources allocated to him for achieving a task or an objective. The technical skills of the manager are primarily those associated with some area of specialization, such as engineering or market research. The managerial skills include such functions as setting objectives, structuring an organization, and designing and implementing controls. Interpersonal leadership skills encompass such concepts as motivation and an understanding of human behavior.

These skills are required in varying degrees depending upon the managerial level in the organizational hierarchy. Exhibit 1 illustrates these relationships in a three-dimensional diagram. The heavy dash line shows that top management requires a relatively small degree of application of technical skills and headship ("telling" rather than "persuading"), but a high degree of managerial and leadership skills. The converse would be true for the lowest level of management. Many managerial problems are caused by the failure of the manager either to shift his skill mix as he rises in the managerial hierarchy or to develop his managerial and interpersonal skills to the degree required for managerial success.

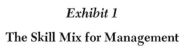

Exhibit 1

The Skill Mix for Management

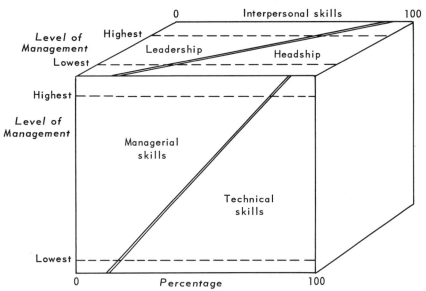

All too often the manager is inclined to treat human and technical resources in an identical manner. An illustration of this confusion of skill application is the comparison of plant layout and organization structure, both of which involve the positioning of resources to achieve coordination and effective production. The analysis techniques of both plant layout and organization structure are more or less similar. The flow of work in the layout of the plant and the flow of orders in the organization structure are the first considerations in such analyses. The next step is to conduct motion and time studies in the flow of work and to develop responsibility and communication patterns in the flow of orders.

In one case management is dealing with machines and in the other with people. When a machine is placed in one spot to do a particular job, there is a high degree of certainty that it will perform just as planned. But when an organization structure assigns work to the individual whose name is in a box in the chart, the degree of certainty found in the machine placement no longer applies. The fact that people are different from machines seems obvious, but there are many managers who have not yet realized this very important fact of organizational life. An organization structure operates because people want it to operate. The major consideration in structuring an organization can still be the assignment of work, but such assignments must be tempered with a knowledge of the human factor and what part it can play in the success or failure of the manager. This comparison of plant layout and organization structure well illustrates the importance of the correct mix of skills for the manager.

COORDINATION SKILLS

While coordination and management may be considered synonymous, each has its special connotation. The coordination skill requires an understanding of the integrative nature of an organization and of how the parts relate to the whole. Management, or managerial skills, is the encompassing term for a whole set of skills of which coordination is but one part.

The manager considers not only the coordination of his subordinates but also the cooperation that he himself must give to both his superiors and other managers in the organization. The complexity of the average organization is so great that relationships must be established throughout to permit the manager to achieve his objective.

There are countless relationships that must be established merely to buy a gross of pencils for an office. The individual requiring pencils reports the fact to his supervisor, who in turn contacts an office manager. The office manager then assigns an inventory clerk to make out a purchase requisition and send it to the purchasing department.

The purchasing department buyer contacts the requisitioner to find out what specifications he has placed on the purchase. The buyer then gets in touch with a vendor, perhaps requesting a sample of the product. This may take a number of contacts. The buyer issues a purchase order to the vendor and sends a copy of the order to the requisitioner to inform him that the order has been placed. The purchase order requires an acknowledgment by the vendor—another paper contact. The buyer will follow up on the order before the delivery date, initiating another contact to insure delivery of the products.

When the pencils are received, a receiving inspector checks to see whether they meet the specifications noted on the purchase order. He completes a receiving report and distributes a number of copies, one of them to the buyer, to indicate that the goods have been received. The buyer may then inform the requisitioner, or the receiving department may send the pencils directly to the requisitioning department, along with some form of move ticket. And the transaction is not finished yet, since the accounting department must match the purchase order, the vendor's invoice, and the receiving report before issuing a check in payment.

This procedure may seem unduly complicated merely to purchase a gross of pencils, but unless the purchasing department has made special arrangements for small purchases, such a procedure would be the normal one, because of the extent of the coordination problems and the interrelations in the average firm. In this example the normal purchasing procedures were applied so that the buyer could assure the requisitioner of the right quality and quantity on time. It was necessary to have the purchasing department buy the pencils in order to centralize control over all purchases in one function. The control by the accounting department was necessary to insure against collusion between the buyer and the vendor and to see that the company received what it ordered.

A problem of coordination exists whenever a task is divided among a number of individuals. For coordination to be effective, there must be an exchange of information among the parties so that no one person will take any action that will prevent the others from performing their part of the task. One manager is given the necessary responsibilities and organizational authority to coordinate the actions of all concerned; the organization hierarchy is clearly defined to permit all concerned to predict the behavior of others; and an objective is decided upon and accepted by all.

The Skill of Formulating and Managing by Objectives

Every organization—and, in fact, every activity—requires a formulation of objectives to provide direction and purpose. Objectives exist for all levels of management and need not be restricted to corporate objectives. Just as the individual driving an automobile must know where he is going, so must the manager know the objective toward which he is coordinating his resources. Unfortunately, the day-to-day pressures on the manager tend to result in his failure to develop and utilize the skill of formulating and managing by objectives.

All too often a manager will not recognize the importance of objectives. But how can he exercise judgment in choosing among alternative courses of action when he has not formulated goals that should be accomplished by such action? While it is true that most managers know what they are doing even without a specific promulgation of objectives, it is also true that there is a great risk of lack of direction without such specific promulgation.

Objectives are formulated for every level of management and related upward to those of the next part of the organization, so that eventually all the objectives are in accord from the corporate level to that of the first-line supervisor. It is necessary to narrow objectives down to the point where each man can visualize what his own are and what action is required to reach them. In other words, the co-ordinating function of the manager can never really be exercised effectively unless the objective itself is understood by him and by those he is coordinating. The manager is a decision maker responsible for making all the decisions necessary to carry out his assigned task. Many such decisions have alternates which are as good as the one chosen by the manager but may be based on different premises or different objectives. The more the manager understands the importance of objectives and their relationship to his assigned task, the better his decisions will be. He can now relate his decisions to the objectives, discarding those decisions that may serve the present purpose but fail to assist fully in the attainment of the longer-term objectives.

An illustration of the failure to formulate and manage by objectives is a conflict of interest that developed between manufacturing and research and development in a large subsidiary firm that was attempting to build up its overall capabilities, not only to service the R&D groups for prototypes and limited-run production, but also to permit large production runs for the parent corporation. The vice-president of manufacturing and the company president had both accepted this objective, but information about the objective had not been disseminated throughout the organization. As a result of the lack of understanding of objectives on the management levels below the vice-president rank, operating management continued to base its decisions on the premise that the manufacturing facility was essentially an arm of the R&D group. Because of this failure of communication, both the R&D engineers and the manufacturing managers agreed to subcontract any work for which they might otherwise have had to build permanent facilities or tooling, and the manufacturing managers made a practice of not increasing their personnel quotas, in order to avoid overstaffing when subsequent R&D efforts would not need the manufacturing facilities.

The result of this confusion or lack of objectives was that the subsidiary firm failed to build the necessary production facilities and the parent corporation was forced to use another subsidiary company for the production runs of products developed by the R&D facility of the subsidiary. The parent corporation lost as well as the subsidiary, since there would have been much better coordination of research and development and manufacturing if both facilities had been under the same roof.

A clearcut definition of objectives is imperative if the executive is to fulfill his management function. Every action of the manager should be directed toward and related to the objectives not only of the entire organization but also of his subsection. Recent experience of successful managers has indicated not only that executives work more effectively when objectives are known and accepted throughout the firm, but also that the setting of objectives or tasks for employees results in higher productivity and morale.

Objectives for managers have a far longer time-horizon than do those for nonmanagers. But objectives translated into tangible goals for workers utilizing much shorter time-horizons can provide the same incentive toward achievement as they do for managers. An example of this use of tangible objectives is the case of a small stamping firm that did not pay incentive wages to its employees, although it had set standards for all operations. The president of the firm was of the opinion that incentive wages would result in endless bickering and poor morale. However, he was also optimistic about what well-motivated employees could accomplish.

Although the majority of the workers were unskilled and poorly educated, the president felt that they could be motivated to be proud of their jobs and do their best for the company. As part of the general motivational program, the president decided to introduce a profit-sharing retirement plan. Simultaneously, he decided to make greater use of the standards set by the company for all stamping operations. Records indicated that the employees in total had been producing at 37 percent of theoretical optimum, although some individual employees produced at about 80 percent of the standard set for individual jobs. The firm's productivity record had previously been based on performance as a percentage of the theoretical optimum, which had been posted weekly, but the president concluded that employees did not understand this figure and therefore would not be motivated to exceed it. He decided, instead, to consider the average productivity of employees as the 100 percent figure for posting on the bulletin board weekly.

At this point, the president called all his employees together to tell them of the profit-sharing plan and what it would mean to each employee. He told them that the productivity figure of the combined production of all employees would be posted weekly on the bulletin board and that, if they exceeded this figure, the firm would make more profit, with a greater share for each employee. He indicated that the standard for each job was to be given to each employee so that he could determine for himself whether he was creating additional profit for himself and his fellow employees.

For the first few weeks of the new plan, employees averaged between 90 and 95 percent on the new scale. Soon a number of the older employees started to question some of the foreman's assignments and to pressure the setup men to set up the machines more quickly. The materials handlers became more conscientious about finding the right materials and moving jobs from one machine to the next. Within a month the index had exceeded 100 percent. Within three months it had risen to 110 percent. At the end of six months the index stood at 131 percent.

Here was a case where employees were given a definite objective. Yet rarely is profit sharing in itself an effective incentive wage, because the employee cannot see his personal reward for his effort. The employees in the small stamping firm were not working for the profit-sharing incentive but were working toward a stated objective, which in this case was the weekly posting of the efficiency index.

ORGANIZATION SKILLS

The manager must work within the organization structure to achieve his task. Although the individual manager, except on the top management level, is rarely in a position to decide where his section or department is to fit into the overall structure of the organization, he is usually able to determine the structure of his own department. One of the most important tenets of effective management is the right of the manager to exercise authority over his part of the organization, subject only to whatever constraints or limitations are necessary to permit effective coordination of all parts of the organization.

The purpose of organization is to assign the tasks necessary to achieve the objective. An organization is divided into parts that are assignable to individuals. These parts, each under the command of a manager, must fit together like a jigsaw puzzle so that the end result of the actions of the individual manager will fit in neatly with that of other managers to achieve the objective set for the enterprise.

The purpose of organization may be clearly seen in the building of a product. The organization structure permits specialization of function to insure the presence of the technical abilities required for the completion of a task. For example, one form of organization structure is the functional division of responsibilities into engineering, production, and sales. In the building of a product, the first step after the decision to make such a product is design, and the design function is assigned to engineering. But the engineers cannot work in a vacuum; they must design a product that the production department can manufacture at the requisite cost and that the sales department can sell. The organization structure demands of the managers who command each part that their work be coordinated with that of the other managers to insure that the product is well designed, manufactured at low cost, and readily marketable.

In this illustration, the organization structure might be designed differently to permit greater coordination of the parts with less specialization of function. The important consideration is to remember that the purpose of organization is the assignment of tasks in the best possible way to achieve the objective of the firm. An organization can be structured by product, clientele, process, or function with certain advantages and disadvantages accruing to each, but each type of structure has as its basic purpose the assignment of tasks to achieve objectives.

A problem sometimes encountered in organization structures is subservience to the organization structure as the primary objective rather than to the objectives themselves. The organization structure should not be considered sacred, but merely a means to the end of coordinating resources. Worshiping of organization for itself may be the result of a basic human desire for security and abhorrence of change. The organization structure is intended to facilitate work and has no raison d'être in itself. If an organization structure hinders the accomplishment of tasks that will achieve the objective, then the structure must be changed. The only caution, of course, is that change in itself is costly and hence any organization changes must not be considered lightly.

A major factor to remember in structuring an organization is that the structure also serves as the formal communication pattern for the enterprise. Setting up an organization by assigning a manager to be in charge of a particular section automatically names that man to be the channel of communication for all formal information to and from that section. Informal channels of communication immediately spring up in any organization and are often necessary to make an organization structure work. But often such channels are not trustworthy, since they may be used to achieve personal, non-company-oriented objectives. It is important to consider the design of the communication channels when the organization structure is designed, so that official channels will supply the network of information required for effective coordination of all parts of the organization.

THE SKILL OF PLANNING FOR RESULTS

Understanding and effective use of planning skills are critical to managerial success. Most managers recognize this need for planning, but few are really effective planners. First of all, most managers do not realize what is involved in the planning process. Second, the day-to-day pressures of operating problems make it difficult for the manager to find time to plan. Third, the manager's ego often leads him to believe that he can solve problems as they arise and that there is no need for detailed planning. Finally, there is an attitude among the lower levels of management that planning is an activity that takes place on the corporate level but is not indigenous to the lower levels.

What is planning, and what makes it so difficult? Planning is the predetermination of events, through prediction and decision making, in advance of the need of action. The manager marshals his resources and predetermines their allocation and use. When the actual requirement occurs, the decisions have already been made and all that is necessary is to follow the predetermined plan.

An example of the planning process may be found in any simple inventory control system. Top management has decided what level of inventory is to be maintained in absolute dollars. The sales department has issued a sales forecast, which in turn provides the information to the manufacturing department for the development of a production schedule. The production schedule calls for the manufacture of a certain number of different classifications of products over the next 12 months.

The inventory planning section has to decide how many parts of each type or part number must be carried in inventory, as determined by the production schedule. However, because thousands of parts may be required, and because a firm normally maintains a perpetual inventory, the inventory control section utilizes a maximum-minimum automatic reorder system. This system provides a minimum point at which the inventory clerk automatically reorders, using a reorder quantity or a formula system for calculation of the amount to order. All that is necessary is for the formula or the reorder quantities to reflect the information from the production schedule.

In a simple inventory control system, considerable planning is required on the part of top management to determine how much money the firm can afford to invest in inventory and where to obtain such funds. The sales department has to make a market research study to determine how much volume of what products will be sold in the coming year. The manufacturing department must translate the sales forecast into production schedules and determine whether additional plant capacity is required. The inventory control section must plan for the effect of such a production schedule on the inventory of parts and must balance the need against the inventory level in absolute dollars established by top management. The planning process is particularly complex here because each part of the organization must project its plans before the remaining parts can plan.

A manager's plea that he does not have enough time to plan is not valid. If he has excessive responsibilities and tasks, he must either demand a realignment of work in the organization or reorganize his own activities to provide for greater delegation to his subordinates. This takes planning in itself, but unless the manager does such planning he will never be able to be effective.

The manager who feels that he has the necessary abilities to solve problems as they occur, rather than spending his time in planning for such occurrences so as to minimize their effect on the organization, may find that there are times when preliminary planning would have avoided the difficulties. Alternatively, he may find that insufficient time is left to solve the problem. An illustration of this failure to plan is the case of a manager who had abandoned elaborate and detailed planning when he found that there were emergencies regardless of how well he planned. He decided that his time could be better spent supervising the men completing the project. Although some days were hectic, he found that he could keep on top of his jobs and handle any decision that had to be made. He did find it hard to keep subordinate managers, however; they transferred to other crews whenever a vacancy occurred.

On one particular job, a number of design and specification changes were made while the job was in progress, which only reinforced the manager's opinion that detailed planning was not worth the effort. He did not calculate the effect of the changes on the normal processes of the job because he knew that in the past he had been able to handle such factors as they occurred. As the job progressed he came to a number of design and specification changes that were quite different from any he had seen before. On closer examination he found that a number of parts needed some special plating. This was available only through a government-approved source that required a lead time of six weeks, compared with the normal lead time of less than two weeks for similar parts. The end result of this lack of detailed planning was a late delivery of the job and a setback for the manager in the eyes of top management.

An important consideration in planning is the factor of acceptance by subordinates. Planning is a major vehicle by which the manager coordinates his activities with others, but plans must be acceptable to subordinates if they are to be carried out effectively. This point of view may be questioned by the inexperienced manager, who will state that it is the subordinate's job to carry out the plans and that the subordinate therefore has no alternative but to accept them. Nothing could be further from the truth. If the subordinate passively accepts the superior's plans while really objecting to them, he may not take corrective action when the plans are not working, since he really did not accept them in the first place. But if the subordinate has been involved in the planning process, he will do everything in his power to make sure that the plans work. The technique employed to insure such success is *participation.*

"Participation" can be an overworked word and an overworked concept, but a manager's failure to recognize its worth may often lead to disaster. The importance of participation is illustrated in the following example.

A management consulting firm had been hired to evolve a new production control system and had appointed a brilliant young man to do the job. The consultant spent considerable time with a number of the company managers. Many of the younger managers in the firm had been aware of the deficiencies in the production control system for some time and, unbeknown to top management, had partially evolved a new system. Since these managers were interested in having their plan adopted, they told the consultant about the plan.

After the consultant had been given the information that the younger management group had collected on the new production control system, he no longer consulted them in any way. After some time, he presented to top management a plan that contained the major elements of the plan presented to him by the younger managers, *without giving any credit whatsoever to them.* Predictably the new plan did not work.

In this illustration, not only did the consultant commit the cardinal sin of idea theft without recognition of authorship, but he failed to involve in the planning process the very people who were to implement his plan. Little wonder that the younger managers in the firm sabotaged the plan, even though it hurt the company as well as the consultant.

THE SKILL OF CONTROLLING MANAGEMENT ACTION

The term "control" conjures up the picture of a policeman watching every move to catch an individual in some wrongdoing. Nothing could be further from the truth, if industrial control is used properly by the manager. Control is any necessary action or corrective measures taken to insure that a plan is being carried through to attain an objective. Information for control may be collected by staff personnel other than the line operating manager, but such information is communicated to the manager in order for action to be initiated. Much of line management's distrust of control has resulted from the misuse of information collected by the staff agencies to assist line management in taking corrective action. Such abuses have resulted in making control punitive rather than corrective.

Modern criminologists often shock the general public with some of their views on criminal acts and suitable "punishments." One criminologist, in commenting on a recent murder trial, said that the alleged murderer should not be punished. It was not that his crime was justified or that he was innocent; it was that the criminologist felt that the exact circumstances under which the man murdered his wife would have little probability of reoccurring. Since punishment has as its rationale the prevention of crime or the rehabilitation of criminals so that such men will no longer commit crimes, there was no need for punishment in this case.

Industrial control more nearly fits this modern criminologist's pattern than that of normal criminal or military discipline. The important factor in any business enterprise is to accomplish a task through performance according to plan. Control consists of whatever mechanisms are necessary to insure that the plan is being carried out. Control is designed to achieve action to correct any deviations from plan, not to punish nonconformance. Industrial discipline, when associated with control, must also serve to achieve corrective action, not to punish. Punishment for the sake of punishment has no place in the industrial scene.

The effective manager is one who designs his control systems to bring deviations first to the attention of the man responsible for the action, and to the superior only when the man fails to take corrective action. This control process starts when the superior delegates a task to his subordinate manager. The manager formulates a plan that includes various control points, which he checks with his superior to insure that the plan will work. He communicates his plan and its control points to a separate staff agency, which typically may be a production planning and control group in manufacturing. The control points may be inspection or schedule points for the completion of parts or subassemblies. When the control information staff agency finds that there is a deviation from the plans or standards set for the job, it immediately communicates such information to the manager responsible for immediate corrective action. The corrective action taken will be reported to the control information staff agency. Only if the manager fails to take corrective action is such a deviation reported to the superior so that he in turn can take whatever action is necessary to bring the plan back under control.

The organization must be protected from the vagaries or shortcomings of its members. It cannot depend upon any one individual completely in any situation. It must take the position that no man is infallible. Such a philosophy of management may be unpalatable to many individuals who feel that this is a negative view of human nature and that a man who knows he is not trusted will shirk responsibility or perform badly.

This philosophy of management does not assume that managers cannot be trusted, that human nature is such that individuals will fail to do their duty unless they are watched closely, or that the organization cannot depend upon individuals to carry out their assigned tasks. Rather, it assumes that the individual manager requires feedback on his performance to insure that any deviation from plan or required performance will be corrected. These controls are exercised to assist the manager in the performance of the job, but at the same time to assure the organization that the plan is being carried out to attain the prescribed objectives. The individual manager still has freedom of action to make the decisions he thinks are best to solve problems. Except for the constraints exercised by the organization to insure conformity and predictive behavior in intraorganization relationships, the individual manager has the necessary authority to organize and manage as he pleases.

The control system provides a double assurance. It assures the manager that his performance is according to plan, and it assures the organization that tasks of the subparts are being accomplished. Such assurance cannot come from the manager alone but must come through a control system independent of the manager. The control system then serves both the individual manager and the organization: It reports deviations from standard to the manager for corrective action, and it reports uncorrected deviations to the organization. In this way the manager still retains his freedom of self-determination, while the organization retains its assurance of effective performance.

LEADERSHIP SKILLS

Human behavior skills. Leadership skills require an understanding of both human behavior and organizational behavior. The latter differs from the former in relating human behavior within the organizational framework of task assignment and accomplishment. The lack of understanding and experience in exercising leadership skills particularly plagues the newly promoted manager who is over-anxious about his responsibilities. He is in a quandary about how to treat his subordinates and how to fulfill his task of providing leadership and direction. Often his lack of experience makes him inclined to direct and supervise his subordinates too closely, with the reasoning that the organization has designated him to be the manager and leader and that the employees must therefore turn to him for answers to their problems. With this philosophy he assigns his subordinates quite detailed responsibilities, demanding that they check every part of their work with him. Since he takes his responsibilities so seriously, he rarely understands the resentment such actions foster in his employees. He finds that no matter how much time he spends in supervising their activities, difficulties arise constantly. Yet as he ponders his problems he still comes to the conclusion that he is providing true leadership and direction.

The manager in the above illustration has failed to consider the human factor in his provision of direction. What do subordinates want of a leader? How can the subordinates be motivated to accept leadership? Another newly promoted manager may take quite a different view of his task of supplying leadership and direction. He may look upon his subordinates as equals. He may reflect upon the fact that just a short time ago he had the same responsibilities, tasks, and interests as they, and that there must really be little difference between the responsibilities of the manager and those of the non-manager. Such an outlook is particularly common among production workers who have been promoted to first-line supervision or among professional employees who have been made supervisors. The newly promoted manager still identifies with his fellow workers of yesterday and considers that his outlook remains the same as theirs. Rarely does he stop to think that he was promoted because he evidenced some particular talents, one of which was undoubtedly a high sense of responsibility, and that, in fact, his outlook and that of his subordinates are probably quite different.

This new manager's leadership style will be to treat his subordinates as he would have liked to be treated when he was a subordinate himself. He assigns work in a casual manner, expecting that the conscientious employees will define their jobs in the best interests of the organization. He does not exercise controls, since he trusts his employees to do a good job and considers that an employee who needs help will come to his supervisor for assistance.

His unit of the enterprise is likely to be one of the happiest in the organization. His employees practically sing at their work. Conflicts are rare and as a manager he seems to have little to do except complete the necessary forms and paperwork. One day a conference is called on the progress of the jobs under his command, and he has to obtain progress reports from his subordinates. He asks his people how they are doing and whether they will meet delivery dates, receives affirmative answers to all his questions, and blithely goes to the conference. His superior asks for a progress report, but does not accept the rather general comments offered by the manager. He asks for specific details—which the manager is unable to supply. As a result, the superior seems quite unhappy with the progress of this manager, whom he had recommended for the position, and schedules a private appointment to see if he can provide some help.

The manager returns to his unit determined to find the answers his superior wants. As he investigates further, he finds that a number of his subordinates have not carried out their tasks. There is considerable confusion among the men as to who has what assignment. In a number of instances the projects are in trouble, but no one has realized this. The manager learns very quickly that he has failed to supply the direction and leadership his subordinates required and that the happy crew is not necessarily the most efficient crew.

In these two illustrations, one manager has supervised too closely, failing to recognize the need for room for growth and latitude in assignments for his subordinates. The other manager has made the mistake of identifying the motivations of his subordinates with his own. Both managers have been ineffectual leaders and have failed to provide the proper direction for their subordinates.

Effective leadership requires proper balance between excessive supervision on the one hand and lack of control on the other. The leader exercises command and yet simultaneously permits his subordinates self-determination. He elicits participation without relinquishing his authority. He provides some technical input where required, since his entire job cannot be merely that of assigning tasks to others. He fulfills his responsibilities to his subordinates and has their interests at heart.

Most managers master managerial skills more easily than leadership skills. Few master skills without much trial and error and heartbreak. It is necessary for the manager to recognize the importance of understanding human behavior and motivation. Then and then alone can he become a truly effective leader and manager.

Evaluative and appraisal skills. The final task of the manager is to evaluate his own performance and that of his subordinates. Such evaluation is designed not to punish subordinates for ineffective performance but to use past performance as a training device to improve future performance. It has been said that experience is the best teacher, but a teacher cannot teach unless the pupil is willing to learn. Every day the practicing manager has countless opportunities to learn how to improve his performance, but all too frequently such lessons go unlearned.

An apocryphal story circulated in industrial circles concerns the promotion of a bright young man to a higher management position. A colleague of the bright young man had 18 years' service in his department compared to but one year's service for the young man. When a supervisory vacancy occurred in the department, the bright young man received the promotion, much to the consternation of his older colleague. The older man went to the superior complaining that he should have received the promotion—after all, he had had 18 years of experience in the department, and the younger man had had only one. The superior answered that it was true that the man had been in the department 18 years, but as for experience, he had had one year's experience 18 times.

How may the manager carry out this important task of evaluation and appraisal? Who is to do the evaluation and what bases may be used for such appraisals? The most important consideration for the manager to remember is that the purpose of the evaluation is to improve performance, both his own as a manager and that of his subordinates in carrying out planned activities. This is important since it will determine what attitude the manager carries into such an evaluation session. If he uses the evaluation session to allocate blame among the responsible parties, each individual will spend his time protecting his interests by either blaming someone else or making excuses for poor performance. If the manager can genuinely convince his subordinates that the purpose of the evaluation session is to have everyone learn where he made mistakes and how such mistakes may be prevented in the future, he will be in a position to use such conferences as a realistic and effective training device.

This type of performance appraisal is not to be confused with rating systems that evaluate the total performance of subordinates. The performance appraisal relates to the evaluation of planned performance to sharpen managerial abilities. It is essentially a day-to-day training device that permits personnel to obtain the maximum benefit from experience. It need not be a formal session, since such evaluation should be a constant, almost daily task for the manager.

An illustration of the need for constant evaluation is the case of an engineering manager in charge of professional engineering employees. He had organized his section into electrical and mechanical subsections in order to obtain the maximum specialization of function. The projects to be completed by this section had both mechanical and electrical engineering components, although in general the electrical engineering elements were more important to the functioning of the project. It was necessary for the electrical and mechanical managers to cooperate as a team in the design of the product. Technically, the electrical engineers required mechanical engineering clearance in the design, although in practice the electrical engineers often failed to consider the mechanical problems. Because the company was in the electronics industry, the electrical engineers had greater status in the firm than did the mechanical engineers.

To solve the problem of coordination, the engineering manager suggested to his subordinates that teams of electrical and mechanical engineers be formed to work together on the design of the projects. One such team was formed of one man from each group, but shortly after the formation of the team it was obvious that the men's personalities were not compatible, with the result that constant conflicts arose on the technical design level between electrical and mechanical engineers. Such conflicts were noted by both men to their superiors, but the electrical and mechanical supervisors were unwilling to arbitrate these differences, so no action was taken. As the situation worsened, costs increased and little attention was paid to schedules. When the situation eventually came to the attention of the engineering manager, he was perplexed as to how to solve the problem.

This is an illustration of the need for constant evaluation. The engineering manager recognized the problem of coordination between the mechanical and electrical units and took a particular action; that is, constituting a team. Here was an important decision with far-reaching effects on the organization, and yet it was not followed up by any form of appraisal or evaluation. The engineering manager blithely made the decision and never tried to find out whether the decision was the right one. The end result was that in trying to solve one problem he created a greater and more difficult one.

This overview of managerial skills has been selective rather than exhaustive. It is not the purpose of this book to enumerate a long list of skills, but rather to provide the manager or prospective manager with a realistic appraisal of his job and a selective set of managerial skills. It is intended that the knowledge provided here will give the manager an understanding of the component skills that he must exercise to be effective. Such understanding cannot be by rote or by formulas, because the pitfalls in application are numerous and constant even for the experienced manager.

Subsequent chapters develop in depth the managerial skills outlined in this chapter so as to provide sequential understanding of the total managerial process.

2

Corporate Objectives
and Long-Range Planning

THE ACCEPTANCE of time horizons and of the need for purposeful behavior directed toward highly specific goals is what differentiates
the successful manager from the mediocre one. The development of
managerial skills in the formulation of objectives and strategies provides the tools to implement an understanding of time horizons and
goal-seeking behavior into organizational realities.

All too often it is taken for granted that objectives have been set
and strategies have been developed in a company. After all, people
are working, schedules are being met, and the company may be
profitable. But these actions may or may not be appropriate in light
of optimum goals, resources, and environmental constraints.

An example of the failure of a company to develop viable objectives and strategies is a small firm in a closely knit industry. From its
leadership position in 1875, it had declined to the point of holding
less than a 5 percent share of the market some 90 years later.

When the firm's executives decided to formulate long-run corporate objectives and examined the history of the firm, they found that

at no time since 1875 had the firm set forth any long-range plans or concrete objectives in terms of market shares and the like. At one time in the history of the firm, the sales manager had implicitly decided on his own to set forth the objectives of the firm by concentrating his sales force on one sector of the market. Unfortunately, his choice was ill made, since the particular sector that he chose declined from something like 50 percent of industry sales to less than 5 percent, and the firm declined with the market sector. The lack of attention paid by the firm's management in the past to the formulation of objectives had resulted in the drastic decline of the firm's position in its industry.

THE FORMULATION OF OBJECTIVES

The formulation of objectives is one of the basic skills for management, since objectives are required before the manager can apply his other skills. But in order to formulate objectives, the manager must have extensive knowledge not only of the objectives of his superiors and of the corporation but also of the resources and abilities available in his subpart of the organization. He is necessarily constrained by the demands of the organization in terms not only of the corporate objectives but also of the resources he is given in order to achieve his part of the corporate objective.

The job of management is to insure that objectives are formulated at all levels from the top to the bottom of the organization. It is important not only that the objectives be formulated but that they be visualized by the individual manager. The time span of objectives varies considerably with the level of management if the rule of visualization is to be observed.

Managerial level	*Time span of objectives*
Board of directors	5 to 20 years
Corporate management	1 to 5 years
Operating middle management	12 weeks to 1 year
Operating first-level management	1 to 12 weeks
Professional employees	Project basis: 1 week to 1 year
Production employees	Daily task

Unless the concept of visualization of objectives is accepted, the formulation of objectives will not serve as an effective aid to operating management. It will be quite difficult for lower levels of management to recognize their contributions to the organization unless the objectives of higher levels of management are translated into concrete tasks for the individual manager and are related to the attainment of sectional, departmental, and corporate objectives.

The Need for Clearly Defined Objectives

It is necessary to pay attention to objectives not only on the corporate level but also on every other level of management. The lack of clearly defined objectives at any level results in waste motion and inefficiency. Each manager must have a goal. Each manager must relate his goal to his own actions and to those of his subordinates.

When objectives are not specifically formulated, the manager will either set his own objectives or vacillate because of the lack of direction. An example of the high cost of failure to set appropriate objectives is the case of a large research and development corporation which was organized functionally within the research and development sector to permit a high degree of specialization of function. Concurrently with this functional organization, the research and development director utilized product development groups. These groups competed for the common facilities provided by the functional organization.

The product development groups had very definite objectives, which were defined by their assignments from top management to develop a particular product by a certain date within certain budget limitations. Although the product development managers rarely considered the formulation of objectives any more than did the other managers in the firm, the nature of their assignments resulted in very specific objectives. The functional groups had no such built-in factors for the formulation of objectives. Top management had promulgated some general policies in regard to the relationship between the functional and product development groups, stating that the former were to service the latter while simultaneously contributing to the state of the art in their particular specialties.

Because the major pressures came from the product development groups to obtain design services from the functional areas, the latter normally fulfilled the "service" function quite satisfactorily.

But their contributions to state-of-the-art research were quite limited, because the functional managers had not defined their objectives and submitted them to the product development managers and top management for acceptance. As a result when the product development manager had alternative designs—a superior design at a higher cost that would contribute to the state of the art or an adequate design at a lower cost that would not make such a contribution—he would always choose the lower-cost design. This resulted in the firm's losing all the major contributions that such a functional organization would have made because one area of operating management failed to formulate the appropriate long-range objectives and involve other areas of operating management in their implementation.

No manager can be successful and effective unless he formulates objectives. Not having clearly formulated and understood objectives is tantamount to not knowing what is to be done. It leaves subordinate managers to decide for themselves what their tasks are. It makes the manager's problem of coordination most difficult and his task of planning almost impossible. Finally, it fails to provide some standard of performance for appraisal and evaluation.

The sequencing of the use of managerial skills calls first for the manager to formulate objectives; all the other skill applications are predicated on the existence of viable and appropriate objectives or goals. The manager cannot provide leadership for his subordinates unless he himself knows in what direction to go. He cannot plan until he knows what objective he is planning to achieve. He cannot control the actions of his subordinates to achieve the objective unless such an objective is known and recognized. He cannot make effective decisions unless they are related to the attainment of some task or objective. He cannot evaluate performance that must be measured on the attainment of the objective.

SETTING OBJECTIVES

The first step in the management process, then, must be the formulation of objectives. How can the manager set objectives? What are objectives, and how can they help the manager to be more effective?

Before operating management can formulate its objectives, top management must have formulated the organizational or corporate objectives. On the theoretical plane, there has been considerable discussion as to whether the business firm has really only one objective—to maximize its profits. There is considerable evidence that, although firms still have an objective of making profits, they do not maximize profits in the traditional sense. The trend to professional management as the controlling element in business enterprise and away from the entrepreneur with his strong profit motive has led to a changing outlook on corporate objectives.

Economists since the time of Adam Smith have based economic theories on the premise of profit maximization by the entrepreneur in a free enterprise economy. Price theory and the theory of the firm relate the decisions of the businessman to maximizing his profit without any other considerations. When economists observe any action on the part of the businessman that does not seem to be based on the profit maximization principle, they either consider that the man is not acting rationally or redefine the concept of profit maximization. For example, if the businessman provides benefits for employees that are not required by law or by unionization and that have the effect of reducing the net profit of the enterprise, the economists state that the businessman is still maximizing his profit *in the long run*. They say that the benefits paid to labor today will accrue as increased profits in the future through better worker-management relations and that therefore the businessman is still maximizing his profits.

Is profit *the* objective of business enterprise? Is it the overriding objective of business? To answer these questions we must take a new look at the corporate entity. A corporation makes decisions only by having its management make decisions. It is therefore necessary to study the motivations of management in order to ascertain the motivations or objectives of the corporation. The control of the major part of American business in terms of net assets and net sales is in the hands of professional managers. The professional manager is defined as one who does not have a major ownership interest and therefore sells his talents to the corporation for a salary. The owner-manager has a major ownership interest and receives the reward for his talents through profits. This simple dichotomy does not take into account the special case of professional managers who receive a major portion of their income in the form of stock options or profit sharing.

What is the motive or objective of the professional manager? Certainly, it is profit; but is it profit maximization? Is the motive a social consciousness of the obligations of a business enterprise? Or is the motive one of personal gain through the corporation? Realistically, all these elements are present in the motives of the professional manager, except that realistically the concept of profit maximization changes to one of profit satisfaction. In other words, the single goal of profit maximization changes to multiple goals, which are more socially acceptable, as long as the firm remains reasonably profitable.

The private enterprise system with mobility of investment funds will allocate funds to the most profitable firms. But investment funds seek not only short-run profit but also long-term growth and stability of earnings. In fact, the securities market defines preferred investments in terms not only of immediate profits but of long-term growth and stability of profits. In the business cycle, profitable performance attracts investment and retained profits serve as the base for further growth and stability. With such a critical role for profit in a private enterprise economy, how can there be any doubt that firms maximize profits?

The professional manager is still subject to the will of the investors, but such investors are so scattered and numerous in the average large corporation that rarely do they control his actions. The investors will take action to remove the professional manager only when he fails to generate profit. Obviously, the professional manager must have profit as his objective for the corporation, but rarely can the widespread ownership of the publicly held corporation effectively demand a true maximization of profits. Rather, the definition of profit goals will depend upon the particular industry, the stage of the business cycle, and the personal desires and motivations of the professional managers directing the corporation.

General Motors averages a return of more than 25 percent on invested capital before taxes. But the sophisticated investor discounts this very respectable profit because the automobile industry is not a growth industry and is subject to fairly heavy cyclical fluctuations. General Motors common stock will not sell for the same multiple of earnings as will a so-called glamour stock in a glamour industry. Does this mean that professional management in General Motors will be removed by stockholder action? The answer is definitely no! The firm produces what is considered a satisfactory profit. Could top management of General Motors increase company profit, particularly in the short run? Here the answer is undoubtedly yes, but the motive of the professional manager in a firm such as General Motors is not solely to maximize profits. If General Motors were to maximize its profits at the expense of the other automobile manufacturers and thus greatly increase its share of the market, there is a high probability that the government would break it into a number of smaller companies as it did with Standard Oil many years ago.

The professional managers in large corporations are certainly profit-oriented, but rarely are they completely oriented toward a true maximization of profits. In the General Motors example, it can be argued that the company is in fact maximizing profits by not increasing its share of the market, since such action could mean the end of the corporation. It is much easier to recognize the reasons for certain actions and motives of the professional manager when profit is seen in its proper perspective. The primary motive in a private enterprise economy must still be profit, even though such a motive is tempered in terms not of the maximum profit but of a satisfactory profit.

One motive of the professional manager, then, is profit satisfaction. This is also one factor in attracting investment funds. Are stability of earnings and growth, the other two factors responsible for attracting investment funds, also the motives or objectives of the professional manager and of the corporation? Stability of earnings means reduction of risk. The professional manager is inclined to avoid risk and uncertainty to a much greater degree than the owner-manager. The owner-manager receives the full reward for risk taking—that is, profit—although he also bears the full brunt of failure in risk taking. The professional manager, on the other hand, gains little in risk taking, compared with the loss that he may suffer personally through failure of the risk-taking venture. Certainly, then, the professional manager will consider the corporation's stability of earnings to be one of his objectives.

The passing of the era of the risk-taking entrepreneur may have serious consequences. The large corporation can be considered too security-minded in its inclination to avoid risks. As the large corporations controlled by the professional managers throughout the Western world hold most of the free world's natural resources and hire most of the wage earners, their actions have a considerable effect on world economy. If such corporations are no longer willing to take the risks of the entrepreneurs who built the great businesses that produced the national wealth and economic well-being of the Western world, how will progress take place?

The professional manager's objective of stability may exact a high price in lack of progress. Although it is the large corporation that can best afford the risk-taking function, it is the small, owner-managed firm that is motivated to take such risks. Government-owned and government-controlled firms are usually much more conservative than private business; the reward-and-punishment system in government tends to punish innovation and reward conformity.

There is constant criticism of the growth of strong and powerful central governments. Yet even in the United States the large corporations look to the federal government for protection and insurance against risk. Almost all progress in the United States in electronics and aviation, as well as in many other industries, is heavily subsidized by the federal government through its defense expenditures.

The third factor affecting the attraction of investment funds—growth—is also an objective of the professional manager. A strong psychological motivation for man is the act of creation, of building something for posterity. Many American executives are almost hypermotivated by work. The depiction of the executive as a driver, as one who places his position in the business enterprise above everything else, is common in novels about the business scene and is not far from the truth.

An apocryphal story about the visit of a South American businessman to the United States well illustrates this hypermotivation of the American executive. When the South American was asked his opinion of his North American counterpart, he answered that he found it difficult to understand the actions of the American executive. In his country, men work to earn money to enjoy leisure, but in the United States, the executive tolerates leisure only because it insures him enough energy and health to work. He concluded that it is an odd state of affairs, indeed, when a man's objective is work rather than play!

Although some executives do carry their personal work objectives to extremes, it must be recognized that a man's major activity is work and that his greatest satisfactions come through the act of creation in work. The professional manager receives twofold benefits from his objective of growth. The first is that growth as a corporate objective will attract investment funds and, by keeping the stockholders content, permit the professional manager to retain control. The second is that growth of the corporation is a reflection on the personal ability of the professional manager and satisfies his psychological need for creation and work satisfaction. The personal objectives of the professional manager are amply satisfied if the corporation takes as its objectives satisfactory profits, stability of earnings, and growth. The attainment of such corporate objectives serves to attract and retain investment funds, which are necessary for the continuity of the corporation and of its professional management.

What about the highly publicized objective of service, so commonly advanced by corporations as their major objective? An examination reveals that service cannot stand as *the* objective of a business enterprise. Is this service rendered to the customer, to society, or to the state? Unless a firm has a natural monopoly granted by the state, such as public utilities or a monopoly through patents, customers always have complete freedom of choice whether to buy a product or service. Are not the "service" factors, then, determined by competition and therefore related to the profit motive? The concept of service to society has greater rationale, although it too might be questioned, since society under the private enterprise system should determine the allocation of resources through consumer choice and not through conscious control on the part of the business enterprise.

A further consideration about service as an objective is professional management's obligation to investors or stockholders, even if such an obligation is only one of continuity of the corporation and therefore continuity of the positions of the professional managers. It is hardly necessary to note that service can never be a primary objective, but must be secondary to profit, stability, and growth. This logic applies to other highly publicized objectives such as employee satisfaction, customer relations, and the like, all of which either are directly related to the primary objectives of profit satisfaction, stability of earnings, and growth, or are actually secondary to them.

Social Responsibilities as a Corporate Objective

Corporate objectives, since they are decided by professional managers, will be related in some way to personal objectives. The chief executive and corporate officers of large firms have normally had long tenure as executives. They have worked as employees, as sub-managers, and as managers. Their experience has led them to value the worth of good employees and managers and to recognize the needs and rights of such men and women. They think of themselves as employees of the corporation, and they think of the corporation as an entity to which they owe loyalty.

The professional manager considers the corporation to be an extension of his own personality and expects it to act in a responsible way. He wants the corporation with which he identifies to be moral and ethical, to be a respected part of society. If he had to make a choice between an immoral or unethical act and the failure to satisfy the primary objectives of the corporation, there is little doubt that he would choose the latter. But the decision as to what is moral and ethical is not always easy to make. What are the social responsibilities? What part must the corporation play in society?

An example of the dilemma facing executives in fulfilling corporate social responsibilities is the case of a textile firm in the Northeast. The firm was the mainstay of a small New England community facing potential bankruptcy because of high labor costs. Four generations of employees had worked for the mill. The firm was not only the economic base for the community but its social base as well, since the owners had traditionally been the social leaders. When the textile industry declined in New England, the owners sold the firm to one of the new combines so common in the industry. The new professional management sold the inventory of the firm, moved its better machinery to other plants, sold the remaining machinery, and put the buildings up for sale. Eventually, the governor of the state declared the town a depressed area. All the young men drifted into the larger cities to work, and the older men exhausted the unemployment benefits available to them.

Here is a concrete case of the problem of a corporation's social responsibility. Undoubtedly, from the point of view of society, the closing of the mill produced a great deal of human suffering. It destroyed a town. But the economist may argue that if the mill was a marginal operation, its closing did benefit society as a whole. This is because the textile industry could produce textiles more cheaply than the marginal mill, with a resulting economy of natural resources and a lower cost of living. Furthermore, the surplus labor could be used in another industry where its production would be greater. But the economist also adds a rider: "in the long run." The statement attributed to Lord Keynes, "In the long run, we will all be dead," certainly applies to the small New England town, which will take a long time to die.

The sociologist would decry the action of professional management in closing the mill because of its effect on one local segment of society, regardless of the economist's contention that such an action was necessary to raise the standard of living of society as a whole. The sociologist would note the effect of such unemployment on the moral fiber of the town and on the people who lived there. Here the social scientists would disagree on what action they would have taken if they had been the decision makers. The sociologist would undoubtedly have voted to continue the mill in the interests of society locally, whereas the economist would have voted to discontinue the mill in the interests of society as a whole.

Was there any justification for the action of the new professional management in closing the mill? Didn't the corporation have social responsibilities to its employees, who had loyally served it for generations? To answer these questions, we must project what might have happened to the firm had it continued in operation. The firm was a marginal producer, perhaps producing a profit only because its machinery was fully depreciated. Since the firm had higher labor costs than firms in the southern United States, it would be unable to make a satisfactory return on investment in the long run. The original owners could have subsidized the mill by utilizing the family fortune, but the mill would attract investors only through its liquidation.

The question becomes that of whether there was any choice open to the professional managers. If the mill had not been closed then, it would have been only a matter of time before the fully depreciated equipment broke down or was no longer economically competitive, even without machinery cost. Inevitably, it would have been necessary to close the mill. The professional management may very well have recognized the social responsibilities of the corporation, but was unable to fulfill them.

There is also the question of social responsibility to individuals in the firm. Does long service in a corporation automatically entitle an employee to some form of retirement or disability benefit? An example of the problem of social responsibility to the individual employee is the case of a small firm with fifty employees and three principal executives. The ownership of the firm was concentrated in the hands of the president and vice-president, although the general manager shared in the executive decisions of the firm.

The general manager became ill with Parkinson's disease, and over a period of time his disability sapped his energy to the point where he was able to carry less and less responsibility. The president and the vice-president had to assume more and more of the work that had previously been done by the general manager. Now the firm had only two effective executives, and a number of functions went untended. But the profit margin was not sufficient to permit hiring another high-level executive.

The president and vice-president were quite perturbed over the problem; they felt that it would be unfair to the general manager to dismiss him, yet on the other hand it would be unfair to the company to keep an ineffective executive. Furthermore, since the two men had the ownership interests, it became almost a personal question for them. The firm continued to carry the general manager, but finally it could no longer afford to be without an additional executive assistant. With great reluctance the president dismissed the general manager and provided as much severance pay as the firm could afford.

Here was a question of the responsibility of the corporation to an individual member of the firm. The corporation could not accept its responsibility to one individual without neglecting its responsibility to all members. If the company in question had continued to keep the disabled executive, it would have jeopardized its very existence. Can special treatment of one individual be allowed to jeopardize the jobs of all the company employees? Although the answer to the question must be no, the individual will still suffer, and there will continue to be a feeling that the corporation has failed in its social responsibilities.

The problem of the acceptance of social responsibilities is not an easy one to resolve. Certainly the fulfillment of social responsibilities must be considered as a corporate objective, but the implementation of such an objective is extremely difficult to carry out.

OBJECTIVES AND PLANNING

Objectives must be attainable to be useful. Do the very general objectives of growth, stability of earnings, and a satisfactory profit serve the important purpose of providing direction for executive action? It is necessary to translate the more general goals into specific objectives that may serve as guides for corporate action and permit measurement of performance.

At one time it was considered that the objectives of a corporation would be limited by its bylaws to a particular industry and type of business. This is no longer true in an age when diversification is the rule rather than the exception. A corporation can no longer be guided in perpetuity by a set of bylaws in its charter. Rather, it must reconsider and structure its future through a constant reevaluation of its objectives. If necessary the bylaws can be easily amended.

In order to formulate specific objectives, management makes a thorough study of its resources, its abilities, its markets, and the economy. Such a study is often called long-range planning, in which a corporation attempts to formulate short-, medium-, and long-range objectives after investigating its past record and projecting future trends in its industry and its position in the industry. Such long-range planning investigations have many similarities to a market research study, but extend beyond the immediate market potential into all the internal and external factors affecting the firm.

LONG-RANGE PLANNING

The objective of any long-range plan should be to set forth a blueprint or roadmap for the firm to follow for a five- to ten-year period. Of course, it is important that the long-range planning project receive sufficient attention to insure that the plan is worth following. Since it is impossible to foresee all possible events pertaining to the growth of a company, the long-range plan should anticipate the unexpected. In other words, the plan should be sufficiently flexible that it is not abandoned completely at the first unanticipated event. Even if the plan has high enough priority to warrant an adequate budget and the time and energy of key executives, there is still one important pitfall: the plan may not be action-oriented and hence will remain in the locked top drawer of the chief executive.

It is imperative that all major decisions be made in accord with the plan. If major decisions do not conform to the plan, then the plan must be amended, which in effect means that the entire long-range planning process must be repeated. If this is not accepted as an integral part of long-range planning, it is a waste of time and money to formulate a plan.

Long-range planning involves the following steps:

1. Determination of both the company objectives and those of the plan itself.
2. Determination of the scope of the plan and its budget.
3. Determination of the timetable for implementation.
4. Evaluation of the research of various staff specialists.
5. Implementation.
6. Periodic evaluation.

A serious problem confronting management in formulating a long-range plan is a built-in prejudice regarding past actions, which may make it difficult for the executives to be sufficiently objective and daring in their approach. Formulating a long-range plan permits management to consider a wide range of potential directions in which the firm may go. There should be a certain amount of star-gazing before management grapples with the realities of budget and other limitations. If the firm is in a moderately growing industry, what range of possibilities exists to take advantage of such company strengths as the availability of an executive team, the similarity of manufacturing processes to those of an allied industry, the use of the same sales force for different products, and so on? Specifically, the company objectives should be reexamined in regard to the following points:

1. Should the firm remain in the same industry?
2. Should the firm continue to operate in the same market segment of its industry?
3. Should the firm attempt to grow through acquisition or internal growth?
4. Should the firm consider operating with a greater degree of calculated risk in order to grow at a faster rate?
5. Should the firm become essentially a manufacturing facility or a marketing firm, abandoning the other facilities?

The basic objective of any long-range plan is simply to determine what types of input are required to attain a given goal. To translate this objective into specifics, a firm should consider the following.

Rate of growth. What rate of growth does the firm want to achieve? How practical is this rate of growth, considering the experience of this company and others in the industry? Does the corporation have in mind a slow initial rate of growth with an accelerating rate after certain points in the long-range plan have been reached?

Market share. Is the company to be satisfied with its present market share, expecting any growth to be the result of population growth? What market share does the company want to develop, and in what market segment of its industry or another industry?

Return on investment. What return on investment is required to attract investment funds? How will this affect the rate of growth? Is it necessary to increase the equity capital to finance this growth? What effect will this have on control of the firm? What other sources of capital are available?

Diversification. This is a common objective in the plans of many firms these days, small and large alike. What avenues are open for diversification? Is there sufficient management strength to absorb other firms? If the company is not listed on a securities exchange, is it planning to obtain such a listing so that it may grow through exchange of stock for acquisition without cash investment? What is the objective of such diversification—profit, marketing advantages, production advantages, overhead absorption?

Survival. Are there factors on the horizon that point to a problem of survival for the firm? What changes are forecast by the firm in distribution patterns, cultural patterns, consumption patterns, and manufacturing techniques?

In order to ascertain whether the objectives set forth in the long-range planning process are realistic, management must examine the resources and character of its firm. An illustration of such a process is the case study of a small firm that did a thorough job in long-range planning by examining the various objectives of rate of growth, market share, return on investment, diversification, and survival. After considering the factors involved in such objectives, the firm's next step was to make a realistic appraisal both of its present resources and of the additional resources required to implement the objectives set forth in the long-range plan. The company executives set forth eight major factors to consider in the evolution of a long-range plan.

1. Capital requirements and available capital. Although capital requirements depended upon a number of other factors, the executives decided that, to keep the planning realistic, some estimate had to be made of how much capital would be required to carry out the long-range plans.

2. Organizational requirements. It takes considerable time to build an organization, and the existing organization of this firm was considered to be one of the major limiting factors in any long-range plan. The availability of top executives was severely limited, so a redistribution of functions would be necessary if the firm was to assume larger responsibilities. The company's management decided that a plan for the evaluation and development of executives would be necessary before any major expansion could be considered, and it recognized the need for compensation plans for executives and the introduction of some form of retirement or deferred compensation.

3. Sales organization. This particular company depended to a great extent on its sales force, so long-range planning for the sales organization was of particular importance. Such planning included consideration of the following factors:

- Territorial distribution of the sales force.
- Selection and training of salesmen.
- Motivation and compensation of salesmen.
- Evaluation and control of sales.
- Long-term sales forecasting.
- Marketing strategy (including determination of market segments).
- Classes of customers desired by the company.
- Product lines.
- Product development.
- Overhead distribution and relationship to sales volume.

4. Sales promotion. In the area of sales promotion, the major problem was to decide what kind was best and how much money to spend on it. The company executives felt that there were three major factors to be considered:

- The relationship of the advertising dollar to sales volume.
- The type, frequency, and cost of advertising.
- The development of special customers or classes of customers.

5. *Assessing competition.* A major factor in any long-range plan, and particularly in the plans of this firm, was the assessment of competition. The appraisal considered what actions competitors were likely to take in present markets and in the building of future markets. Another important consideration was the reaction of competitors to successful penetration of their markets.

6. *Manufacturing facilities.* Were there any actions that the firm could take to reduce manufacturing costs? As a solution to seasonal fluctuations, could the company do subcontracting work? What effect would this have on costs and prices? Should the firm consider eliminating its manufacturing facilities and becoming solely a distributing company? Could it move its manufacturing operations to an area with cheaper labor costs? The company executives considered answers to those questions as an integral part of long-range planning.

7. *Product development.* The company decided to reconsider its methods and procedures for the development of products. Among the questions asked by the executives were these: How much innovation was acceptable in the market? What relationship should exist between sales and product development? What long-term investment was required to develop products required of the industry leader?

8. *Management controls and evaluation.* What management controls were necessary to permit top management to monitor operations and to anticipate difficulties? How could the performance of supervisors and executives be evaluated during the various growth stages of the firm? What financial figures were necessary, and how should they be used? Company executives considered controls and evaluation of performance to be of considerable importance to the success of any long-range plan.

The small firm's long-range planning committee examined each of these questions in turn and evolved a plan designed to increase the firm's share of its market from 5 percent to 10 percent over a period of five years, to increase return on invested capital by 100 percent, and to increase profits as a percentage of sales by 50 percent.

CORPORATE OBJECTIVES AND MANAGEMENT BY OBJECTIVES

Few managers can be directly involved in charting the destiny of an organization by formulating corporate objectives or directing a long-range planning study. But it is imperative that all managers be cognizant of the process, since they will be directed in their actions by the corporate objectives. It is no longer valid to assume that all a manager has to do is be efficient in the performance of his job. He also has to be sure that the activity he performs so efficiently is contributing to the attainment of corporate objectives.

An approach to engineering design, called value engineering, well illustrates the concept of management by objectives as compared to managerial efficiency. In the design of an automobile, a great deal of engineering design effort goes into perfecting the drive shaft from the motor or transmission to power the rear wheels. Value engineering would study not the drive shaft but the problem of transferring power to the wheels, which could be accomplished by a rear-drive engine, front-wheel drive, or use of individual electric motors at each wheel. The economies that could be effected by perfecting the drive shaft could not equal those potentially provided in the value engineering approach of studying the function. Similarly, the emphasis on management by objectives to relate the activities of a subgroup to the overall objectives of the organization will produce far greater economies of time and effort than the narrower accent on efficiency alone.

3

Management by Objectives

MANAGEMENT BY OBJECTIVES is a philosophy of management as much as a skill. It provides direction and purpose for every managerial act and allows greater discretionary powers to lower levels of management throughout the organization.

At the corporate level, objectives are determined after an examination of resources, market position and opportunities, and managerial capabilities. At the operating level, such corporate objectives are accepted, and subobjectives or strategies are decided on to implement them. Each level provides objectives for the next lower level of management, but permits the determination of objectives by the lower level within prescribed limits. Since the objectives of the next higher level of management prescribe what limits of discretion are permitted to subordinates, there is need to have subordinates participate in the setting of objectives.

Few executives would dispute the need for corporate objectives and for their implementation by operating management. But is it practicable to have operating management formulate objectives? What uses can lower levels of management make of objectives? The answer to these questions is that an understanding of corporate objectives permits each member of management to measure his ambitions and capabilities against those of his organization. Furthermore, such an understanding prevents the sidetracking of management and managerial resources into courses of action that are not in accord with corporate long-range objectives. Full use of objectives at all levels of management can provide tasks that can be visualized by the individual even down to a daily task for the production worker. Furthermore, the formulation of objectives permits the manager to have some rational basis for the design of his organization structure. If the manager wishes to emphasize one factor more than another in order to attain his objectives, he can organize his division or department in such a way that this factor receives more attention, greater funds, or better management through organization.

A most important use of objectives is as standards of performance by which to appraise management. For an objective to be useful in achieving results, it must be capable of being visualized by the manager and it must be attainable. The manager's performance in attaining the objective is a realistic and measurable means by which his ability and worth to the organization can be ascertained. The use of participation and the discretion permitted the manager in formulating his own objectives will provide full acceptance of the objective as a standard of performance by which he may be judged.

There are a number of practical problems involved in both the formulation and the implementation of objectives. One of the major problems is to determine the objectives of a department or subsection of the organization. The formulation of corporate objectives presents different difficulties from those of the formulation of objectives by the middle manager. What is the difference between the objective of a section and the function of the manager heading the section? What are the differences among objectives, functions, and responsibilities?

An example of the difficulties in formulating objectives for middle management occurred in a workshop seminar for middle management in a moderately large firm. The participants were asked to indicate the objectives of their departments or sections. Preliminary to the meeting they were to present their working papers. The budget director of the controller's division described the objectives pertaining to his job as follows:

1. Provide the organizations (manpower) to discharge assigned responsibilities.

2. Define and interpret policy for those reporting to me.
3. Promote better communication and liaison with other departments.
4. Develop managerial talent.
5. Execute special assignments.
6. Recommend systems, methods, and procedure improvements so as to promote and develop the controller's function and the company's operations.
7. Participate in company and community activities.
8. Keep abreast of new developments in the accounting-controllership area.

When the budget director presented these objectives to the workshop seminar, he was immediately asked to define his responsibilities, to which he replied that his major responsibility was the coordination of the budgeting activities. Then each of the objectives that he had noted was in turn eliminated as an objective, mainly on the grounds that they were either responsibilities or functions of the man's position. In other words, they were the means by which the objective was to be attained rather than objectives in themselves.

This tendency to confuse functions and responsibilities with objectives is all too common at all levels of management. In order to see objectives in a correct perspective, one must understand the relationships among objectives, functions, responsibilities, and organization.

OBJECTIVES AND THE DESIGN OF THE ORGANIZATION STRUCTURE

Each member of management must relate the objectives of his section or department to those of the broader organization substructure of which his section is a part, as well as to the corporate objectives. It is not necessary to repeat the objectives of the higher levels in the objectives set forth by the manager for his particular section; such objectives should be readily available and understood by all concerned. Since the objectives of the next higher levels of management serve as the basis for the particular organization structure used by the corporation, all levels of management should be able to understand both the objectives and the rationale for the organization structure.

Objectives should be formulated first, and the organization structure should be designed to facilitate their attainment. This procedure is necessary no matter what level of management is involved. The design of the organization structure takes into account the authorities and responsibilities that are to be assigned. Objectives then become the overriding consideration, and the manager will determine organization, responsibilities, and functions only after he has formulated his objectives.

Although objectives should be relatively stable for the corporation, they must be subject to change in any dynamic business situation, and they should be determined annually for operating management. In the workshop seminar discussed earlier, one of the participants noted as one of his objectives a cost-reduction goal of 5 percent per year. At this rate, the firm would be remarkably competitive over the next decade! An objective of 5 percent might be attainable in the first year, but would probably have to be revised up or down in subsequent years. As new personnel are added, there should undoubtedly be a reconsideration and most likely a reassignment of functions and responsibilities, but there is usually little reason for a change in objectives.

An important consideration in the formulation of objectives is that they should be attainable. When the objectives are specific and realistic, it is possible to measure the progress a manager is making toward the attainment of his objectives. Since the manager himself is responsible for both the formulation and the attainment of his objectives, it is a fair method of evaluation of his ability and performance.

FORMULATION OF OBJECTIVES AS AN ORGANIZATIONAL AUDIT

It is odd that more attention is not paid to the formulation of objectives at all levels of management, since it is often standard practice for corporations to issue corporate objectives. But all too often firms stop with setting forth job descriptions for management positions, assuming that such a definite assignment of responsibilities is all that is required.

The formulation of objectives by all levels of management can perform some very special services for the firm, including an organizational audit as a byproduct of the determination of objectives throughout the organization. The first step is the setting of the corporate objectives, after which each level of management below the corporate level formulates its own objectives and presents them to the next higher level of management for approval. As this procedure works its way through the organization, the formulation of the objectives of each higher level serves as a guide for the next lower level.

It is imperative to note at this point that the objectives are formulated by the particular manager for his own operation and are *not* formulated for him by his superior. The subordinate uses the objectives of his superior only as a guide in considering how his objectives relate to those of the larger entity of the organization. This is how the objective formulation can serve as an organizational audit. In the structuring of an organization, top management makes certain decisions on the assignment of responsibilities to achieve the corporate objectives. Top management then assigns responsibility and authority through the formal organization to operating management. Operating management in turn attempts to carry out its assigned responsibilities but, in order to get the job done, places different priorities on actions and responsibilities than were originally intended by top management.

An example of how the original intent of top management can be changed by operating management over a period of time is that of a manufacturing firm where product development was considered important enough to be accorded equal status with the other major functions of sales, manufacturing, and controllership. In the day-to-day operations within the firm, operating management, faced with the problem of implementing the objectives of the company by working within the organization structure set forth by top management, found that an entirely different de facto organization was necessary to achieve results.

The president was extremely cost-conscious, but was willing to let the sales vice-president make all decisions on what would sell in the market and what actions the firm had to take in product development. The president therefore pressured the controller to keep a close watch on costs, but the controller found it much easier to control the product development group than the sales group. The product development group was under constant pressure from sales to bring out new products and from the controller to keep development costs at a minimum. Manufacturing had no say in product development or sales, but was forced to adapt facilities to whatever products the product development group assigned to it. Oddly enough, this was an excellent arrangement and permitted the company to operate quite profitably. Yet it was a far cry in practice from what was depicted on the organization chart.

In the heat of battle to get a job done, operating management often takes whatever liberties it can to achieve its objectives. Such actions are not conscious derelictions of responsibility but merely what is expedient to get a job done. Once a workable channel or method is established, such a channel becomes the traditional one that is followed without reference to the original organization structure. This is not to be condemned, but many times there is waste motion at the corporate level of management, which is likely to pay attention only to the formal organization, without realizing that battle stations have been changed to permit more effective coordination.

If objectives are formulated at all levels of management and then approved by the next higher level, it is possible for the superior to see the actual assessment of responsibilities that his subordinates have recognized. In other words, no matter how the superior has originally organized and set forth the responsibilities of his subordinates, there is considerable likelihood that over time such an assignment has been changed without conscious approval and recognition by the superior. Again, this is not to be condemned but in fact to be commended, as it indicates that the subordinate has had sufficient initiative and managerial ability to take action to get a job done. The only problem lies in the possibility that the subordinate has misunderstood his job and that the superior and the subordinate have different perceptions of what is being done. The superior should fit together the objectives of all his subordinates to see whether such a formulation permits him to carry out his objectives and those of the corporation. He should guard against an overlapping of objectives by his subordinates to insure that there is no duplication of effort. He should consider the restructuring of his part of the organization and a new assignment of responsibility and authority in order to permit his section and those of his subordinates to attain their objectives.

The formulation of objectives by means of communication between levels of management provides an audit of the organization structure, of the assignment of responsibilities, and of the perceptions that individuals have of their jobs. Not only does the formulation of objectives at all levels permit each manager to formulate his objectives and obtain counsel on his formulation; it also gives the manager the right of self-determination and participation in decisions affecting his role in the organization.

OBJECTIVES AND STRATEGIES FOR MANAGEMENT ACTION

The formulation and dissemination of objectives do not in themselves insure effective management action. All too often, charting an organization structure or formulating and disseminating objectives become the responsibility of a staff manager and are considered by the line operating manager to be but another fad. The line manager reluctantly fulfills his requested task but rarely considers that he might benefit from formulating objectives. Like many of the techniques available to the manager for carrying out his management tasks, the formulation of objectives is considered to be an additional burden on him rather than an important tool to assist him in the management process.

OBJECTIVES AND DECISION MAKING

The operating manager must recognize that his day-to-day actions and decisions are not isolated from one another. It is not enough to make a decision to plug a hole in the dam without considering how to strengthen the dam so that no more holes will occur. The manager cannot be effective if he makes opportunistic decisions rather than relating his decisions to the objectives of his section and of the organization. Unfortunately, even the most conscientious manager, when faced with difficult problems requiring quick decisions, may make such decisions without considering how they may help or hinder the attainment of long-term objectives.

Objectives are the first step in the planning process. In the case of long-range planning, the process is directly related to the formulation and implementation or attainment of objectives. On the corporate level, the actions of top management to attain objectives can be likened to the strategies of the military in achieving a military objective in time of war. (See Table 1.) The military general staff de-

Table 1

Comparison of the Military and Corporate Organizations

	Nature of decision		Decision-making level	
	Military	*Corporate*	*Military*	*Corporate*
Overall objective	To deter enemies from war	To build profit, stability, and growth	Executive and Congress	Board of directors
Specific objective	To build weapons for massive retaliation	To capture and hold certain markets	Department of Defense	Top management
Strategy	Creation of the Strategic Air Command and air bases with nuclear weapons	Building of a sales force and intensive national advertising	Air Force	Operating management
Tactics	The plans of S.A.C. to man aircraft, build bases, and fly missions	The plans of the advertising department and the sales force to capture the market	Strategic Air Command	Middle and lower levels of management

cides what objectives must be taken in order to win the battle or the war. The next step is the formulation of strategies to permit the taking of the objectives. Similarly, the corporate management or the board of directors decides upon the objective. Now the plans or strategies required to achieve the objective must be formulated.

The analogy between military operations and corporate action can be carried through all the ranks of management. Each part of

the military or business organization must play its part in the formulation of objectives, strategies, and tactics if the final or overall objective is to be achieved. In the business organization, the board of
directors is responsible for setting the corporate objectives; top management, the strategies; and operating management, the tactics.

THE ROLE OF PARTICIPATION

Participation is a means by which employees and subordinates
can be motivated to feel a part of the organization and executives
can make better decisions on the basis of more realistic information.
In the formulation of objectives, participation has been recommended only to the extent of the determination of the manager's own
objectives. Why shouldn't the subordinate participate in setting objectives for the entire division or corporation? To answer this question it is necessary to consider the role of participation in the business
organization. Any organization is a hierarchical pyramid with each
level of management responsible completely to the next higher level.
This hierarchical pyramid sets forth responsibilities and authorities
to establish a decision-making hierarchy for the resolution of conflict. Without such a hierarchy, there would be no organization—
only anarchy and chaos.

The concept of an industrial democracy is a myth. Managers do
not receive their positions of authority on the basis of a popular vote.
While it is true that, to be effective, the manager must obtain the
cooperation of his subordinates, this is not to say that he must be
elected as their own choice of leader or that he would necessarily
have won an election in a democratic form of organization. Basic to
the concept of organization is that organizational needs are paramount to the needs of any individual member. Individuals are free
in a private enterprise economy to choose whether they will give
their allegiance to an organization, but once an individual is a member, his needs become subservient to those of the organization.

Once the organizational objectives are determined, the objectives
of individual managers must be related to the attainment of overall
organizational objectives. Participation in these circumstances must
be severely limited. In the first place, a fundamental rule for participation is that the participating individual must possess a certain
knowledge or expertise so that his contribution will enhance the
ability of the group. The specialized knowledge and abilities re-

quired for the formulation of corporate objectives are not present anywhere except at the highest level of management. Individual opinions or advice or knowledge will be garnered from all levels of management, but lower levels will not participate in the actual formulation of corporate objectives. A second rule for participation is that involvement must be genuine and not used as a manipulating device. Since limited experience in and knowledge of developing corporate objectives precludes the participation of lower-level managers, any move to foster their participation in these circumstances would lead to manipulation.

Although the formulation of objectives at the higher level of management does not involve formal participation by subordinates, this does not mean that subordinates should not advance their ideas and concepts. A subpart of any organization must accept constraints on its action inherent in the limited frame of reference at lower levels of management (compared with that at the corporate level). But each level of management should have the right, privilege, and obligation to formulate ideas, plans, and objectives for submission to the next higher level. Once an objective has been formulated, communicated, and accepted, management at all levels must accept it and work toward its achievement, regardless of the individual manager's personal evaluation of the action of higher management. The objectives provide the direction and the raison d'être for actions of all managers. The organization cannot tolerate the substitution of other objectives on the part of any manager because organized and coordinated effort would then disappear, to be replaced with disorganized effort proceeding in all directions and resulting in ineffective management action.

STRATEGIES AND TACTICS

The corporate level of management appraises the resources and capabilities of the firm to develop corporate objectives. Since the development of strategies to achieve the corporate objectives requires the participation of all levels of management, a major consideration in the evolution of strategies is an appraisal of the managerial abilities available for the implementation of the strategies. Other factors in the evolution of strategies include an evaluation of the organization structure for the assignment of authorities and responsibilities, the priority rating of projects, the assessment of manufacturing facilities, the assessment of the marketing facilities, the construction of realistic budgets and statements of financial needs, and the evaluation of the specialized technical abilities required to carry through the plans. Each of these factors requires the participation of subordinate managers, perhaps in the actual formulation of parts of the plans for the strategies, and certainly in the provision of specialized advice and assistance.

The implementation of strategies is delegated to operating management. Strategies are usually broad enough to permit discretion to operating managers both for the development of further detailed planning and for the implementation of the strategies themselves. These detailed plans might be called tactics, since they are subordinate to the strategies—as in a military operation—and normally involve only a smaller part of the organization. Like strategies, tactics also involve participation, although the number of factors affecting their formulation is smaller than for strategies.

The factors in tactical planning that involve participation by subordinates include an appraisal of the available managerial and technical abilities in the subparts of the organization, a realistic approach to the problem of budgets and timetables (although the major responsibilities lie more in the area of time budgets than in that of money budgets), and finally a recognition of the need to assign authority and responsibility. As much as possible, the superiors should leave the formulation of tactics to their subordinates through the delegation of authority and responsibility. The superiors can still provide direction, but such assignments should sufficiently involve the subordinates to permit individual growth and development.

Operating management's evolution of strategies and tactics is dependent upon the action of corporate and top-level management in developing realistic objectives; these must in turn be coupled with the delegation of the requisite authority to operating management, in terms of finances and marketing and productive facilities, to achieve the objectives. Corporate management, in its determination of objectives, considers what limitations or constraints should be placed on operating management in order to insure the profitability of the company. The strategies and tactics of operating management must be within the cost, time, resources, and other limitations placed on it by the corporate level.

Limitations on resources are often misunderstood by lower levels of managers. For example, unless corporate management has brakes on the spending of R&D funds, the cost of product development will skyrocket. But such action on the part of management is often misunderstood by the researcher, who has different objectives from those of the corporation. The researcher wants to make a contribution to scientific knowledge by publishing his results so that other researchers may gain from his experimentation. This is true in applied research as well as pure research, although it may not be true for the design engineer who translates the work of the researcher into a practical product.

One brilliant research scientist, on his first job after completion of his Ph.D., was assigned a research project that was an extension of his work for his doctoral dissertation. He worked on the research for six months and felt that in another six months he would be able to complete it. At this point, the director of research called him into his office to discuss the project and informed him that another firm had developed a product similar to the one that would result from this research project. The director added that he was prepared to assign the research scientist to another interesting project. The scientist's reaction was almost violent when he told the director that the project would be complete in six months and that his research would be invaluable to the entire scientific community.

The research director tried to tell the scientist that companies operate with limited funds and must confine themselves to projects with commercial applications, but the researcher stated that the research director just didn't understand how important the project was to science. The scientist shortly thereafter went to another company, and then to still another when the situation repeated itself.

It could be argued that the management of this firm was quite wrong in not understanding its scientists and their needs. Yet, corporate management has to place certain constraints or limitations on the research and development function. It is unfortunate that such a limitation in this case undoubtedly robbed the world of some excellent fundamental research and deprived a brilliant scientist of his will to contribute to science within a corporate structure.

The operating manager must accept the constraints placed on his actions in formulating strategies; he cannot take action that would contravene these constraints. He in turn must insist that his subordinates accept the constraints, since he cannot give greater freedom of action to his subordinates than he himself has in formulating his strategies.

THE THEORY OF CONSTRAINTS

The theory of constraints holds that (1) constraints must exist at all levels of management; (2) the delegation of authority and responsibility decreases from the top to the bottom levels of management, with delegation being made only to those qualified to accept it; and (3) the organization must limit the impact of its mistakes. The board of directors is constrained in its action by the investors, corporate management is constrained by the board of directors, operating management is constrained by corporate management, and so on. Each level in turn delegates less authority than it has itself, so that from the top to the bottom of the hierarchical pyramid the impact of mistakes lessens.

One of the most difficult things for the newly promoted manager to understand in the management process is what he considers to be its inflexibility. There seem to be innumerable instances in which the manager is thwarted when he tries to do what he knows is best and necessary for the organization. He wonders whether the very concept of the organization is to make management take stupid actions that "any fool can see" are not economic.

A typical example of what the individual considers to be uneconomic in the average business enterprise is the need to issue purchase requisitions and purchase orders. A manager may be in charge of personnel whose weekly payroll exceeds $10,000 and a project involving hundreds of thousands of dollars, yet he cannot sign a purchase requisition for more than $500. The manager feels that if the organization can trust him with such a large payroll and charge him with the responsibility for products selling for hundreds of thousands of dollars, why must he obtain not only his superior's but his superior's superior's signature on a purchase requisition?

In this case the constraints seem meaningless; the manager finds it time-consuming and uneconomic to follow a procedure that corporate management considers necessary. Furthermore, the manager may very well find that his superiors merely pay lip service to the procedure, since they sign without question any requisitions he brings them. Although it may be arguable whether this is an effective control or constraint, nevertheless the concept is readily explainable; that is, such signatures relate responsibility, not to the project over which the individual has control, but to the position the individual holds in the organizational hierarchy.

The theory of constraints with approval limits is essentially that of unit control, which assumes that control over the limits on individual units gives control over totals. This is debatable, since it might be better to utilize control over totals through budgets and thus have control over the units as integral parts of the budget. In other words, the individual manager would have a budget that, once approved, would serve as authorization for any expenditures contained in the budget. But many firms use both budgets and approval limits so that one will serve as a check on the other. It is not possible for the superior to relax the constraints for his subordinates when he himself is bound by them. He can delegate directly to his subordinates whatever authority he has, but he cannot delegate greater authority than he possesses.

Management must recognize that although the theory of constraints is basic to any theory of business enterprise, overzealous use of constraints will produce an inflexible, ineffective organization. All too often, most public agencies operate on the extreme use of constraints. Legislatures spend considerable time passing detailed legislation to cover every exigency. Such detailed legislation leaves little or no discretion to the public servant responsible for its implementation. The lawmakers and the higher echelons of the public agency have spent all their energies in detailing every aspect of the legislation so that the job of the local manager will be completely constrained. Furthermore, the organization penalizes initiative, and the public servant who makes exceptions to the law, no matter what the circumstances, is likely to be punished. Is it any wonder that public agencies have difficulty attracting high-caliber personnel and are so maligned by the general public? Unfortunately, the tendency in many corporations parallels that of public agencies in their excessive use of constraints and the destruction of initiative on the part of the lower levels of management.

Properly used, the delegation of certain authorities and responsibilities, coupled with recognized and understood constraints on the actions of the manager, permits the organization to obtain the conformity and predictable behavior it needs and gives the manager the opportunity to exercise initiative within the prescribed limits. Such a clear and specific assignment facilitates the delegation process as well as defining the conditions under which the superior is to provide direction.

Excessive constraints on the action of the individual manager destroy the concept of delegation and therefore destroy initiative. The greater the constraints, the less likely it is that individual managers will be encouraged to exercise greater initiative and become more effective managers. In addition, the more elaborate the constraints, the less flexibility there will be in the organization to change direction to meet new exigencies.

Management at all levels must observe the proper balance between the constraints necessary to obtain coordinated effort and the freedom of action required to permit the individual manager to develop and the organization to have flexibility. The organization, like the governmental public agency, cannot legislate every act but must depend upon its managers at all levels to exercise the initiative and discretion necessary to give the organization life. There must be some latitude and room for mistakes, since only through mistakes can management be developed. The skills of management can be learned, but their application can come only through experience, which means the opportunity to make decisions and hence to make mistakes.

The organization structure by its rigidity and permanence is a major constraint in the implementation of management by objectives. The organization objective can work at cross purposes with management by objectives because of the failure to take into account the dynamics of environmental and internal changes in personnel, product mix, and a host of other factors. The structuring of an organization is a complex matter requiring a deep understanding of human behavior, rigidity patterns, and the difficulty of legislating interpersonal relationships. The next three chapters develop an understanding of the skills involved in the structuring and design of an organization.

4

Structuring the Organization

BUSINESS ENTERPRISE, or any organizational entity, must rely upon an organization structure to achieve its objectives. Management is the ingredient that gives an organization structure life. But, as an integral part of the organization, management is also responsible for designing the organization structure. Management, then, is both master and servant of the organization structure.

The development and use of an organization structure is a basic managerial skill. The formal responsibility and authority relationships that permit the manager to achieve his objectives are the direct product of the organization structure, and the structuring of the organization is a formal act determined by management action.

An organization is the framework within which work takes place; its major function is to facilitate work. The accent on the term "facilitate" is necessary, because all too often the organization structure itself is considered to be the all-important factor in a business enterprise. The organization structure cannot be the end; it can only be a means to the end of achieving the objectives formulated for the business enterprise. The objectives must be the determining factor in structuring the organization.

An example of the importance of relating the organization structure and corporate objectives is the case of a firm that had defined its objectives in terms of market share and product lines for extending its present limited line of consumer durable products into a full line. Corporate management felt that such an extension of the company's line would permit the establishment of exclusive franchises for retail outlets, and hence insure better control of the corporation's market. The corporation consisted of two quite separate product divisions, each of which had its own sales force, manufacturing facilities, and so on.

In order to implement the objectives of developing a full line of products, corporate management had to make some basic decisions on organization structure. The product divisions' organization structure had the advantage of permitting the divisional managers to exercise their own judgment on matters affecting their particular product lines. Corporate management had recognized that there was duplication of sales forces, but it felt that such duplication was worth the extra expense in order to provide a concentration of sales effort on each of the product lines.

The organization structure was drastically changed in order to implement the new corporate objectives. Management decided to organize the company into functional areas of sales, finance, and manufacturing and to eliminate the two product divisions, although this meant losing some considerable flexibility in the organization and probably some amount of concentration on the individual product line. Management recognized the shortcomings of the new structure, but felt that such disadvantages would be overcome by the considerable advantages of lack of duplication of the sales force and the possibility of having a more coordinated line of consumer durable goods.

The organization structure may be likened to the human skeleton. The human skeleton permits action when the nervous system calls for such action. If a person wishes to pick up an object, the object must be within grasp of his arms, which receive messages from the brain through the nervous system to grasp the object. If the object is beyond the grasp of the arms, a person cannot take action unless the position of his skeleton is changed. The organization structure, like the human skeleton, comes to life only when management—its nervous system—takes action. Just as the human skeleton has a nervous system for the communication of messages from the brain to the various parts of the body, so does the organization structure in an enterprise serve as the channel for communication from management. The organization structure constrains what can be done, and if action requires coordination that is not possible with the existing structure, the structure must change, just as the position of the human skeleton must change if it is to grasp an objective beyond its reach.

It is important to recognize that action can take place only within the organization as defined. When the organization structure is too limited to take the actions required by management, new appendages or informal organizations grow up within the general framework of the organization structure to achieve results.

FUNCTIONS OF ORGANIZATION

It is the function of the formal organization to set forth the ground rules within which operating management must manage, since it defines formal authority and responsibility in the entire business enterprise. This means that a management and hence the company itself can be no more effective than its organization structure. An organization structure should be as dynamic as business itself, and it must be shaped and reshaped to facilitate the attainment of objectives and the implementation of the strategies and tactics of management.

The major function of organization is to facilitate the attainment of objectives set forth for the enterprise or for one of its parts. Such a function is achieved through organization structure by the division of tasks, which in turn becomes an assignment of responsibilities. In other words, top management uses the organization structure to break down the total task of attaining corporate objectives into subtasks and subobjectives that can be assigned to all levels of management.

Effective organization structure can aid the manager considerably by simplifying his job of coordination. It does this by the compartmentalization of the entire organization into separate sections, each of which is assigned a particular responsibility or task. The very act of creating the organization structure results in the assignment of tasks and responsibilities, as well as the setting forth of a hierarchy for reporting on work accomplishment. Such coordination of functions is possible only if the structure is well designed.

Difficulties arise in organization structure when it is not possible to delineate tasks and responsibilities in a way that will make coordination an automatic byproduct. It is often impossible to organize an enterprise to achieve all the objectives set forth for it. Often the organization structure decided upon must be a compromise that will create additional problems in coordination. Within a simple functional organization structure encompassing sales, manufacturing, financial, and engineering divisions, a company achieves specialization of effort in each of the separate divisions, but has created problems of coordination between divisions. When the engineering division designs a new product, what formal relationships exist to insure that the product can be manufactured and sold? The product development group may very well design a technically excellent product that would be too difficult or too expensive to manufacture.

Part of the problem of coordination can be solved by setting forth specific objectives. For example, the product development group would have as one of its objectives the manufacturability of the product. Nevertheless, the separation of the enterprise into functional areas will result in an organizational identification with the particular division rather than with the company as a whole.

In a company organized by product divisions, there would be separate product development groups containing manufacturing, sales, financial, and others within each product division. This would certainly solve the problem of coordination among the functional areas within a particular product line, but would create new difficulties where there was an overlap between product lines. Furthermore, the lack of functional specialization would result in the weakening of such functions as engineering, possibly with a resulting loss in product innovation. This would create different problems of coordination from those that existed in the functional organization, but there would still be problems. Undoubtedly, it would be difficult to coordinate the common use of manufacturing facilities, if such existed, and there might be a need for a single marketing effort in distributing all the products.

At first sight, the structuring of organization seems fairly simple. The manager, once he has decided upon his objectives, merely has to consider what responsibilities are to be assigned and structure his organization accordingly. Such action assumes, however, that there is one perfect organization structure to fit every situation. Unfortunately, such is not the case. In many ways the literature on organization does a disservice to the practicing executive. It sets forth a number of principles or concepts that are to solve the problems of organization if the manager applies them correctly. Nothing could be further from the truth. Many of these so-called principles are in themselves contradictory. Furthermore, such principles disregard any consideration or assessment of the human beings involved. The implication is that effective coordination and operation of the organization are dependent solely on the drawing of an organization chart.

The organization structure by its very nature is inflexible. Just as it is necessary for Congress or any legislative body to repeal old laws before the government can stop enforcing them, so it is necessary for corporate management to change the old organization before operating management can stop heeding it. This inflexibility of organization structure is both an asset and a liability. It is a liability because of the difficulty of the organization structure's adapting itself to new situations quickly, and it is an asset because such inflexibility means there can be greater predictability of behavior within a relatively unchanging organization structure. It is difficult to picture the inner workings of an organization structure, but they may be likened to the mechanism of a watch. A watch cannot run unless all its parts mesh and work together to fulfill its function of telling time. An organization, like a watch, has many parts, all of which must work together in coordinated effort to achieve the objective of the enterprise. If one part of the watch breaks down, the watch stops and it is not possible to tell time. If one part of the organization fails to carry out its assigned duties and responsibilities, it will be impossible for other parts of the organization to carry out their responsibilities, and so they will fail to attain the objective.

An organization is even more complex. One part must perform its function without definite knowledge that another part is performing *its* function. Each part is basing its actions on the assumption that the other parts will carry out the assigned responsibilities so that coordinated effort may be attained. It is the need for this coordination of effort that makes the organization demand conformity and its attendant predictability of behavior within the organization structure.

ORGANIZATION DESIGN

In order to attain skills in structuring an organization, the manager must be cognizant not only of the purpose of organization but also of some fundamentals of its design. Since the purpose of the organization structure is to facilitate the attainment of objectives and coordination through the division of tasks and assignment of responsibilities, the formation of objectives becomes an important decision that must precede the determination and design of the structure. The objectives will determine the major division of the tasks that are to be accomplished. Furthermore, the manager should realize that the way in which he structures the organization may have a marked effect on the relative emphasis given to the various objectives.

ORGANIZATIONAL GROUPINGS

There are four fundamental ways to group activities in an organization structure. Rarely are such groupings mutually exclusive; most business enterprises use two or more in combination.

Functional grouping. A functional organization, usually consisting of sales or marketing, production or manufacturing, finance or treasury, and similar groups, will be found in every enterprise—if not at the highest level, then at lower levels. It is the most natural grouping, since breaking an activity into functions is the very essence of specialization. The functional organization permits specialization of effort, although it may create problems of coordination if there is a need for some common effort of the enterprise to be the product of the coordinated effort of all functions.

Product or project grouping. Organization by product or project permits a high degree of specialization on a product or project, with the possibility of greater coordination within the product or project divisions. Organization by product, product class, or project is becoming relatively more common as the concept of decentralization of authority spreads throughout industry. If major problems of coordination are to be avoided, there should be a relatively large volume within a product line or project so that facilities within the grouping can be completely independent. It should be noted that product grouping creates a dilution of effort within a functional specialty since it spreads the functions throughout a number of product or project divisions.

The ultimate in organization by product or project is the setting forth of a completely separate organization with its own profit and loss controls. At this point, the real purpose of the larger corporations might be questioned if the product divisions are to function as separate companies. The common use of corporation money and facilities will nevertheless aid the product division and therefore give it an advantage over the small, one-product corporation. But if the corporation does not give the product division sufficient autonomy of action, there will be problems of coordination between the corporate and divisional levels.

Geographical grouping. The use of a geographical organization requires little explanation. The major reason for such a grouping is that the corporation or enterprise has a number of scattered locations. The difficulties of distance in managing geographically separated locations are usually such that it is more effective to grant local autonomy to such plants or branches. But within the geographically organized structure there is usually a further breakdown into organization by function or even by product line.

Clientele or customer grouping. The marketing-oriented firm is often organized on a clientele basis to service particular classes of outlets. The major reason for organization by clientele is to provide a high degree of specialized treatment of the customer, often with a different sales force for each class of customer.

The manager's design of the organization structure will depend upon his assessment of the objectives of both the entire corporation and his part of it. If the objectives stress one activity, such as individual projects, the manager will prefer the type of organization that best satisfies this set of objectives. It must be emphasized that there is rarely a pure organization structure that involves only one grouping; since each organization adapts its structure to its peculiar needs, there is usually some form of hybrid organization structure.

The peculiarity of the objectives and the historical development of an organization will dictate the particular type of organization structure best suited to its needs. But it is not enough to set forth the major divisions of an organization structure. It is also necessary to consider what else is involved in the design of an organization to permit effective management action. Essentially, an organization structure reflects the division of tasks. It must therefore have as one of its primary objectives the assignment of responsibility, which insures that the various subtasks will be carried out to achieve the total task or the objectives.

The Organization Chart and Its Limitations

When the organization structure is set forth with assignment of responsibilities, there is theoretically an automatic assignment of authority to carry through such responsibilities. The organization chart, as the mechanism by which the organization structure is displayed, would seem to indicate by its boxes not only responsibility but also authority. It charts the formal channels of communication and formal relationships. If assignments of responsibility and authority are automatic by the design of the organization structure, why does the average business enterprise experience so many difficulties in the exercise of authority and responsibility?

The organization chart can be considered the map of a territory of management interaction. Yet the organization chart, like the standard roadmap, is not a sufficient guide to insure that the traveler will reach his destination or goal as he plans. For example, the typical roadmap does not show contours. The uninitiated driver who wishes to go from Denver to Salt Lake City or from Zurich to Milan may consider it possible to drive at high speed between the two cities. But when he leaves Denver or Zurich, he soon finds a number of mountain ranges between him and his destination, and his average speed varies considerably from his plan.

When the uninitiated explorer of an organization structure reads the organization chart as his roadmap, he will find that it, too, is not a true map of the territory. The organization chart is a mechanistic approach to charting what the organization structure should be or what it is in the minds of top-level management. What it is in practice is something else again, because middle management changes the organization structure to fit its own needs. The uninitiated person soon finds that in order to understand the organization structure he must explore the territory personally to find short-cuts and quicker routes to the destination or goal.

In the average business enterprise, the organization chart represents the structure designed by top management to assign to various parts of the organization the tasks necessary for achievement of objectives. Such assignments are both initiated and accepted in good faith. But rarely does this procedure recognize the personal objectives of individual managers or their differing philosophies of management. The organization demands and obtains predictability of behavior from its members in terms of servicing the organization as a whole. But such conformity in behavior does not extend to the way in which the individual manager coordinates his part of the organization. As long as the particular part of the organization fulfills the task assigned to it by the totality of the organization, there will be no questions asked of its internal management.

It is possible, then, for two identical parts of the same organization to be managed quite differently. In one part there may be a delegation of both authority and responsibility so that one is commensurate with another. In another part, the individual manager may not delegate authority but may nevertheless pin responsibility on his subordinates. While one part of the organization may be more effective than the other, both may still achieve the tasks assigned to them.

ORGANIZATION AND THE INDIVIDUAL

The organization structure is not a structure of impersonal positions in a hierarchy. It consists of individuals with different personalities and methods gathered together in a common undertaking to achieve a common objective. The manager who does not realize that the human factor is predominant is making a great mistake. He must recognize the human factor and build the organization structure around the peculiarities and personalities of the human beings who constitute the organization. This entails recognition of particular or peculiar motivations of some individuals, as well as differences in the design of the structure.

Organization often results in a conflict of objectives. Such a conflict may exist not only between the individual manager and the organization but also between separate parts of the organization. The effective manager recognizes these conflicts and attempts to resolve them. This may involve a change in attitude on the part of a manager or, alternatively, a change in the organization structure to reflect individual motivations.

An example of the importance of recognizing the particular contributions of individuals in organization structure design is the case of one multidivision corporation that had divisionalized in order to decentralize authority and responsibility to each division and, as a result, had created some organizational problems. Although there were some common corporate facilities, each division was in fact quite autonomous in its operations.

A particular technological advance that took place in the industry cut across the divisional lines. The corporation could best adapt to this technological change by coordinating effort in a number of its divisions to turn out the new product. Corporate management believed any major reorganization that put an end to the autonomy of the divisions would be chaotic and not achieve the best results. The alternative of creating a special division to handle the new technological advance was also vetoed as particularly expensive and time-consuming.

In a general staff meeting, one of the divisional heads suggested a compromise that would permit the attainment of the objective of coordination across all the divisions. He recommended the appointment of a coordinator on the corporate staff level with the responsibility to investigate and coordinate all the activities required for the particular product, regardless of which division was to perform such activities. In the staff meeting, one divisional head expressed his opinion that the use of a coordinator was risky and that, furthermore, he would support the recommendation only if the particular man he had in mind could be given the job. He stated that this manager was brilliant enough to grasp the totality of any situation and persuasive enough to obtain the required coordination without authority. The divisional head went on to say that this man had no special ambitions to be a divisional head, although he had the necessary capabilities and qualifications for such a position, and that here was an excellent chance for the corporation to make the best use of an excellent manager by recognizing his motivations and desires.

This is a fine example of a large corporation's opportunity to adapt its organization structure to a particular individual. There were alternative methods of coordinating this technological advance throughout the various divisions of the corporation, but the one that required the least organizational change involved having just the right man for the job. If this man had not been available, a special coordinator could not have been utilized unless the organization structure had been adapted to different managerial qualifications.

ORGANIZATION AND EXECUTIVE DEVELOPMENT

It has been said that the truly effective business enterprise does not produce or provide services; it builds management. The major

ingredient in the success of any business enterprise is its management. The business can take action only through its management,
and hence its management is in reality the enterprise itself. Although it is possible to recruit on the outside for qualified managers
at all levels, it is more common for firms to develop their own managers. Yet many businesses pay little attention to management development, assuming that the individual who has sufficient interest
and motivation will develop himself or seek training from a special
management development staff.

Although self-motivation is critical, and management training
programs are helpful, the major development of the manager comes
in the course of his work experience. This experience is dictated by
the organization structure much more than by what he himself can
do. While the individual will not necessarily be developed by assignments of jobs or positions through the organization, usually
such experience is the major factor in developing managerial skills.
Although the manager is in a position to dictate to a considerable
extent how he is going to manage his own activities, the formal
organization structure can still be a major limiting or facilitating
factor.

If one of the objectives of structuring an organization is the
development of management, the organization structure should be
designed so that there is considerable challenge for the individual
manager. It is possible to structure an organization so that little or no
latitude is given to the individual manager. Alternatively, it is possible to design the organization in such a way that the individual
manager is given considerable latitude to exercise initiative in carrying out his assigned tasks. It is a recognition of how such latitude
can be used to develop managers that is critical in coordinating management development with organizational design.

ORGANIZATION AND COMMUNICATION

An additional element to consider in the design of an organization structure is that the speed of communication within the organization is directly correlated with the speed of action possible in
the organization. It must be remembered that the formal organization structure is also the formal communication structure. All communication must go through the so-called proper channels, which

are those set forth by the formal organization. For optimal speed of communication, there should be as few levels as possible between action management and decision-making management. Alternatively, the organization structure can be more complex, with additional levels of supervision, but then authority should be decentralized so that decisions will be made at lower levels.

The problem of communication is a critical one in large organizations. The limitation on the number of men who can report effectively to one superior, or the span of control, tends to add echelons of management and slow down the communication process. The pyramiding of managerial echelons can be avoided only by some approach to decentralization and perhaps autonomous divisions.

The structuring of an organization is a critical managerial skill that requires an understanding of such factors as individual differences, the purposes of organization structure in assignment of tasks, communication, management development, and particularly the limitations of organization structures in effecting managerial action. But additional knowledge is required in depth about line and staff, the subject of the next chapter, before the actual planning of an organization structure.

5

Line and Staff Relationships

THE PAST HALF-CENTURY has seen major changes in the role of government, the state of technology, consumption patterns, and ownership in industry. Management has had to devise ways and means to adapt the organization and operation of the firm to these changing conditions.

There has been a major change in the role of government in business from that of a laissez faire attitude to that of considerable governmental intervention in the operation and management of firms. This change has been evolutionary rather than revolutionary, growing out of the demands of society for such things as government guarantee of employment, protection of the consumer, and the like. The result is that the federal and state governments have passed legislation on labor relations, minimum wages, social security, transportation rates, depreciation allowances, and many thousands of other factors affecting business. The government has assumed responsibility for full employment, price stabilization, and economic growth. The role of government has so complicated the business scene that rarely can the individual manager make decisions without seeking the advice of a special staff trained to comprehend the impact of government action on the business enterprise.

Another factor complicating the business scene is an increasingly complex technology. The advances made by science are so rapid that a scientific discovery today may very well make an entire industry obsolete within a very few years. No longer is it a matter of companies within the same industry competing—industries themselves are competing. Aluminum competes with steel; copper competes with aluminum; plastic competes with steel, copper, and aluminum. The ever advancing state of technological progress makes it difficult if not impossible for the manager to remain abreast. One solution to this problem is the development of a special staff to advise the manager of technological advances and to keep an enterprise current in exploiting them.

This century has seen constant change in distribution patterns. The one-price policy in the retail trade no longer seems inviolate. The supermarket has become a variety chain. The variety chain has become a drug store. The department store has become a discount house. Every day sees new patterns of distribution, any of which may undermine the plans of the manager. To deal with such dynamics, a company may require specialists trained in distribution research to provide information for management decisions.

Every year there is greater concentration of resources and greater diversification in industry. As large firms grow larger, they look to other industries and other markets to develop outlets for their excess energies and resources. When one large firm spills over into the markets of another, there will be considerable complications in the industries concerned. The trend to diversification and conglomerates, with the attendant mergers and acquisitions, will suddenly bring the strength of a large corporation to a small firm, with subsequent disturbances in a particular industry. To keep companies current on such trends, management often turns to staff specialists to help the manager comprehend the significance of such moves.

THE EVOLUTION OF STAFF

The staff function is one that proffers advice or specialized services to the line but does not act in formal authority over the line. The line function is one that exercises command over the resources of the enterprise to attain its objectives. In the organization structure, the staff is always an adjunct to the line.

The origin of the staff function concept is credited to the military. The term "line" comes from the military concept of the regiment of the line, which had responsibility for direct action in fighting battles. In the Middle Ages, armies were small and were expected to forage in the countryside for supplies and to carry all the weapons required for battle. When Napoleon enlarged the scope of war to include armies of hundreds of thousands of men, the problems of logistics, intelligence, and supplies often became the decisive factors in victory or defeat. No longer was it possible for the field officer to have sufficient information to fight the enemy or sufficient supplies to maintain his forces. To solve these problems, a staff was created with the responsibility for completing the necessary planning to supply the field or line officers with information and supplies, permitting the officers to perform their major function of fighting.

As the business enterprise became more complex, a similar situation was created. It was no longer possible for the line manager to have extensive knowledge of a number of diverse functions. It became increasingly apparent that a high degree of specialization was required in so many areas that no one manager could be fully qualified in all of them. In addition to specialized advice, there was the need for specialized common services for all line managers in such areas as purchasing and accounting.

THE ROLE OF STAFF

The staff role is commonly misunderstood in management circles, and the popular explanation of the role of staff often contributes to this confusion and misunderstanding. Staff has been characterized as the *thinking* role and line the *doing* role. The line man naturally will resent such a characterization, especially when he considers that normally line managers are more highly paid and that they have the final decision-making authority and responsibility.

The role of staff is to take whatever action is necessary to assist the line manager in the performance of his function. The accent must be on the staff's *servicing* of the line. In an important empirical study conducted on the organization structures of a number of large firms, the authors noted the role played by staff:

> As the managerial process grows in complexity, the time, abilities, and comprehension of single executives become increasingly inadequate and must be supplemented by staff agencies able to furnish specialized assistance and advice. An adequate staff organization, designed to take full advantage of specialized knowledge, concentrated attention, unified effort, and definite accountability for results within its appropriate fields, can go a long way toward relieving the burden and increasing the effectiveness of management. Such an organization may be relied upon (a) to determine needs and formulate appropriate plans, objectives, and controls; (b) to review, coordinate, digest, and pass expert opinion upon proposals; and (c) to keep executives informed of significant developments and thus make it possible for management to concentrate its attention upon matters requiring its consideration.*

The theoretical designation of an activity as line or staff depends entirely upon whether it exercises authority and assumes responsibility for such exercise of authority. (Within a staff organization, staff managers will exercise authority over other staff personnel but never over line managers.) Yet the designation of an activity as staff or line is not the important consideration. What is important is the role that the activity plays in the management process. Is it assigned specific responsibilities for action that *must* be performed if the firm is to attain its objectives? Is the activity in the mainstream of the management process or an adjunct to assist the line manager in the performance of his function?

The staff role exists to facilitate the work of the line. In the simplest of organizations there would probably be no staff. The functions performed by staff in the larger organization are performed by line in the smaller organization. Staff may be considered as more or less a subdivision of the manager's job without the necessary authority to make decisions.

The job of the foreman in a manufacturing concern illustrates the building up of the staff to perform a number of adjunct functions for the foreman. In very small firms, the foreman may very well be

---

* Paul E. Holden, Lounsbury S. Fish, and Hubert L. Smith, *Top-Management Organization and Control* (New York: McGraw-Hill Book Company, 1951), p. 36.

responsible for recruitment, selection, training, engineering, inspection, materials handling, and many other functions. As the firm grows larger and the problems of coordination with other parts of the company grow more difficult, a number of separate staff functions will be added. These staff functions will be responsible for the planning process, but will not have the authority to make final decisions, which must be reserved for the line officer or, in this case, the foreman. The basic role of the foreman to achieve production, meet schedules and costs, and so on is unchanged in the largest concern. But functions such as recruiting, selection, and engineering are assigned to staff where greater expertise is available. The role of the staff is not to supplant the foreman in the performance of his function but either to carry through planning in greater depth than the foreman himself can do or to provide specialized assistance that will permit the foreman to function more effectively.

When the role of staff is merely to permit the subdivision of the manager's tasks, the question may be raised as to why such functions should be staff rather than line. Why shouldn't authority be delegated to the individual who has been designated to carry through the particular function, rather than have the individual in a staff advisory position? It would seem that the concept of staff involves the assignment of responsibility without authority, or with neither responsibility nor authority.

The director of market research in a large company is considered to be in a staff position normally advisory to the vice-president of marketing. When a decision is to be made on the introduction of a new product or a change in pricing policies, the market research director is assigned the task of conducting a survey to determine what reaction the consumer will have to the new policy or product. After the market research director has completed his survey, he reports to the vice-president of marketing and normally makes specific recommendations.

The concept of the staff role is that the director of market research is considered to be an expert in market research but not necessarily able to see the broader implications of product lines, effects on sales volume, and so forth. The decision to introduce a new line or a change in a price must be left to the line officer, in this case the vice-president of marketing.

This is a classic case of the role of staff. If the vice-president of marketing had the specialized ability and the time to conduct a market research survey personally, he would be in a position to use the survey information in making his decision affecting the attainment of the firm's objectives. But time limitations and perhaps lack of technical knowledge make it necessary for him to depend upon specialized staff—in this case, the director of market research. The staff manager's knowledge and experience outside his specialty are usually not extensive enough to make a decision that has ramifications beyond his own function. The vice-president of marketing has limited knowledge of the market research function but is able to relate staff recommendations to the broader function of marketing.

The role of staff is not always so clear-cut. The foreman in a manufacturing concern is charged with responsibility for quality. It is a commonly heard axiom in manufacturing that "quality cannot be inspected into the product, but must be built into it." Yet the question of quality is decided not by the foreman but by policy-making management, perhaps even the board of directors. The engineering department translates the quality standards set by policy-making management into the specifications that are to be followed by the manufacturing division. These specifications cannot be rejected by the foreman, so part of his job is actually removed from his jurisdiction.

To insure adherence to specifications or quality standards, a special staff agency called "quality control" is created. This staff agency determines what manufacturing specifications are required to meet the overall engineering specifications. The term "control" appears in the title of this agency because it does have a control function. The quality control agency is charged with the responsibility of insuring that quality specifications are met. Here is a possible conflict of responsibilities: the foreman is held responsible for quality, and yet there is a special staff agency also charged with this responsibility.

To insure that the quality specifications are met, the quality control agency or even another staff agency of inspection will perform an inspection function. The job of the inspector is to interpret whether a particular part has met the specifications called for and to pass or reject the part. Although the inspector is considered staff, his advice on whether the part meets specifications is so strong that in fact it becomes authority. He has a direct line of communication to the chief inspector and quality control and, through these managers, to the vice-president of manufacturing. If the foreman fails to heed the "advice" of the inspector, the vice-president of manufacturing can give the foreman a directive to do so.

In this illustration, is the inspector performing a part of the foreman's function or is he performing a function independent of the foreman? Is the inspector truly in a staff—and therefore advisory—position to the foreman? If the inspector is wrong, does the foreman have the necessary authority to countermand his decision? The authority of the inspector is actually the authority of the specifications, which were set forth by top maagement. In his staff role the inspector is performing two separate functions: (1) control for top management and (2) inspection for the foreman. Such a dual function can confuse the concept of staff in the mind of the line manager to the point where he feels that he no longer exercises authority in the performance of his function.

Application of the staff concept in organization has led to considerable confusion in the day-to-day operation of the firm. Regardless of such confusion, line and staff organizations are found in a majority of firms. Staff is widely used in a number of different roles in organizations, including control, service, coordination, and the provision of advisory assistance.

A common function needed by all levels of management is likely to be centralized in a staff agency. An example is personnel services; these are normally centralized in the personnel department, which assists operating management in such areas as employment, wages and salary administration, and job evaluation. The centralization of employment in a personnel department relieves the line manager of much of the tedious and routine work of employment and provides the specialized assistance and help of the staff specialist. The personnel department performs an important function for the corporation as well as for the line manager. It sets forth the standard routines and methods for hiring which, after acceptance by top management, become commands to and control over line personnel. Should a line manager fail to adhere to established hiring procedures, the personnel department can give him no direct commands but will communicate his disregard for the procedures to top management. Control is exercised by line personnel, but the information concerning performance that deviates from the standard is collected by a staff agency.

The term "control" connotes command. Yet staff has been defined as a facilitating function, not one of command. Can a staff agency be charged with the function of control? In order to answer this question, we must first define control. As the term is commonly used by management, it does not differentiate between the collection of information and the exercise of the command resulting from such information. For example, cost information relating to the performance of line against a budget is collected by accounting personnel. When actual performance deviates from performance planned according to the budget, such deviation is reported by accounting to top management. Is accounting then exercising control? If it were, the budget director would demand corrective action on the part of the line officer responsible for the deviation.

The budget director is not trained in the line function and does not know the reasons for the deviation. If the budget director were exercising control directly, he could demand slavish adherence to the budget regardless of circumstances. But he does not have the competence to decide whether the budget must be changed to adapt to new circumstances; his competence lies in collecting information that can be used for control by top management, and only in this way can he be said to exercise control. It is the responsibility of the line to exercise control on the basis of the information collected by the staff agency.

Using staff for control purposes can provide greater specialization of function in such areas as personnel and accounting. Because such staff functions serve all line officers, there must be a standardization of procedures, systems and policies for staff, all of which must be approved by top management so that enforcement will carry the highest authority. Through design of control systems, staff facilitates the function of control more than it controls.

The Role of Staff as a Service Agency

A staff service agency is created wherever a number of line operations must share common facilities. It is differentiated from staff as a control function by serving essentially as a facilitating function rather than a reporting function.

In practice, it is difficult to distinguish between the role of staff as a service organization and as a control organization. A purchasing department is organized as a service department to centralize purchasing for an entire organization. The purchasing department provides expert knowledge through its buyers and saves the time and effort of line management. Purchasing extends its services to any line department simultaneously performing a control function for the organization. Only authorized personnel may sign a purchasing requisition, which is an order to purchase. If specifications are set by engineering or a similar function, line production managers may find that purchasing is exercising control over their actions by turning down purchase requisitions that do not fit the original specifications.

In this illustration, the purchasing department obviously serves operating departments but also serves the corporation through the implementation of purchasing policies and procedures. Unfortunately, there is a tendency for service departments to consider that their function is a primary rather than a secondary one. They are inclined to be overzealous in their adherence to system when what is really important is recognition of a common objective with the operating department.

In structuring an organization, the problem arises of whether the service departments or staff should be centralized or decentralized. Should the staff activity report to operating management in each division or department, or should it report to top management through its own staff activity head? A high degree of centralization of a staff activity in a service department permits specialization. But it may also sow the seeds of distrust among operating management. Physical proximity enhances good personal relations. Having the highly centralized department physically separated from the operating departments it serves to create a sense of aloofness that is often fostered by the service department itself, with its highly specialized and highly trained personnel. The attendant distrust of the staff agency may result in poorer management and coordination. The loss of expertise through decentralization may be more than offset by the added acceptance of the staff agency when its subsections work directly with the operating management they serve.

At the start, a service department is created to facilitate the work of operating management. As an enterprise grows in size, the service departments are likely to grow at a much greater rate and to hire personnel with an ever-increasing degree of specialization.

Unfortunately, the more highly trained the individual is in his own specialty, the less breadth and interest he will have in activities not directly related to his own profession. All this serves to split an organization. On one hand, staff pushes highly specialized skills down the throat of operating management; on the other hand, operating managers resist the intrusion of staff into operating affairs. A service department may soon consider that it is sufficient unto itself and may even reach the stage where it fails to recognize that it exists only to serve other departments. It is imperative that top management recognize this tendency in service departments and take whatever steps are necessary to remind them of their primary function: to facilitate the work of operating management.

THE ROLE OF STAFF AS A COORDINATING FUNCTION

It is difficult to structure an organization in such a way that coordination is effected automatically. Each department or division is set up as a specialized activity in order to attain the highest degree of competence among its personnel. This specialization creates problems of coordination, as was the case in a corporation where the research and development function and production were organized as separate line departments. This was done deliberately to attain the highest degree of specialization possible in both departments, although it was recognized that such specialization of effort would make it difficult to achieve the integration and coordination required for the final product.

As a solution to the problem, top management evolved a third function called product planning, which was responsible for coordinating the two functions. In order to retain as much autonomy as possible for each of the functions, product planning was organized as a staff function, with product managers for each of the major products or product lines. These product planners worked closely with their counterparts in production and in research and development, as well as with sales, to insure that each product was salable, manufacturable, and well designed.

The role of the staff manager in a coordinating capacity is a difficult one. He is often charged with the responsibility for insuring coordination, and yet he cannot be given authority. Such a role requires a very special type of personality. The individual must be somewhat ingratiating and persuasive, yet practical. The manager who can handle such a role successfully will prove his worth and will undoubtedly be slated for an important line job. This is contrary to the normal progression of staff personnel.

Staff managers are rarely transferred or promoted to line operating positions. Although the ranks of staff may include the best educated and often the most brilliant men in an organization, rarely is this reserve of managerial personnel tapped for important line positions. Staff jobs are all too often dead-end positions. The starting salary for staff may be higher than for the counterpart in line management, but the top salary rarely approaches that of operating management. The spread between the starting and ending salaries is often limited in staff, as is the opportunity to become president or chairman of the board.

Most of the young men and women in university business schools are training for staff positions rather than completing general management programs. Even in the standard M.B.A. program, with its accent on training for general management, there is a tendency for students to demand training in an area of specialization. In part this may be because most entry jobs in business used to require specialized training. Today, however, more firms are recruiting for management trainees or generalists.

Top management of leading corporations can make more effective use of this reservoir of highly qualified staff personnel. One answer to the problems both of line and staff conflict and of greater utilization of staff executive talent lies in rotating managerial personnel into both staff and line positions. This would remove the stigma of "dirty hands" from the status of the operating manager, would give the operating manager a much better concept of how to use staff most effectively, and would give staff an understanding of line problems.

THE ROLE OF STAFF AS AN ADVISORY FUNCTION

Perhaps the "purest" role of staff is that of adviser. The management of the business enterprise today has many faces and has, as a result, an ever increasing need for specialized advice. When the staff manager is permitted to assume this advisory role he is in a position to develop his own specialty as an end in itself. He owes no special allegiance to any group or function in the enterprise. He can offer his advice and recommendations, realizing full well that his greatest worth to the organization lies in his independence of thought and action.

The proper use of staff in an advisory capacity can assist the line manager in resolving many of his problems. The most important consideration is to permit the staff manager sufficient freedom of action and opportunity to exercise initiative to keep him from feeling that the line officer wishes to hear only the advice that is palatable to him.

The staff role may take many forms in an organization, from that of a control agency to that of a general adviser. In every instance the limitations of staff must be recognized. By its very nature, staff is highly specialized. But the staff member has neither the breadth of knowledge nor the breadth of viewpoint of the line manager, so he cannot make decisions affecting the entire enterprise, even when the knowledge required to make such decisions must come from him. Top management recognizes such limitations in structuring the organization and hence never gives authority, either implicit or explicit, to staff.

THE CONCEPT OF FUNCTIONAL AUTHORITY

The concept of functional authority pervades staff-line relationships. Functional authority exists when the staff manager responsible for a staff activity has control over some part of the activities of a subordinate staff manager who performs the same function in another section of the enterprise, but who is not in a direct subordinate relationship.

A corporation with separate divisions might have both a corporate director of budgets and a divisional budget manager. Since the corporation requires that all budgets be prepared in the same manner, the corporate budget director is given functional authority over the divisional budget manager, even though the latter reports directly to the divisional vice-president. All matters pertaining to the *method* of budget preparation are decided by the corporate director of budgets through functional authority granted by top management. Decisions relating to the *content* of the budget are made by the divisional vice-president and communicated directly to the divisional budget manager. Adherence to the systems and procedures for budget preparation on the part of the line manager results not so much from the relationship as from the delegation of functional authority to the budget director.

The concept of functional authority recognizes that certain staff functions require line compliance with procedures, methods, and systems if staff is to make a contribution to the management and organization of the enterprise. Again, this is a matter of compromise. Ideally the organization structure should be designed with clearcut definitions of authority and responsibility, without the need for special coordinating or control activities under the direction of staff. Yet it is because of these very inconsistencies in organization structure that the staff role was created. Budgets well illustrate this problem of compromise and the need for staff in organization. The president of the corporation is responsible for coordinating all the activities of the enterprise to achieve the objectives. The president delegates the budgeting function to a specialized staff manager with training and experience in budget preparation and supervision. The budget director cannot be a line manager, since his services are essentially an adjunct to the operation of the enterprise rather than an integral part of it.

The president charges the budget director with responsibility for the preparation of budgets. He indicates that, should any difficulties arise, the budget director may turn to him for assistance. He purposely does not give the budget director any authority over the line managers. When the budget director presents his plan to the line managers, they know that it bears the stamp of approval of the president and recognize that they must therefore cooperate with the budget director. Here is the anomaly of the situation: what the president has given the budget director is essentially functional authority over the preparation of budgets by line managers, rather than direct authority.

In this illustration, it is obvious that there can be confusion between line and staff in regard to authority. The line managers are more likely to consider that the budget director has intruded upon the authority granted to them by the president. The budget director probably thinks he has been given a task without the necessary authority to insure that it is performed. Such is the case with functional authority.

The trend toward decentralization of authority and the granting of greater authority and discretion to operating managers has made the problem of functional authority all the more acute. If there is true decentralization of authority, is part of the operating manager's authority usurped when functional authority is granted to staff specialists? The trend is to give greater functional authority than ever under a decentralization-of-authority concept to insure uniformity of managerial methods and policies.

Sometimes a zealous staff can overwork functional authority to the detriment of division autonomy and appropriate divisional action. The independent actions of the divisional executives may then be exercised to deny such functional authority. This was the case in one large corporation that had five major divisions, one of which was by far the best managed and the most profitable. In fact, through its absorption of overhead this major division, under a man named Hooper, undoubtedly carried two or three of the other divisions. The corporation had been organized on the basis that each divisional vice-president had complete authority and power over his own division. Of all the divisional vice-presidents, Hooper was the one man who insisted on this full authority.

Often members of the special staff in the corporation head office, perhaps in order to justify their share of the overhead, would dream up special new procedures which they would impose on their counterparts in the division over which they exercised functional authority. Whenever Hooper's division staff received this official advice (tantamount to commands) to introduce the new techniques or methods, Hooper would dispatch what came to be known as "Hoopergrams" throughout the firm. A typical Hoopergram would read as follows: "Thank you for the special advice you have sent to our Mr. Adams. We acknowledge receipt of same. Please be advised that we do not plan to follow it. (Signed) Hooper."

The concept of functional authority is necessary if the organization is to have conformity of behavior in management action. Such conformity is obtained through the use of common policies and procedures, many of which are originated by staff specialists and must be accepted by operating managers. The major problem lies in deciding how to permit the maximum of discretion and decision to the operating manager without destroying the entity of the organization. Perhaps the use of functional authority may achieve such a goal of conformity, but it may do so at the expense of initiative and discretion at the operating level.

STAFF-LINE OBJECTIVES

The major factor inhibiting smooth working relationships between line and staff is the probable conflict of objectives. The objective of the enterprise is translated by line management into working operating objectives. This is difficult for staff. A staff activity is created to provide both a concentration of attention on a particular activity and a high degree of specialization of function. Although it is true that staff exists only to service line, the provision of the necessary specialized assistants to line requires a high degree of development of the staff activity itself.

Within the staff activity there will automatically be a conflict of objectives, even if there is explicit recognition of the primacy of the objective of servicing the line. Staff will recognize full well the need to develop its own activity to service the line better, but may have to do so at the expense of short-run service. An illustration of the conflict of objectives within a staff department is the case of an industrial engineering department in a manufacturing corporation operating as a staff activity under the direction of the vice-president of manufacturing.

The industrial engineering department manager had recommended to the vice-president of manufacturing that the company evolve a standard data system. The vice-president had in turn received approval of this proposal from the executive committee and agreed to give the industrial engineering department the responsibility of converting the firm to standard data.

As the industrial engineering department manager planned the standard data system, he decided it was necessary to make a number of selected time studies in order to collect sufficient observations for the application of least-squares and regression equations. Although he had requested a special budget for additional manpower, he was told that he would have to evolve the standard data system without any increased budget. He recognized that there would be a conflict of objectives in the short run, since the collection of necessary observations for the system would mean that the department would not be able to render all the services requested for the operation of line departments. Yet he, and obviously top management, felt that priority should be given to the standard data system even though other services would necessarily have to suffer.

Shortly after this policy had been established, the product costing manager from the sales division asked for tentative standards on some new products. The industrial engineering manager said he would be able to provide such services, but the standards would be estimates and there would be a short delay in supplying the information. The product costing manager felt that he was not receiving essential service from the industrial engineering department and complained to his boss.

Shortly thereafter, the standard costs department manager asked the industrial engineering department for a number of restudies of existing standards to ascertain whether some revision in standard costs was necessary. Again the industrial engineering manager indicated that he had given high priority to the new standard data system and that he would be unable to provide this service except where the requested studies coincided with the new standard data system.

Here is a concrete case of a conflict of objectives arising from what the industrial engineering department wished to do in order to provide better services in the long run for operating management. Even if a larger budget had been provided there would have been difficulties in servicing other departments, since the more experienced personnel may have been assigned to the standard data system.

Such a conflict of objectives plagues staff departments. If they become subservient to the demands of line, they will not be carrying through the objectives assigned to them for the development of their specialties. On the other hand, if they fail to provide the necessary services for the line department, there will be a feeling that staff is not servicing line properly. It is indeed difficult to have the line accept the fact that such a conflict of objectives exists, just as it is difficult for staff managers to resolve such a conflict.

The Role of Staff and Usurped Authority

The dictum governing the staff role is that authority may be granted only to the line. Yet the maxim "knowledge is power" may deny this pronouncement. There is no symbol differentiating the status or position of the staff manager from that of the line manager. Both are managers and both exercise command over subordinates. If there is more prestige attached to one job than to the other, often it is the position of the staff manager to which such prestige accrues. In the solution of day-to-day operating problems, rarely is a distinction made between the authority of the staff manager and that of the line manager. Although the organization structure may designate that staff is not to exercise authority in the making of line decisions, actual practice may dictate quite a different view. The strength, ability, and personality of any individual manager may transcend the limits of his job to the point where he may act quite differently from what was originally intended in structuring the organization. There is no way to guarantee that staff managers will not have strong personalities or considerable managerial ability; in fact, such qualifications may be required for the job.

An example of a staff manager's usurpation of line authority took place in a medium-size concern in a marketing-oriented industry that relied quite heavily on market research for the formulation of its marketing strategies. Owing to the heavy market orientation of the industry, the firm was organized into only two divisions, sales and manufacturing, with product development under the jurisdiction of the sales division.

As the company grew, the role of market research increased in importance. Eventually, the vice-president of sales decided to hire a top-notch experienced executive as director of market research. The new director was a dynamic, brilliant man with considerable experience in sales. Since the position had never been clearly defined in the firm, much of the definition was left to the new director.

The new director quickly assumed an important role in marketing decisions. He used the information collected from market research not only to the advantage of the firm but also to his own advantage. Because the information was so vital to the continued success of the firm, both the ability of the new director and the weight of the knowledge he gleaned through market research gave him a position of considerable prestige and status in the organization. The situation soon reached the point where no individual, including the vice-president of sales, could take effective action without this information. Eventually, the new director became the de facto decision maker on marketing strategy.

In this illustration, the vice-president of sales could have taken measures to control the director of market research, but perhaps to his own detriment. There was a high degree of dependence on market research, regardless of its head. Circumstances combined in such a way that the staff usurped line authority.

STAFF-LINE CONFLICTS

One of the major difficulties in a staff-line organization is that the staff function is forced on operating management. The line manager does not necessarily see the need for a staff function or know how he can use it effectively, but top management has decreed that such a staff function be created. The line manager is frequently reminded that staff can have no authority and that all authority rests with the line. In practice, he finds that the staff managers have access to top management and the opportunity to exercise pressure on line managers to follow the dictates of staff.

All too often in the modern industrial organization, the staff manager is so involved with his own specialty that he forgets his primary function: to aid operating management in the fulfillment of its responsibilities. The staff man acts rather like a small boy who, when he is unable to bend the will of his playmates to his own purpose, turns to some higher authority, either a parent or a bigger boy, to assist him. The staff manager has a high degree of specialized knowledge and ability that can assist the line manager. But instead of interesting the line in his project, he may present it to higher management for implementation and enforcement.

Staff is not always to blame. In numerous instances, line managers resist and resent the advice and help of staff. There is also a feeling among line managers that staff really makes more work for the line rather than reducing its load. They look upon staff as the agency causing the manifold increase in paperwork and are often unwilling to make the investment in time that staff requires to simplify the operating manager's job.

Line and staff often misunderstand each other's roles. One remedy adopted by some companies is to insist that the staff "sell" itself to the line. But this is not always possible. The staff agency must deal with many line managers in such a way that it can fulfill its own responsibilities while simultaneously serving the needs of the line.

This requires a certain amount of conformity which it is not possible to "sell" to every manager. The resolution of staff-line conflicts must rest in education. Each must become cognizant of the role of the other. Each must recognize what is required for the other to do an effective job. Perhaps the way to obtain such understanding is to rotate line managers into staff jobs and vice versa.

REAPPRAISAL OF THE STAFF CONCEPT

A reappraisal of the staff concept by management theorists and practicing managers is long overdue. The recent trends in organization toward more decentralization of authority, increasing concentration of resources in fewer and larger concerns, and greater dependence on staff specialists require a reevaluation of the role of staff.

The original tenets in the creation of staff were threefold. The first was that the use of staff would make it possible to subdivide the functions of the operating manager without decreasing either his authority or his scope of activity. The second was that specialized and expert assistance would be provided to the line manager in order to broaden the knowledge that he needed for his decisions and actions. The third tenet was that the use of staff to serve management through a common facility could provide the conformity required by organization without decreasing the scope and authority of the individual line manager. These tenets still apply to the role of staff today. The major problem lies in the area of authority. Though it is basic that staff may never be granted authority over line, there are numerous breaches of this rule. Staff does have authority over line even if only in specific instances where the organization demands conformity by line managers in utilizing staff services.

In many instances, the right of the line to deny the staff is more fiction than truth. When top management condones the actions of staff over line, isn't it fooling itself in saying that staff is always in an advisory position? Isn't it a fiction when top management insists that the foreman must authorize the rate set by the industrial engineer by signing his time-study form? What alternative has the foreman? If the foreman is given the right to veto the standards set by the industrial engineer, top management is saying in effect that the foreman knows more about standard setting than the engineer does.

Top management knows this is not true, for if there is a dispute, rarely will the foreman win the argument over the industrial engineer.

What is in order is the redefinition of staff or, alternatively, the designation of a number of staff agencies as line. Some management theorists have subdivided staff into staff agencies and service departments. The service department is considered to be more a line than a staff organization, with control over those activities strictly within its own province. The major factor is the reconsideration of the staff role and the possible redefinition of some staff agencies into line.

The personnel department exemplifies the confusion of line and staff authorities. The director of personnel in many corporations is increasingly unsure of the role his department is to play. One of the major functions with which he is charged is employment. Top management looks to the personnel department to insure that corporate policies are followed. In order to do an effective job in employment, personnel projects manpower needs. Such a projection is dependent on the cooperation of line management. In order to carry out the process of selection, the personnel department needs job specifications or a listing of the qualifications required of applicants for the job. Personnel must look to line management for this information. The personnel department screens applicants for each job, possibly utilizing psychological tests, before deciding whether the individual is qualified or not. When a number of satisfactory applicants have been found, the personnel department asks the line manager to select the man who seems likely to do the best job for him.

In all steps in the employment process, the efforts of the line manager and the personnel department must be coordinated. The line manager can rarely defy the authority of personnel in each of these steps. He does not have alternative methods of hiring open to him. Although it is true that he may reject all the applicants, it will still be necessary for the personnel department to process additional applicants for the line manager's final choice.

Does the personnel department have authority and jurisdiction over the line manager? Indications are that within the personnel function the personnel department exercises authority over the line. It could be argued that this is the standard role of staff and that the authority is not that of personnel but of top management in authorizing the procedures set up by personnel. How, then, does this situation differ from that of any line manager who also receives his authority from top management?

One possible solution to this impasse between line and staff is to give many of the present staff departments what might be considered a functional role. Each functional department, whether it be personnel, purchasing, or research and development in a manufacturing company, would have complete authority over its own function and matters relating to the performance of that function. This would not destroy the authority of the line manager over his own operations, since he would still be entitled to accept or reject the services provided by the functional department. Line would not have jurisdiction over the functions performed by the functional department.

If the purchasing department were treated solely as a functional department, all matters relating to purchasing, such as vendor relations, gift practices, and negotiations of contracts, would be subject solely to the authority of the director of purchasing. The relationship between the functional department—in this case purchasing—and the line department would be that all purchases must be channeled through the purchasing department. The purchasing department might insist that its procedures be followed, but it would not have the authority to reject any duly authorized purchase. While it is true this is what is done in practice in most purchasing departments, purchasing is considered a staff function or, in some companies, a service department. In reality, purchasing is as much a line department in a manufacturing concern as is research and development.

If such departments as personnel, purchasing, and accounting were designated as functional departments rather than staff, there would be less misunderstanding between these departments and operating management. The true staff agencies such as legal counsel and market research would then be expected to act solely in their advisory capacity. The function of control so despised by operating management when exercised by staff would now be relegated to the functional departments, which might have as their primary objective that of control. Designating certain staff groups as line functional organizations will not in itself solve the problems of organization created by the innovation of the staff-line concept. It could be argued that this functional concept is already an organizational reality, no matter what terms are used.

Technology and management will not become simpler in the decades ahead; on the contrary, they will become much more complex. The generalist or line manager will have greater need for the advice and assistance of staff specialists. The increasing size of the corporation will also create new problems of coordination in utilizing the massive resources of the parent to sharpen the management of the subsidiaries.

Though there is no simple solution to line-staff problems and companies have no alternative but to use staff functions, perhaps the increasing sophistication of computers and of management methods and skills will uncover new forms of organization structure. One such structure might entail the designation of all parts of an organization as functional, as displayed in Exhibit 2.

Central management would evolve the corporate strategies in conjunction with the long-range planning group and program them

Exhibit 2

The Computer-Based Organization Structure of the Future

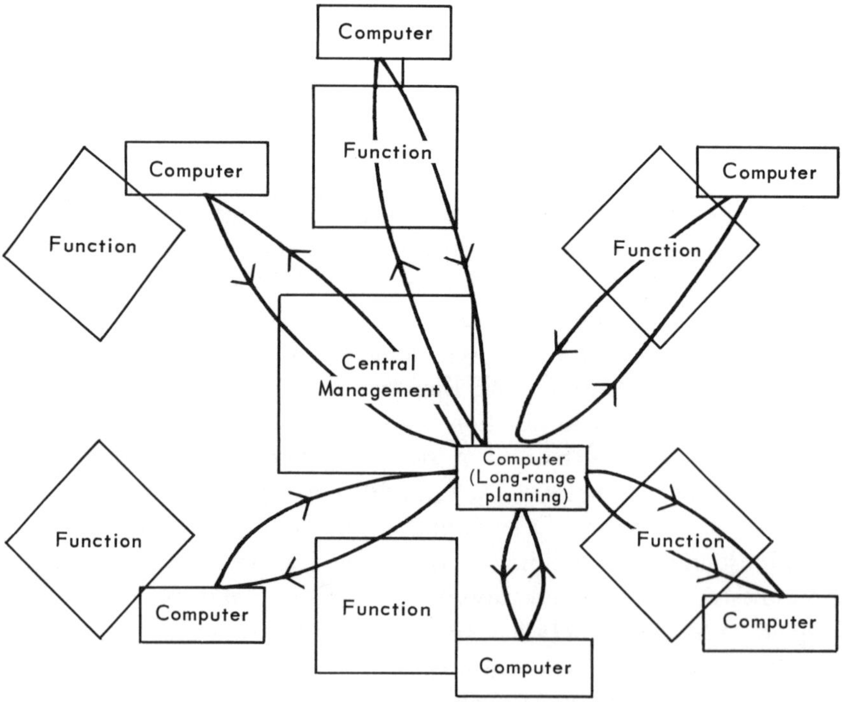

into the central computer. Each functional area, such as engineering, marketing, and finance, would evolve operating plans; these plans would be programmed on the functional computer, which would in turn correlate with the central computer. Unfortunately, until another generation or two of computers and management has passed, companies will have to design organization structures within present limited knowledge and information, with all the existing problems of line and staff.

6

Organization Structure and Delegation of Authority

In DESIGNING an organization structure, the manager is torn between building a tight organization for conformity and control and building a loose structure to permit initiative and discretion at lower levels of management.

An organization must be so structured that management can operate effectively in all conceivable circumstances and situations. It must also provide for the coordination of all separate tasks to attain the corporate or organizational objective. Not only must the various parts of the organization intermesh to achieve the objective, but the separate parts of the organization must be able to function effectively.

Most firms must make a choice between tight controls and centralized decision making, at the expense of individual initiative, and discretionary decision making at lower levels, at the expense of coordination.

There are countless firms at both ends of the spectrum as well as at a number of intermediate points. The increasing complexity of business is pushing organization structure both toward the highly centralized firm, which results in greater speed of communication, and toward the highly decentralized firm, which permits the manager on the local level freedom of action to adjust to local conditions. Which route should the manager take?

CENTRALIZATION VERSUS DECENTRALIZATION

In a highly centralized organization it is necessary not only to refer decisions to higher authority for action but also to provide the information that will permit higher echelons to make the decisions. The information and the need for a decision must be communicated upward in an organization. What is to be gained by making the decision at the higher level? The manager at a lower level must cull the information that he thinks is required for making the decision. Yet the very fact of censoring the information may modify the decision. In other words, the individual who controls the information really controls the decision.

The advocate of the highly centralized organization will emphasize that a better decision will be made at the higher level, where there is greater ability and experience. The higher-echelon manager is undoubtedly more capable and experienced than his counterpart on the lower level, but this does not necessarily guarantee that he will make a better decision. The manager at the lower level knows a great deal more about the particular situation than the higher level manager. Furthermore, he has the opportunity to discover what his subordinates will accept or reject as a decision. Although the manager at the higher level may have a better grasp of corporate objectives and policies, he should communicate such information to the lower levels of management rather than centralize decision making. Operating decisions that will affect the first-line supervisor are best made by him rather than by higher levels of management. The problem is for the first-line supervisor to know when the decision is really one of policy that should be referred to higher management for action.

The following is an illustration of the problem facing the first-line supervisor in determining whether a decision is one that he can make. Excessive absenteeism during a wave of illnesses had put a department behind schedule. The first-line supervisor had to decide how to make up for the lost work and get back on schedule. In the past he had sometimes made the decision to work overtime and sometimes—when he felt that overtime was not the best solution to the problem of meeting schedules—asked his superior for help, in effect referring the decision to higher management. But this time he did not really know whether the authorization of overtime was an operating decision to be made at his level or whether he should refer the decision to higher management, since it might be in the firm's best interests to subcontract the work outside rather than authorizing overtime.

Decisions should be made at the lowest level at which they can be made satisfactorily. The basic premise is that savings or income from the decision must exceed the costs involved in its implementation. But management must estimate the dollar cost of making decisions as well as the dollar savings resulting from them. The question of referral of decisions to higher management is then related to the savings and cost that will be involved.

There are two factors in determining who should make a decision. The first is the cost of making the decision itself. If the president of the firm makes a decision, there is a cost for his salary during the time required to make the decision. But a more important measure of the cost is the income the president could generate by spending his time on other matters. The second factor may be termed the cost involved if the president does *not* make the decision. The issue becomes one of relative magnitude or priority to determine where decisions should be made in the firm.

These cost factors are significant for organization design. To make the optimum use of managerial resources, decision making should be allocated on the basis of the cost of the decision. Decentralization of authority for decision making thus becomes a matter of cost alternatives, not a philosophy of management.

DELEGATION AND DECISION MAKING

Another major factor in the delegation of authority for decision making is the personality or ego characteristics of managers. The manager who insists that all decisions be checked with him is all too common in business. Such a man considers the job of the manager to be that of supervising his subordinates in the performance of their jobs. His motto: If you want a job done properly, do it yourself. He personally checks every part of every job to insure that there are no mistakes. He meticulously collects every possible statistic and completes all reports himself. He complains frequently about being overworked and about the failure of his subordinates to understand their jobs. He takes work home, arrives early on the job, and stays late. In his own eyes, he is the epitome of a good company man. He usually fails to understand why others are promoted when he is not, especially when such individuals apparently do not take the personal interest in their jobs that he does.

Such a manager does not understand the relative costs of decision making. He insists on making decisions that are more expensive for him to make than for his subordinates. He fails to utilize his subordinates to the limit of their abilities, but is inclined to consider them no more than other pairs of hands, which need his brain to operate them. He does not understand the job of managing.

Such personalities are to be found in most organizations, and often the organization structure reflects the same kind of thinking. True, the organization structure itself may not be at fault; the problem may be in the managers who operate within it. Nevertheless the assignment of duties and responsibilities within the organization structure must bear part of the blame. Structure and job assignments determine where and how decisions are made in the organization. A stable firm in a static industry can standardize routine decisions by issuing detailed procedure manuals that permit a high degree of centralization of authority and control. The existence of detailed instructions does not preclude the need for interpretation by the individual responsible for the decision. If decisions have to be continually referred to higher management, such decisions will be time-consuming and hence wasteful of managerial talent in the higher echelons. Even under the most static conditions, it is almost impossible for top management to anticipate all the kinds of decision situations at operating management levels.

This high degree of centralization is an attempt on the part of the designers of the organization to attain maximum coordination, an attempt to condition the reflexes of the organization to provide maximum predictability of behavior. It fails because such centralization leads to rigidity and the eventual inability to adapt to new conditions except through centralized action. So much communication is required that the channels become clogged and sluggish.

Advocates of the highly centralized organization believe high-speed computers will permit the communication of relevant information instantaneously to the central decision-making body. Theoretically, the higher degree of knowledge and sophistication at the head office, coupled with this rapid digestion of data, will provide the necessary flexibility and speed of decision within the highly centralized organization. What is missing in this model is a recognition of the realities of organization structures. The operating manager controls the information needed by the system and may decide to use it for his own ends.

A report from the U.S.S.R. on the effects of a high degree of centralization may serve to illustrate the dangers of overcentralization. In the central planning agency's organization of transportation facilities, a manager was placed in charge of shipping oil in tank cars from point A to point B. The manager was required to submit a report periodically on the number of tank cars he had shipped, compared with a quota that the central planning agency had set for his section.

Trouble in the oil field prevented the refining of the oil for the transportation manager to ship from point A to point B. The manager was in a quandary; he knew there would be an investigation if his periodic report indicated that he had failed to meet his quota, and any falsification of the records would be caught by the check of the railroad's figures against his own. His answer was to fill the tank cars with water and ship them from point A to point B, thus fulfilling his transportation quota.

The Russian manager in this illustration failed to obey the spirit of the law in fulfilling his function. His discretion was severely limited by the central planning agency. He had not been taught to understand the objectives of his job, but only to pay attention to the form. The highly centralized business organization, by depersonalizing and hence failing to develop qualified, reasoning managers, is likely to develop similar errors to the ones found all too frequently in totalitarian countries.

DECENTRALIZATION AND HUMAN MOTIVATIONS

The design of the organization structure must recognize that it is *people* who implement the objectives of the enterprise. It must recognize that the organization must satisfy the needs of the individuals who constitute it if they are to work effectively within the structure. Every person wants to be an integral part of some organization, but not as an appendage to a computer feeding information to a central agency which in turn will make decisions affecting him. He wants to be creative. He wants responsibility. He wants the right of self-determination. These human motivations cannot be satisfied by the highly centralized organization structure.

Because the highly centralized organization structure has the major faults of inflexibility and the inability to satisfy the motivations of those who constitute it, what it gains in management satisfaction and growth, it loses in coordination. Wherever common facilities or responsibilities must be shared in the attainment of a specific objective, the problem of coordination makes the decentralization of authority difficult.

A major motivation for managers is the right of self-determination and personal pride through accomplishment. This concept is contrary to the thinking of many managers in many organizations, who believe that the more authority given the individual, the greater the chance for him to make a major error. Yet somewhere in any organization there is someone charged with the final responsibility for making decisions. Is he infallible?

Man is a strange creature. Fail to trust him and he will not be trustworthy. Trust him and he will go out of his way to justify that trust. This is not to say that every individual should be given the right automatically and immediately to exercise authority and accept responsibility. Such privileges must be given to those who earn them and who are qualified to accept them. But even in some small measure, management and its organization structure should challenge every individual by giving him the opportunity to be trusted and to assume responsibility.

DECENTRALIZATION AND CONTROL

There is no position in a business enterprise that is not subject to constraints, even in the most highly decentralized organization. Such constraints must be held to a minimum if the manager is to feel that he has freedom of action to do what he thinks is necessary to fulfill his responsibility. There must still be coordination of effort within the organization with such decentralization of authority, resulting in the need for balance between centralization and decentralization.

One of the major problems in a decentralized organization involves management's control over subordinate management when there is a high degree of delegation of authority and responsibility. Control sounds rather like the antithesis of decentralization of authority. But delegation does not absolve the organization from responsibility for insuring that each part has completed its task. Control is a major factor in the design of the organization structure, since it is the means for assuring coordination of the activities of the separate parts of the organization. Without control, what assurance is there that the tasks and responsibilities assigned through the organization structure will be carried out? The more standard forms of control are rarely applicable to decentralized management. It does not seem to be in the spirit of decentralization of authority to ask a manager to submit detailed plans of action, especially if veto power is given to the higher managerial levels; this would seem to defeat the very purpose of decentralization of authority. How, then, can control be exercised over decentralized operations?

The best control is no control. This rather dogmatic statement demands explanation. The exercise of controls over plans, decisions, and actions of the decentralized section of the organization will result in an excess of dependence by the manager on the censoring body. It is a fundamental concept of decentralization that the local manager is better qualified than anyone else to make decisions affecting his part of the organization. The exercise of tight controls over his actions denies this concept and defeats the original purpose of such an organization structure. This leaves unanswered the question of how to control decentralized operations. The answer is that controls over decentralized operations must be exercised *on the basis of results*. In a business enterprise, the best such control would be separate records and separate financial statements.

One example of the use of separate cost and other figures for control over decentralized operations is a small company whose products are distributed nationally through 40 branches. The president of the company was a firm believer in the concept of decentralization of authority and designed his organization structure to reflect his philosophy. He wanted to have specialization of effort in such areas as sales administration and sales training, but did not want to interfere in any way with the authority he had given his branch managers. Considering decentralization of authority to be the overriding consideration, he made staff positions of all those in the head office, including the vice-presidential posts, and thus made them advisory to the branch managers. The president remained the only superior to whom the branch managers were responsible.

Each month, complete financial and operating statistics were issued for each branch, including such ratios as inventory turnover and return on investment. Not only did each branch manager have his own figures, but he was given those of all the other branches, although such branches were not identified. The president considered that each branch manager was capable of doing whatever was necessary to make his branch profitable and gave him complete authority to take whatever actions were required to do so. This firm practiced complete decentralization of authority, even to the point of stripping the head office of any power of veto over the branches. The president was also careful to insure that such delegation of authority was complete even in his own relations with his branch managers.

For example, the behavior of newly promoted branch managers in this small firm followed a fairly predictable pattern. After the first few days or weeks on the job, a new manager would usually phone the head office and ask the president what to do to solve a problem. The president would counter with a question: What did the branch manager think he should do? After much discussion, the manager would realize that the president was not going to give him an answer and that it was up to him to solve his own problems. Seeking advice from other head-office officials or other branch managers would have the same result; they too would throw the problem back to him. When asked about his tactics the president said he really meant it when he put his new branch managers in complete charge. He noted further that if he were to solve one problem for them, they would turn to him for answers to all their problems, in which case he might just as well be running all the branches himself.

In this firm, how did the president exercise control over his branch managers? He exercised control by studying monthly financial and operating figures closely and watching to see whether a branch was getting into trouble. When he found that a branch was getting out of control, he could obtain further information from his staff personnel, who were in constant contact with the branch, or visit the branch to see for himself what was happening. He made it a point to visit branches periodically anyway, so a visit was not considered the kiss of death. On his visit he acted rather like an inspector-general, asking questions that would point out to the branch manager what sort of problems he had. But the president would not supply direct answers or take direct action, since he felt that this would rescind the authority he had given his branch managers.

Top management can exercise control over decentralized operations as long as such control does not deprive any local manager of his right to make decisions regarding his own operations. The major control over decentralized operations is through evaluation of results on the basis of financial statements. Such evaluation involves measurement in terms of profit, operating ratio, or other financial ratios that constitute effective management. Once a standard of performance is set and is accepted by the local manager, top management may exercise control by observing the performance of the local manager and comparing it with the standard.

A possible danger not necessarily present in the highly centralized organization is that the control factors on decentralized operations will come into effect only at the end of the period. This greatly increases the danger of loss from ineffective management. However, offsetting such a danger is the fact that the decentralized operation normally is more efficient, because local management can adapt to local situations quickly and effectively.

ECONOMIES OF SCALE AND DECENTRALIZATION

The decentralized organization structure with separate autonomous divisions may not have the same advantages of size as the centralized operations. The large organization has a highly specialized staff to provide services to the entire organization at a much lower cost. If there is complete delegation of authority, as is necessary for maximum effectiveness in a decentralized organization, what advantage is there for the larger corporation with autonomous divisions? Is the corporation to become essentially a holding company or investment company, to garner and dispense funds for the separate divisions? Have the larger corporations grown beyond the optimum size? Certainly a major problem is to keep the advantages of size and yet gain the advantages of managerial effectiveness through decentralization of authority. Perhaps priority should be given to the effectiveness of management under the decentralized organization structure rather than to the advantages of size inherent in the more highly centralized organization.

A number of large corporations have attempted to retain the advantages of size with a decentralized organization structure through the utilization of a corporate staff. According to this concept, the specialized staff at the corporate level has functional authority over its counterpart in the division. The right to command remains with the divisional manager, but there is a line of advice between the staff specialists at the divisional and corporate levels. It is difficult to utilize the corporate staff concept without overemphasizing the power of the staff on one hand or the autonomy of the decentralized division on the other.

In some companies with a corporate staff organization, the divisional staff spends considerable time and effort to avoid doing what the corporate staff recommends. The divisional staff may be of the opinion that the corporate staff knows little or nothing about local conditions and therefore provides little useful advice and help. Often the corporate staff level issues directives which, although they are not commands, have the blessing of corporate top management. Unfortunately, sometimes the corporate staff takes such actions as a move to justify its existence to top management.

This problem of the retention of expertise is a thorny one for the decentralized organization. Ideally, the provision of specialized services at the corporate level without charge to the divisional level should result in retaining the advantage of size without sacrificing managerial initiative. Unfortunately, the separation of the corporate and local staffs by distance and by custom often makes it all but impossible for the corporate level to provide such specialized services.

Multinational companies find it particularly difficult to balance the need for regional and national autonomy and the desire to provide autonomous divisions with the expertise of a highly specialized staff. The very complexity and size of a multinational company complicates communication and decision making; the autonomous divisions must have access to the technological and managerial know-how of the total corporation. But if profit responsibility is highly decentralized, there is a problem of reward or lack of reward for the unit supplying such technological and managerial know-how.

One solution is to designate part of the corporate staff group as formal agents of the decentralized division. For example, the South African division of a Netherlands-based company would have two or three men working in the Netherlands research and development group but on the payroll of the South African division. These men would be constantly searching for technological applications for the division.

Conglomerates also have difficult organizational structure problems. A conglomerate can be considered primarily as a financial manipulation device, but its long-run success depends upon its managerial strength. Since conglomerates are engaged in multiple industries rather than single industries, the usual pattern is to allow a very high degree of individual subsidiary freedom of action and autonomy. But unless the conglomerate greatly strengthens its total management, including the subsidiaries or divisions, its initial earnings growth probably cannot be sustained. The conglomerate will eventually find itself in the same position as the multinational company with the need to strengthen its corporate staff but keep the decentralized autonomy of its subsidiaries and divisions.

The design of an organization structure is a critical managerial skill requiring knowledge not only about the technical considerations of organizational structure but also about human behavior. The next chapter blends these considerations to show how to plan the organizational structure.

7

Planning
the Organization Structure

ONE OF THE MOST critical decisions facing the manager is the design of the organization structure. The limitations placed on the authority and responsibility of an individual have a major impact on his perception and execution of his job and therefore on his effectiveness. The organization structure can facilitate or hinder managerial effectiveness.

The structure of an organization is a major vehicle for carrying out corporate objectives. Structure is difficult to change because changes automatically involve the commitments and aspirations of individuals. The organization structure is, in effect, a mechanical means of giving order to interpersonal relations. Like morals, interpersonal relations cannot really be legislated, yet more physical proximity and social interaction will lead to closer and perhaps deeper interpersonal relations. When organizational changes are instituted, the consequent reordering of interpersonal relationships is resisted and even rejected by the people involved in the change. Furthermore, inertia caused by the failure of individuals to relate to new situations and new interpersonal connections often results in major inefficiencies as a short-term, although not necessarily long-term, result of organizational change.

The inflexibility of an organization structure and the short-term inefficiencies resulting from organizational change make it imperative that organizational changes be initiated infrequently. To avoid frequent changes, the design of the organization structure must be preceded by a critical examination of corporate objectives. For example, if the firm intends to diversify in the near future, the organization structure may have to be designed so as to create a corporate staff that can permit semiautonomous divisions. Failure to make such an examination of objectives may result in the design of an organization structure with a short life span.

The "Ideal" Organization Structure

An organization structure reflects the individual qualifications, strengths, and weaknesses of management. The tendency is strong to design the organization structure with the major constraint of utilizing the current management group. But this does not permit consideration of all the potential alternatives and severely limits potential effectiveness. To guard against this tendency in organization structure design, an "ideal" organization structure should be designed on the premise that appropriately qualified managers are available.

As will be noted later, the capabilities and motivations of management may affect the organizational plans considerably. The question might be asked: Why consider the ideal organization structure, when in reality it is necessary to consider the available managerial talent? The answer is that planning will be severely constrained if nothing but incumbent management is considered. When this constraint is eliminated, the design of the organization structure can come closer to the ideal.

The first step in forming the ideal organization structure is to determine what responsibilities should be assigned in dividing the total task among a number of organizational subsections. The major problem is in obtaining coordination of the various parts of the organization, since the structure can promote or destroy coordination.

The greater the need for managerial coordination across subsections, the more difficult the job of management.

Essentially, the typical organization structure is vertically oriented in its coordinating function. The assignment of responsibility and authority, with each manager reporting to a superior, permits effective coordination vertically but results in far less effective horizontal coordination. Coordination in the standard hierarchy is obtained vertically through command, but must be obtained horizontally through persuasion. Horizontal communication is made much more difficult by the very strict adherence of most organizational entities to the unity-of-command concept, which dictates that each manager or employee have only one superior. There is little question that such unity of command is necessary. Utter chaos would result if each individual in the organization received orders from a number of other individuals, with objectives, orders, and responsibilities all in conflict.

Exhibit 3

Horizontal Coordination and the Unity of Command

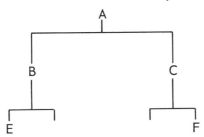

How is horizontal coordination to take place in a vertically oriented organization structure? Exhibit 3 illustrates the necessity for managers E and F to coordinate their activities to accomplish their tasks. In this illustration, E's superior (B) and F's superior (C) both report to A, theoretically permitting A to coordinate E and F through the vertical reporting system. But problems of coordination between E and F would not usually occupy the attention of A. Furthermore, the organization is not structured to facilitate such coordination. It could be argued that if the efforts of E and F need to be coordinated, A should reorganize the structure in such a way that E and F report to one superior, either B or C. But this would conflict with the original rationale of organization, which had a specialized function under B and a different specialized function under C.

One of the most serious pitfalls in the structuring of an organization is the potential conflict between task allocation to assign responsibilities and the overall coordination of functions necessary to achieve corporate objectives. A clear-cut direct assignment of a responsibility may result in the failure to coordinate such an assignment with others; thereby the total task may not be accomplished. This conflict is exemplified by the accent on vertical lines of authority and responsibility to achieve task assignment at the expense of horizontal coordination to attain corporate objectives. Typical are the firms that need close liaison and horizontal coordination between production and sales yet have opted for strong vertical coordination within sales and promotion.

An additional factor in the construction of the ideal organization structure is the problem of control. It is not enough merely to assign responsibilities; the organization, to have coordination of all its activities, must have assurance that all assigned responsibilities are being carried through. This places a heavy responsibility on the organization structure, which must be designed in such a way that control can be readily and easily accomplished.

An example of control's becoming an overriding factor in the assignment of responsibilities is the case of a firm reconsidering its organizational relationships for the purchasing function. This group traditionally had reported to the vice-president of manufacturing. Over time, the corporation lost its place as the industry leader and ceased making a profit. Stockholder action eventually forced the board of directors to replace the chief executive.

Shortly after assuming the position, the new chief executive found that the company was in serious financial difficulties with a shortage of working capital. Further, a great deal of capital was tied up in inventory, much of which was obsolete. As a solution to this problem of lack of inventory control and lack of working capital, the chief executive moved the purchasing function from the manufacturing division to the controller's division. His reasoning was that the company's major commitment for funds was through purchasing, which accounted for more than 50 percent of the sales dollar, and through accumulation of inventory, which ate into the available working capital. The chief executive charged the controller and the purchasing function not only with a reduction in working capital requirements but also with an overall reduction in costs.

Within a year the purchasing function, under the guidance and direction of the controller, had achieved the objectives set forth by the chief executive for the reduction of inventory, use of working capital, and cost of purchased materials. The corporation had changed its organization structure to reflect the need for control as well as for assignment of responsibility.

MATCHING AUTHORITY AND RESPONSIBILITY

A further consideration in the design of the ideal organization structure is the need for sufficient authority to permit the individual manager to carry out his assigned responsibilities. The organization structure as represented by the organization chart is misleading. The charting of the structure is based on the assumption that authority and responsibility are identical and automatic. One of the difficulties in the chart process is to show variations in responsibility and authority for the same general level of management. It is quite possible that one manager will have a much greater degree of authority and responsibility than another at the same level. The organization chart may reflect this by showing this manager in a slightly higher position in the hierarchy, but this is rarely effective. The very nature of a function may be such that a great deal of authority is assigned to an individual whose position in the organizational hierarchy is lower than that of the people he commands.

Examples of the varying problems of functions and levels of management are to be found in military and civilian organizations. In the army, brigades commanded by brigadier generals consist of a number of battalions, each commanded by a colonel. The organizational hierarchy in the military requires that the colonels be responsible to and report to the brigadier general. In the brigade headquarters there is a staff commanded by a brigade major. In some brigades, the brigade major is the tactician responsible for developing the tactics and strategies to be followed in war or war exercises, under the direct command of the brigadier general. The brigade major in turn briefs the battalion colonels on the tactics to be used in each battle. In the military, the rank of colonel is, of course, higher than that of major, but here is the case of a major giving orders to colonels. This is accepted by the military as a typical general staff concept; the brigade major is merely giving orders in the name of the brigadier general.

The problem of levels of management and requisite authority is not limited to military organizations. A manufacturing facility in most organizations will have a production control section responsible for scheduling work through the plant. When an order is received from a customer, the production planning and control section determines what is involved in the manufacturing order and schedules the necessary allocation of men and machines to do the job. Production planning draws up a work schedule calling for the manufacture of certain parts on certain machines at certain times. The schedule is released through a dispatcher on the plant floor. The dispatcher tells the foreman of a particular department what work he is to start, what the completion date is, and what machines to use.

An examination of the organization chart will reveal that the production control section and the dispatcher are staff personnel with no authority over line foremen. Furthermore, the dispatcher is on a much lower level in the organizational hierarchy and is not even a member of management. Here is a further complication in the structuring of an organization by the introduction of staff personnel. In the military, the responsibility for the attainment of objectives belongs to the battalion commanders and to them alone. In the manufacturing organization, the completion of the customer's order is the responsibility of line managers in manufacturing. Is the assignment of authority here commensurate with the responsibility given to the line managers? Unfortunately, even the ideal organization structure cannot solve all the problems of matching authority and responsibility. Solving the problems of coordination may have greater priority than assigning commensurate authority and responsibility. The extensive use of staff in modern organizations is the means by which greater coordination is attained, even at the cost of lessening the authority of line personnel.

An organization structure is a compromise. It cannot anticipate every problem of coordination, assignment of responsibilities, matching authority and responsibility, control, and level of management. The manager must weigh the consequences of one action against those of another. He may decide to give more weight to the control factor, to the assignment of commensurate responsibility, or to other factors in the design of his organization structure. Such an accent on any one factor may make it difficult for operating management to fulfill its tasks. But since the organization structure is a compromise, management must exercise the initiative and ability needed for effective action in spite of the organization structure. This is not to say that management should not try for the ideal in organization structure. But at most the organization structure can aid the able manager in carrying out his task. It can never serve as a substitute for effective management.

Matching Managerial Talents to the Ideal Structure

The next step in planning an organization structure is to modify the ideal structure in light of the availability of managerial talent. Up to this point, the planning has been mechanistic and impersonal, completely disregarding the human factor. But since managers are the lifeblood of the organization, the human factor must be taken into consideration.

In fitting the ideal organization to the existing managerial personnel, first priority must be given to making the most of available talent. In many instances, higher levels of management seriously underrate managers at the lower levels without giving them an opportunity to be tried under battle conditions. Yet if the organization is designed with only the available managerial talent in mind, the result may very well be a second-best structure. When the assignment of responsibility is based solely on what the existing managerial talent is able to handle, the organization will be far different from what it might be if responsibility could be assigned solely on the basis of what needed to be done.

Often, management consultants who are hired to make recommendations on a company's problems find that operating management has already established tentative solutions. In many instances, the consultants merely act as listening posts at the operating managerial level to pick up sufficient information on how operating management would solve the problem if permitted to do so. It is an unfortunate fact that the joke often repeated by business speakers—

that "any manager is an expert fifty miles from home"—is all too often true.

There is far too much dependence on age and status as qualifications for managers, although the practice is not quite as prevalent in the United States as it is in European countries. Perhaps the long apprenticeship required of managers in the average company serves less to train each manager for eventual responsibility than to frustrate him to the point of accepting mediocrity. It is amazing what abilities men show when they are asked to assume responsibilities!

Top management is normally cognizant of the special abilities and limitations of the firm's managerial personnel. When new managers are hired from other firms, the hiring company knows their strengths but not all their limitations. Hiring new managers is not the simple solution to organizational problems that it seems to be. But if qualified managerial talent does not exist in the organization, top management must not hesitate to recruit outsiders for managerial positions. Unfortunately, far too many men in industry have been promoted to positions for which they do not have the qualifications. The organization is always the loser, not only because an ill-qualified manager is ineffective in his job, but also because he must eventually be replaced. Thus the man himself is destroyed, since it is very difficult indeed to accept a position of lower status and lower pay in a company, and the corporation has lost a man who was effective in his previous job.

Just such a promotion of an inadequately qualified man took place in a small firm with national distribution of its products through its own sales force. The company had recently expanded its sales coverage, causing a heavy drain on the time of executives in the head office. The executive vice-president, whose major responsibility was administration of sales, found he could no longer supervise 28 field salesmen. So he decided to promote to the job of sales manager a salesman who seemed to have a good personality, high intelligence, and excellent selling abilities. The vice-president then prepared a job description of both his own job and that of the new sales manager, to permit a division of responsibility and authority between them.

Over a period of two years, it became obvious to the executive vice-president that the sales manager was unsatisfactory. Furthermore, the sales force had been reorganized to include regional sales supervisors. The executive vice-president was at a loss to know what to do with the sales manager. If he was relieved of his position, the company would lose an excellent salesman—perhaps to the competition. On the other hand, if the sales manager remained in his present position, management of the sales function would be ineffective. The vice-president finally solved the problem by establishing a separate sales division with the sales manager responsible for it, but without subordinates. The company continued to pay the sales manager his current salary, although he was really now a salesman rather than a sales manager.

This small company was fortunate in being able to solve the problem created by the promotion of an ill-qualified man without losing the man or destroying the company. But it should have considered the qualifications for the job and selected the man who was qualified to fill it. An opportunistic approach to the structuring of an organization usually ends badly.

When the assessment of existing managerial personnel has been completed and their qualifications matched against the ideals set forth for the organization, the structure can be modified to fit their particular weaknesses and strengths. Not all managers on a particular level will necessarily have reached the same stage of development, so it may be necessary to vary the responsibility and authority assigned to them. Furthermore, the organization structure should be tailored to allow the individual to realize his personal goals as well as those of the firm.

Relating the ideal structure to the realities of existing managerial qualifications and abilities may result in quite drastic modifications, as in the case of a functionally organized company that decided to install a computer and develop computer-based managerial control systems. In assigning the computer and its programming to a particular function in the organization, the president had a choice of the controller, the engineering vice-president, the manufacturing vice-president, or a catch-all vice-president in charge of operations. As he assessed each of the men in turn, the president came to the conclusion that the vice-president of operations had a far greater interest in data processing than any of the other men at his level. Although accounting, under the leadership of the controller, would be the major initial user of the managerial control system, the president decided to assign the computer and programming to the vice-president of operations. He felt that the latter had enough interest in the program to develop a managerial control system that would not be tradition-bound by past accounting methods. In this case the particular function might naturally have fallen under a different head, but the assignment was based on the particular interest and qualifications of the management concerned.

PARTICIPATION IN ORGANIZATION DESIGN

The next step in planning an organization structure is participation by various levels of management in evaluating the plan. The question might be raised at this point whether there can be true participation when the organization structure has already been designed. The problem is to provide both involvement and the expert help needed for organization design. Certainly, there is not enough experience and judgment at lower levels of management to decide what the structure should be for higher levels. Essentially, the participation in this instance is participation by the individual manager in that part of the organization which is directly related to his work. Here his experience and judgment are greater than that of other levels of management, and he should therefore have a voice in assessing whether the structure will permit him to fulfill his responsibilities.

It must be emphasized that the examination of the organization structure by managers at all levels is intended to communicate the prospective decisions of top management in advance of the actual decision, to see whether there are shortcomings from the point of view of the operating manager. The participation of each manager is limited to his section of the organization structure, since subordinates should not pass judgment on superiors, nor should peers judge peers.

COMMITTING THE CHART TO PAPER

The final step in planning the organization structure is to commit it to paper. Organizational planning, manuals, and charts are extensively used in structuring. Although there may be some doubt as to the usefulness of these aids, they are an established part of the organizational pattern of industry.

The organizational chart shows graphically the relationships between functions and individuals in the enterprise. Its main purpose is to define lines of authority, responsibility, and coordination. It is an organizational aid in that it indicates graphically the organizational structure and hence defines executive limits. Most organization charts show only the status quo. They may be likened to a still picture in that they show only the static position of the organization at any one time and cannot reflect its dynamic nature. Of course, the chart reflects the formal or officially sanctioned organization. It therefore does not show all the existing relationships, for merely committing an organization to paper will not define its workings.

THE INFORMAL ORGANIZATION

Three different sets of relationships exist in the average organization, although not all can be indicated by the organization chart. The first set is the formal one of positions, titles, and channels of communication, which are plainly indicated on the chart. The second set of relationships—that of status—is often inferred, because it seems obvious that the chart should indicate the prestige of individuals in the organization structure. However, formal organization alone cannot confer status on the individual; this is something he must earn himself.

The third set of relationships involves the informal lines of communication followed by many managers to avoid red tape. Rarely are these informal lines indicated on the organization chart, because top management either is unaware of them or does not wish to recognize them officially. These informal relationships are tolerated as an alternative to unwieldy lines of communication in a complex organization structure.

The organization chart, although it does not show all three of these important sets of relationships, still performs the important function of defining the formal lines of communication, authority, and responsibility with the firm.

Although the final step in structuring an organization should be committing it to paper in the form of an organization chart, there is some doubt as to whether the chart itself will serve any purpose or will be used once it is committed to paper. However, the chart serves a historical purpose for reference in future redesigning of the organization structure.

An important consideration is communication between those designing the organization and those affected by the design. The structuring of the organization is perhaps the most important direction that top management provides for operating management. Subsequently, operating management will change the organization to achieve its own ends of getting the job done, but, initially, top management has had the opportunity to influence operating management.

Organization manuals and job specifications are important adjuncts to the organization chart. The individual executive is involved in determining job specifications, which delineate authority and responsibility to a greater extent than the organization chart, and also aid in the selection and training of managerial personnel. In some instances, the very preparation of an organization manual and job specifications can expose structural weaknesses and the need for a change in the organization structure.

The organization manual suffers from the same disadvantages as organization charts, since it is essentially a static document that does not portray the dynamic nature of the business enterprise. Operating managers may resent the organization manual, thinking of it as a gimmick required by top management or staff personnel but of little practical use. Yet if used properly it can acquaint a superior with the responsibilities of his subordinates and with any structural weaknesses in his organization.

UTILIZING THE ORGANIZATION STRUCTURE

In planning and developing an organization structure, too little attention is paid to the dynamics of enterprise and too much attention to the statics of the existing structure. One of the most important characteristics of business is its ever changing concept of the role it plays in a dynamic economy. Management is all too likely to consider that organizing is a once-and-for-all function. A manager may devote considerable time and effort to his research and investigation before designing the organization structure, but he rarely considers the need for its revision and rarely evaluates its performance. This is strange, since the manager seldom considers that his operating problems are solved when he has completed detailed planning.

Not only the manager but also the operating levels of management pay little attention to the organization structure once it has been designed. The operating manager is faced with performing under adverse conditions to complete a task. He is preoccupied with the achievement of his goal and, except for specific restrictions on his behavior, he will take whatever path or whatever action is necessary to fulfill his task. When he uses channels of communication other than those established by the formal organization structure, or when he jumps formal chains of command to achieve immediate results, the manager rarely considers that he is in any way breaking the rules. He knows his objectives and those of the organization, and he takes any action that he deems necessary to achieve these objectives.

When the operating manager finds the formal organization structure stultifying in its complexity, preventing him from doing what he feels is right, he merely makes whatever necessary changes he can within his own power. Higher levels of management are inclined to condone such behavior, again because the important consideration is the achievement of objectives. The end result of these attitudes is that the formally planned organization structure does not always serve as the vehicle for achieving results at all levels of management. This means that one of the most important tools available to aid the manager in his acts of coordinating and managing does not necessarily serve the purpose for which it was intended. In some instances, the formal organization structure has become a mockery rather than an effective tool.

How can this important tool be sharpened? How can an organizational structure be designed in such a way that it will be utilized rather than disregarded? The answer to these questions lies in two separate directions. The first is for the managers responsible for the design of organization structures to recognize the dynamic nature of enterprise and constantly revise the structure through appraisal and evaluation of performance. The second is to change the attitude of management toward the concept of an organization structure.

Redesigning the Organization Structure

The organization structure exists to facilitate work. Since work and the achievement of objectives are the major tasks of management, it is the responsibility of management to determine whether the organization structure is in fact facilitating or, as is often the case, hindering work. If the structure makes it difficult for a particular manager to achieve results, he will have to divert his energies to the redesign of the structure on an informal basis so as to get his work done. Any time there is divergence from the formal structure, top management has the responsibility for investigating such divergence and attempting to redesign the organization to permit effective management within it. Effective action cannot be expected in an ineffective organization structure.

It is also possible for the organization structure to be well designed but for the managers to be ill qualified for their posts. This was the case in a medium-size concern that had quadrupled its business over the past decade. During this period of growth, competition in the industry was not sufficient to make heavy demands on the talent of the firm's executives. Since the president of the firm had noticed no particular stresses on his management or on the operations of the company, he maintained essentially the same organization structure with the same executives, even though the workforce was greatly expanded. As more and more firms entered the industry, and as increasing demands were placed on costs and on delivery schedules, performance became steadily poorer.

The president concluded that the executives did not have the ability to manage the larger organization, although they had had excellent qualities for managing the smaller firm. He could now replace his old team with a new team of qualified, competent managers, or he could keep his present management but face the possibility that the situation would worsen. Finally, he decided on a compromise whereby he would keep the old management but bring in younger men to bolster the old management and, if necessary, take command where the older management lacked qualifications. However, this was to be done on an informal basis with the appointment of such men as administrative assistants or assistant managers.

After the president had hired his bright young men and installed them in their positions, he heard rumblings in his organization.

There seemed to be considerable confusion as to which men exercised command under what circumstances. Rather than solving the problem, his action served to create new and more disturbing problems.

This tendency to defer decisions on the replacement of management is all too common in industry. Top management of the firm may have been responsible for promoting the ill-qualified managers in the first instance, but circumstances do change and actions to handle such changes must be initiated at the top. When surgery is necessary in the corporate body, it must be done quickly and cleanly. Although compromise is always a necessary fact of life in any organization, the right to exercise command through organization structure cannot be compromised. When the superior is ineffective, it is next to impossible for the subordinates to be effective.

Whenever there is a change in management personnel, there should be a realignment of responsibilities and hence changes in the organization structure. Personalities do affect the structure, since the organization itself is made up of the interrelationships of people's capabilities and personalities. Often, a change in personnel affords the company's top management an excellent opportunity to realign the structure. What would otherwise have been considered a demotion or loss of prestige for individuals within the organization would now be made palatable if it were known that such changes were necessitated by the promotion, demise, or retirement of a manager. Although an organization structure is a mechanistic attempt to depersonalize an enterprise, the impact and importance of personalities cannot be ignored. The structure should not be considered sacrosanct but should be amended to fit the needs of the personalities who make up the organization.

The organization structure in itself has a number of limitations. One of the most important is that organization structure is not a substitute for good management but only one of its tools. Some managers consider that an organization structure will resolve all problems of management or coordination. Nothing could be further from the truth! It is the manager who must make the structure work, no matter how well it is designed.

Changing management attitudes toward the organization structure is perhaps even more difficult than having top management accept the limitations of the structure. The effective operating manager is action-oriented. He does not consider form for its own sake, but is interested in results. Any organization structure seems to the operating manager more a matter of form than of substance. In other words, all too often he thinks of it as something that hinders him from doing what he considers necessary.

To change the attitude of the operating manager, the structure itself must prove its worth. It must be of such service to him that he is motivated to utilize it. Such an attitude starts with top management, which must make it known that the organization structure will facilitate the work of the manager. This means action on the part of top management and not merely issuing a statement. It means that top management must continually amend the structure to meet the needs of operating management. It is only when managers at all levels recognize the need to utilize the organization structure or abandon it that they will pay sufficient attention to the formal organization structure.

8

Planning
and Organizational Realities

Planning complements other management skills. It is both a prerequisite to and a means of attaining objectives. Leadership involves planning, both to provide a sense of order and decisiveness and to develop the best means of motivating individuals. The organization structure determines responsibilities and authorities for planning and sets the stage for its implementation.

The environment within which planning takes place is a major factor affecting the manager's ability to plan. Planning, like the other management skills, is conceptually simple. It is something that every manager does; it involves timetables, cost factors, and similar elements that must be ordered in a business enterprise. But its simplicity is deceptive. The planning process, or its closely allied decision process, may detail the precedures or processes for formulating plans or decisions. Certainly, it is important to understand these processes and procedures. But mere procedures do not guarantee effective planning or decision making, and planning cannot be merely an intellectual process. Operational difficulties and environmental conditions can often act against both the development and the implementation of plans.

THE PLANNING ENVIRONMENT

An examination of the planning process can be mechanistic and somewhat procedural. Certainly it is important to know what planning is, how it is to be accomplished, and what part it plays in the management process. It is also important to understand the environment within which planning must operate. A recognition of these realities of organization life and their effect on the planning process is an important prerequisite to planning.

Planning in some form is an absolute requirement for effective management. Often it is not even an overt act on the part of the manager. Often it is opportunistic and given insufficient priority. The only way to understand these shortcomings is to understand the realities of organization in a business enterprise.

A manager is charged by his superiors with the attainment of results. As long as he conforms to the practices of the organization, few questions are asked about his methods. He may gain procedural assistance through the creation of staff functions, but, in the short run, this assistance may prove to be more hindrance than help.

An example of such a staff aid might be the centralization of hiring through a personnel department. Its purpose is to relieve the manager of the need to find and test job applicants, thus allowing him more time to carry out his main task of coordinating the resources allocated to him to attain the objective. Yet in reality the personnel department may complicate the manager's job. For example, it may require time-consuming procedural information from him. Delays within the personnel department, or difficulties in writing job specifications, may even delay the hiring process.

It is true that in the long run the special procedures of the personnel department will aid the manager in the attainment of his objectives; but in the short run they may only frustrate him and keep him from performing his tasks. This is not to say that centralized employment procedures should be eliminated; it merely presents a reality of organizational life that may in some way constrain the manager from immediate action.

The organization demands conformity to its procedures and methods to permit predictability. Such conformity, although necessary, creates a high degree of inflexibility within the organization. The price paid by the individual manager for such conformity may be increased difficulty in attaining his own objectives in the process of facilitating the attainment of total corporate objectives.

PERSUASION AND BARGAINING NETWORKS

The manager, when faced with these formal hurdles to action, soon sees that he must find some informal way to attain his objectives. His major weapons are persuasion and bargaining. That is, he must persuade others who are not under his control to assist him, which may involve a certain amount of bargaining, or trading of favors, with another manager so that both may achieve their objectives.

The individual manager is action-oriented. When the organization structure gets in the way of his objectives, he will attempt to create an environment to permit him to fulfill his responsibilities. Is this wrong? Only when it makes the attainment of the total corporate task difficult or impossible. The neophyte in management will insist that the organization structure is not fulfilling its function if individual managers must create special networks in order to achieve the tasks assigned to them. But the organization must serve many masters. The designers of the structure, normally top management, must make a number of value judgments as to which of these purposes has priority over the others. The organization structure is a compromise that cannot possibly meet the organizational needs of all managers or be all things to all men.

A further difficulty for the individual manager is the fact that his plans must involve others not under his control. This problem, when coupled with a lack of overall or master planning, often causes the failure of planning in a firm. For example, there must be a meshing of plans where there is dependence on some common facility. The individual manager may be wasting his time in attempting to plan his activities, unless others utilizing this common facility also plan and advise him of their needs in advance. The failure of one group of managers to plan will make it impossible for others to plan.

Authority and Managerial Hierarchy

At first sight, the rationale of organization—with its precepts about authority, responsibility, the scalar principle, and the like—seems to simplify the task of management. One precept often quoted is that authority must be commensurate with responsibility. Yet even the premise about authority may prove to be invalid. According to this precept, authority is delegated by the organization to its officers, who in turn may delegate to subordinates. This implies that authority is conferred essentially by position. Applying this concept to planning, the manager must be given the necessary authority to plan and must therefore be in a position to carry out his responsibility.

But in application it is indeed difficult to make this authority and responsibility commensurate. This was the case in a firm which had contracts to develop, design, and build defense products. The company's major activity, the one that required the greatest outlay of funds, was design and development. But the contract also called for the manufacture of a limited number of products. Engineering (including research and development activities), manufacturing, and sales were separate divisions, and within each there was a further breakdown of organization by project. Although each project had both engineering and manufacturing components, the organizational hierarchy separated the responsibilities by division. The project engineering manager reported to the vice-president of engineering, and the project manufacturing manager reported to the vice-president of manufacturing. There was no official or formal liaison between the project managers in engineering and manufacturing.

Authority was formally delegated to each project manager in engineering and in manufacturing from his superior. Although for organizational purposes there was a separation of engineering and manufacturing into projects, such a separation was in fact artificial. Whatever the engineers developed and designed had to be manufacturable. No matter how much authority had been delegated by the vice-president of manufacturing to the manufacturing project manager, it would be impossible for him to carry out his responsibility of building a product if engineering did not design the product in such a way that manufacturing could build it with its facilities.

Similarly, the engineering project manager was charged with the responsibilty for the so-called integrity of the product. In other words, the overall quality standards had to be designed into the product by engineering. But in fact it was quite possible that the process chosen by manufacturing to fulfill the specifications set by engineering would not fulfill the integrity requirements. How, then, were these project managers given the necessary authority to carry out their responsibilities? The design of the structure prevented the delegation of the authority needed to discharge the assigned responsibilities. Even under the traditional concept of authority granted by superiors, it is indeed difficult to give commensurate authority and responsibility.

The traditional definition of authority does not admit the existence of a social system in the firm, a system that may or may not accept such authority. But it does exist, and the manager, in his attempts to plan, must deal with it. Equally important to the organization structure is what might be termed the power-and-influence hierarchy, which could also be called company politics. The manager cannot depend solely upon the formal or legitimate structure.

UNCERTAINTIES IN PLANNING

Cognizance of organizational realities is a necessary prerequisite to planning. The meaning and problems of authority, of management levels, and of horizontal integration of plans are all factors affecting the efficiency of planning. But in addition there are a number of what can be called operational difficulties. A parallel exists in the operational difficulties of military planning. The army collects the best possible intelligence about the plans of the enemy and the location of its tanks, artillery, and the like; assembles topographical maps of the territory; deploys its own forces and facilities; and considers problems of supply and logistics.

From this collection of information, army commanders make a plan of attack for an ensuing battle. The plan is disseminated to the commanders of the various parts of the army, and detail plans are completed for other military support systems and logistics. But this is not the end of the planning process. The army commander who commits his forces to battle also arranges for information to be transmitted to his headquarters on the progress of his plan.

During the battle it may be found that the intelligence about the enemy's positions was incorrect. The topographical map may not have been completely accurate. The relative strength of forces may have been misjudged. There may have been certain inherent weaknesses in the plan that did not come to light until the forces had been committed to battle. As reports flow in, the army commander must adjust his plan to deal with the changes in circumstances. His objective is unchanged—to defeat the enemy—but his plan must be constantly changed to insure the attainment of this objective.

In business planning, an assessment of the competition may be incorrect, or the competition may have developed new strategies. The planned manufacturing processes may be inadequate. There may be a strike by suppliers. Every plan, no matter how well formulated, will have such operational difficulties. Additional difficulties include the problem of speed. A high priority given to timely accomplishment of the task may overemphasize the need for action at the expense of planning. Although there may be a detailed plan to handle particular circumstances, the urge to action may cause operating management to overlook the plan and take opportunistic, short-run action. This sense of urgency and need for action often reduces the amount and depth of planning in the firm.

DETAILS AND ERRORS IN PLANNING

There is a tendency toward a high degree of detail in planning. This tendency may evidence itself in an attempt to predict every eventuality and legislate every possible action. The planner may forget that human beings, including himself, are fallible. Planning is itself essentially an aggregate, an integration of the thoughts and actions of many people, and, as an aggregate, it is essentially a compromise.

The aggregative process of planning involves many people and has a high propensity for error. These errors are different from those committed by one individual in preparing a plan. The individual has a tendency to make value judgments that may prove to be incorrect. Usually, aggregative planning corrects for errors in value judgment, but introduces errors caused by compromise and variations in frames of reference.

There are also major errors involved in predicting uncertainties. "Uncertainties" are defined as unpredictable events or factors, unlike "risks," whose predictability permits some form of action to insure against failure. A plan is only as good as the premises on which it is based. If the basic environmental or internal conditions change, the plan is invalidated. The fact is that planning is not exact either in formulation or in implementation. Yet all too often, miracles are expected from planning.

There is a tendency to consider that committing a plan to paper concludes the planning job. But this is not the case, since there are major problems both in the implementation of the plan and in its adequacy to attain the objectives. These errors of aggregation and failures of the plan in spite of elaborate detail incline the manager to abandon planning, at least as an activity demanding his highest intellectual abilities and time priorities.

THE CASE FOR PLANNING

Planning is a time-consuming and difficult task. Most managers find it difficult to allocate time for it and often find the intellectual process constraining. At this point, if a manager finds that planning is not doing all the wonderful things he anticipated, he may decide that his time could be better spent on supervision, control, or other jobs.

But, on balance, planning has more pluses than minuses. It permits the manager to sort out the variables that affect his managing, and it also forces him to attempt to predict uncertainties. In addition, it forces him to consider what relationships must be established with other parts of the organization or with firms or institutions outside the organization. The prediction of the interrelationships involved in operations allows the manager to anticipate the problem of inadequate lead time to accomplish some important aspects of his operations.

The manager, like people in general, is looking for panaceas. The history of management is replete with examples of vanished fads and fancies that were once considered the answer to all problems. Taylor's scientific management was one of the earliest of these fads. Operations research and program evaluation and review techniques

(PERT) are two of the latest. But planning is no panacea. It is merely one of the tools that can simplify the manager's job. If he recognizes the potential shortcomings of planning, he will be in a position to use it more wisely.

ELEMENTS OF PLANNING

In formulating plans, the manager should document his premises explicitly, stating exactly what conditions or premises underlie his plans. He should also attempt to predict the alternative conditions that might come into play in the future and affect his plans. If possible, these predicted uncertainties should form part of the plan, with separate skeleton plans to handle each of them should they occur. At this point, the manager has recognized that his planning is not infallible. He has noted what possible changes might be necessary in his plan when the basic conditions under which the original plan was formulated no longer hold true.

The manager must also be careful not to detail his planning in such a way that, should one detail prove to be incorrect, the entire plan will have to be scrapped. It is difficult for the manager who is precise by nature to accept this condition. He may feel that detail is required in the plan if it is to be sufficiently comprehensive to cover any situation. But the greater the detail, the greater the potential for error and the greater the difficulty of implementing the plan.

The manager must build flexibility into his plans. It is true that he cannot leave sections of the work unplanned, although it may be possible to have the detail in one section independent of that in other sections. One possible solution is to use planning the way top management uses policies. Top management sets policies to serve as broad guides to action so as to permit operating management maximum discretion and flexibility within predetermined limits. Planning can be used in a similar way, except that plans must have greater detail and usually have a shorter life than policies. The planning process becomes the means for delegating both discretionary powers and specified tasks from one level of management to the next. The operating manager develops the details of that section of the plan for which he is responsible.

Since the master plan sets forth timetables, costs, and other limits to delegated authority, the operating manager need not submit his own plans to his superior for approval. He will stand or fall solely on his ability to plan and carry through the discretionary powers given to him through the planning process of his superiors. Planning can be integrated through the evolution of plans at every level of management to carry through the plans of the next higher level of management. This relieves operating managers of the necessity of detailed planning for subordinates and allows more time to consider alternative plans of action and to ascertain whether the original premises hold true throughout the life of the plan.

PLANNING IN ACTION

The manager must understand the organizational environment within which he is planning, if such planning is to be effective, and he must condition his plans and their implementation to fit this environment. But specifically, what is the design of a plan? A good illustration is the concrete plan (greatly simplified here) for the marketing of a commercial application of a military product in a firm primarily engaged in defense work.

In this case, firm responsibility for product planning was vested in a product planning committee whose members came from the functional divisions. This committee reported its recommendation to the president and was then responsible for formulating plans to implement the recommendation. Since a recommendation for new products had to contain all the relevant cost and time considerations, it was necessary to make fairly extensive plans before the recommendation. In the case of one particular product, the preliminary investigations had been completed by the president himself in discussions with company personnel and with two potential customers. The president then asked the committee to develop plans for its introduction or, if the product was not feasible, detailed reasons for its rejection. The product planning committee first evaluated the ability of this product to contribute to the objectives of the firm. The next step was to assess both marketing and cost.

Marketing considerations. The first question was whether the product could be sold through existing channels of distribution. In this case the answer was no, since the product would be sold to a new industry. This involved developing a plan for the recruiting and training of a special sales force. An equally important determination was the market potential for the product, which was considered adequate. Here, as in other phases of the development of a plan, the committee utilized staff services—in this instance, the marketing group.

The products, prices, and services of major competitors were studied. Decisions on price had to be incorporated in the plan: Should the price be higher than, the same as, or lower than that of competitors? A decision also had to be reached on whether maintenance would be supplied cost-free to the customer, partially subsidized by the company, or fully charged to the customer. Another major variable was the quality of the product compared with competitors' products. In this case, there was also a technological question of whether the product, a machine, should be designed to have greater speed of operation than that of the competitors' products, which would involve greater costs and therefore a higher price.

Cost considerations. Operating management of the firm supplied detailed information on manufacturing and other costs involved in the design, manufacture, and distribution of the product. Naturally, the decisions on price, maintenance, quality, and speed of operation all had considerable effect on the costs involved in manufacturing and distribution. A major cost was that of product development, which would have appreciable effect on the total costs. In fact, this was such a crucial area that, had the development costs been too high, the entire project would have had to be discontinued.

Another major cost consideration involved manufacturing. In this instance, manufacturing costs were not as easily determined as might normally be the case. In manufacturing defense products, the cost of components had traditionally been considered less important than design costs, because of limited production runs. But in the manufacturing of commercial products, where a larger production run was contemplated, the cost of components became a crucial factor.

An additional cost was that involved in developing the product quickly enough to capture the market ahead of competition. What would be the cost of a crash program to hit the market with the product before competition could change tactics or products? A high cost requirement for such a program was calculated as one of the variables in the total plan for the marketing of this product. The maintenance costs were also a consideration, since, if manufacturing costs were lowered, the product would require more maintenance. This in turn would depend in part upon whether the market could accept a product that cost more in operation and less in initial cost.

A final cost to be considered was marketing. Was it necessary to develop special salesmen or special promotional devices? Perhaps a lower product price would lower the cost for marketing; alternatively, a higher product price might require a much higher marketing cost.

Personnel considerations. During the planning for the development and introduction of this product, existing personnel had to be measured against the projected personnel needs. Were there any available employees with the necessary technical skills to perform design and manufacturing operations? Were sufficient managerial people available to carry through the project? Would the use of these personnel rob other projects that required their specialized skills? If such personnel were not available in the company, could they be obtained in the general labor market? This required a more precise plan to phase personnel into and out of the program.

Facilities considerations. The initial study of facilities determined whether they were adequate for the new project. But even if the facilities were adequate, it was still necessary to plan their effective utilization and integration with the project needs. Were the research facilities adequate for the design of this particular product? What replanning had to be done on other projects to permit the joint use of research facilities? Would new quarters or new plans be required for the research facilities? Comparable questions were asked in manufacturing. Alternative plans for the utilization of subcontractors were completed should manufacturing facilities not be available.

The planning of installation, sales, and servicing was a particularly complex problem. It was difficult to determine whether the present facilities could be utilized effectively or not. It was difficult even to decide whether the present facilities were being fully utilized and what special training would be required to permit their full use. All decisions depended on the design of the product, and the design itself would not be available for some time. The planning was complicated further by the physical distribution of these particular facilities, which made it difficult to coordinate them centrally until sales were actually made.

This is but the briefest description of the factors involved in developing a plan. The factors themselves of course change with each situation. Furthermore, this summary does not consider such problems as jurisdictional disputes, difficulty of obtaining accurate information, and other organizational realities. But it does provide an outline and some idea of the process and detail of planning.

Planning and Organizational Realities in Review

Planning seems deceptively simple, but in practice it is one of the most difficult of the management skills and in some ways the very essence of management. No manager can lead without some plan of action for his exercise of leadership. Controls themselves are the product of planning.

There is little quarrel with the importance accorded to the development of planning skills. The problem lies, not with the need to priority-rate planning, but with its implementation by management. The effective use of planning is conditioned by what could be termed organizational realities. One such reality is the built-in inflexibility of the organization to deal with the individual manager's problems. The organization is designed to perform services for the greatest number of managers or to give the greatest priority to particular objectives. Furthermore, the structure and its procedures are designed for the long-term operation of the firm. Functional authority will permit the development of standard procedures and the introduction of expertise through staff. But such constraints complicate planning, although they are best for the organization and also for the individual manager in the long run.

A far more important reality is the need for the interdependence of planning and the difficulty of unilateral action. The organization structure and its procedures tie the firm together so that joint action is possible, but it rarely provides for joint planning. Planning is something charged to the individual manager as a task, but, with the exception of what might be called master plans (such as budgets), it is not coordinated through structure and procedures. This may result in one manager's plans being thwarted by the lack of planning on the part of his fellow managers. The existence of a social system within the firm and its effect on the formally constituted managerial hierarchy also complicate planning. The formal structure may call for planning procedures different from those dictated by the informal structure. Here the manager must learn to cope with this ever changing complex of the social system and pattern his planning procedures accordingly.

Planning is a dynamic process affected by changes in external and internal environments. It deals with uncertainties and can therefore never predict with perfect accuracy. But since the job of management is to deal with uncertainties, planning serves at least to reduce the uncertainties to alternative courses of action. The manager can then decide among the alternatives to develop a plan of action.

Planning can also be an aid to delegation, since the plan serves to set forth the limits of delegated authority or discretion. But if planning is too detailed, it inhibits delegation and gives rise to inflexibility. Plans must be constantly upgraded with current information and intelligence, which requires limited detail and great flexibility.

The organizational realities of structure and power patterns, coupled with the problems of uncertainty, competitive action, and the like, greatly complicate the planning task of the manager. But effective planning can mean the difference between success and failure. It can even affect survival of the firm. Effective planning requires information and involves decision making and controls. Subsequent chapters develop these factors in considerable depth.

9

Information Systems
and the Planning Process

THE DETERMINATION and formulation of plans require current, accurate information. Much of this current information is available through the standard, routine collection of information for control purposes. The collection of cost information for financial statements, of standard times for production planning and control, and of sales call reports is usually a standard routine. Although such information may not be in the form required for current planning, it is often available in some part of the organization. But when plans are being formulated to handle a completely new situation, the process may be thwarted because of the lead time required to collect the information on which the planning is to be based.

An illustration of the difficulty involved in planning when input information is unavailable occurred in one firm whose competitor had established a 48-hour delivery on products previously sold on a two-week delivery basis. Immediately, top management decreed a 48-hour delivery to meet competition, and operating management was delegated the task of attaining the new goal.

It was at this point that information became crucial. Although standards had been set on machining time for each operation and on assembly of the products, there was insufficient information on the total time it took to manufacture and assemble the products. How long did it take for products to go from one point to another in the plant? How much in-process inventory would be required? How large a finished inventory would be necessary to meet the 48-hour delivery schedule? What were the seasonal and annual trends of sales on each of the standard products?

This information was not readily available from existing records. In fact, the collection of the information would have gone on far beyond the deadline given to operating management to put the new delivery plan into effect. The end result was a hit-or-miss, trial-and-error plan that left the firm with heavy costs and loss of customer goodwill. In this example, management had not anticipated the action of competitors to the point of planning alternative courses of action. But there will always be instances of insufficient lead time to permit the collection of the requisite information for adequate planning. This is but another illustration of the need for planning.

ACCOUNTING SYSTEMS AND INFORMATION

A wealth of information exists in every organization. There is, in fact, a tendency to collect too much information rather than too little. Although data collection and retention are costly, businesses amass a great deal of miscellaneous information without considering its ultimate utilization or its cost. But the major problem is how to tap this information to obtain meaningful data. It is imperative to have specific objectives for the collection of information or the firm will be burdened with excessive clerical and administrative costs.

A knowledge of the existing information network and the types of information available can be invaluable to management. There are many routine reports that can supply the manager with the basic data for planning. Much of this information is collected by accounting, but for the most part it is not in a form suitable for planning.

There has been much criticism of accounting information. Operating managers often state that accounting information is not meaningful for operating purposes. Certainly it is true that accounting does not necessarily assemble information that the operating manager can utilize in its present form. Furthermore, much of the information is essentially historical in nature and is collected more for tax-recording purposes than for decision making. While all this may be true, not all the blame can be leveled at accounting.

Accounting is a staff activity often restricted in function. It is vitally interested in upgrading its services to management by providing the type of information required by operating management, but operating management must indicate to the accounting division what information it requires for effective decision making. This calls for a great deal of thought and investigation by operating management, a great deal more thought than is common in the average firm.

Wherever possible, operating managers should utilize existing information. Many routine reports can serve their needs. By familiarizing themselves with these pieces of routine information, as well as with the standard information collected by accounting, they can prepare in advance to assemble the information required for detailed operating plans. If a manager institutes his own information collection system without reference to existing systems, he will put the company to great expense.

COMMUNICATION PATTERNS AND INFORMATION NETWORKS

Information networks are widespread throughout organizations. Superimposed on the formal vertical communications network of the organization structure are the cross-relationships essential for the operation of the firm. An example is the cross-relationship between purchasing and the other parts of the firm. Operationally, purchase requisitions are routed directly to purchasing from a requisitioning department. Although the formal organization structure rarely shows any link between the requisitioner and purchasing, the operational demands of the firm require formal communication between these parties. Construction of both the formal and the informal overlay of communications patterns would show definite relationships between many parts of the firm and purchasing. Many of these patterns are a result of formal procedures, but a number of other patterns are set up informally by managers requiring information for planning.

A major distinction is made between communication that requires action and communication that provides information. Action
communication more closely approximates the formal organization
structure than does information communication. The information
communication may not necessarily receive or require formal approval, since it serves as a form of planning intelligence for operating
management. An example of such an informal communication and
information network existed in one firm between the receiving and
operating departments. In this firm, the procedure manual required
that receiving reports perform the functions of informing (1) purchasing that the order had been delivered, (2) the requisitioner that
the order had been received, and (3) accounts payable that the supplier's invoice could be paid. Accounts payable verified that the
original purchase order, the supplier's invoice, and the receiving
report matched.

In this case, the requisitioner of purchased parts was the inventory control section of production control, not the ultimate user.
The paper flow was so involved that information from inventory
control to the department using the materials took a few days. In
many instances, the materials in question were in short supply, sub-
jecting the user department to long and anxious waiting periods.
User departments were cognizant of the inherent delay in the procedures; individual managers in the manufacturing departments
made a practice of checking with the receiving department to see
whether critical items had been delivered. But this was haphazard
and took considerable time. Eventually the manufacturing managers
persuaded the receiving department to reproduce extra copies of
each receiving report, which were then routed to the user department for information. The receiving report gave advance notice
of delivery, permitting the user to bring pressure to bear on inventory control to release the item to the manufacturing department.

In this illustration, the informal organization utilized the procedures of the formal organization to be kept informed. The user departments in manufacturing had difficulty in carrying through their
plans without this specialized information. Since the formal structure and its overlay of formal communication processes were adequate for this purpose, individual managers designed their own
system to utilize the information.

Design of the Information Networks

Ideally, the information and communications network should be a consciously integrated design by top management with the involvement of operating management. But the dynamic nature of business operations precludes such omniscience. Rarely can the formally designed and planned information network anticipate all the needs of all operating managers. Furthermore, since the information network must serve the needs of many managers, it may therefore fail to serve adequately the needs of any one manager. This leaves the manager who is responsible for planning also responsible for the design of the information network to supply him with the information he requires for planning and for the evaluation of his plans. But, as in the receiving report illustration, operating management should first check the formal information channels. In addition, every attempt should be made to have the formal collection agencies supply such information, because the collection of information after the fact is both costly and time-consuming. And there are dangers in permitting the indiscriminate collection of information.

In some instances, information networks may be used to satisfy personal rather than institutional objectives, as was the case in one firm where the director of a particular function had high ambitions. He wished to impress his superiors at every turn with his brilliance and managerial ability, but did so at some expense to the firm itself. This particular director had two clerks in his department collecting information and compiling special reports merely to keep him informed. From the point of view of the company, it was questionable whether this information was worthwhile or whether the procedure was just another trick of the director to curry favor with his superiors by having immediate answers to queries. But this is the exception; most managers collect information to do a better job of planning and control.

Wherever possible, information systems should utilize existing routine reports and collection methods. The tendency is to superimpose a new information system on the existing routine system rather than to redesign the whole system. But this often leads to a duplication of effort, particularly when top management decides that an information network should be put into effect to provide specialized information. This information may already exist, although not necessarily in the form desired by top management. A careful examination of the existing network might permit its redesign to accomplish the retrieval of required information without the institution of a new information network.

The Computer and Information Systems

The computer has had considerable impact on the design and use of information networks. Prior to the use of electronic data processing, laborious hand posting of figures and information was necessary to generate basic data for reports and other formal communication. This work was not only laborious but also costly and slow. It was often necessary to have either duplicate records or a double-check system to insure accuracy.

Although the computer can handle fantastic amounts of information with accuracy, precision, and speed, it does not in itself guarantee a good information network. It is still necessary to determine what information is required, and in what form. And the cost of information collection remains high. Furthermore, there is a major problem in translating the data into computer language. The program required for a computer demands a particular sequence (called computer logic) as well as the punching of information on cards or tape. Such keypunching of information is costly in both time and money, and, like the old hand posting, it introduces the possibility of error at this point in data processing. Within the next decade, scanning devices and, eventually, direct voice command will eliminate keypunching or magnetic tape preparation.

It is still necessary to design the information network. In fact, a more careful design of this network is required when EDP is used. Programming an information network on a computer is time-consuming and costly. Furthermore, it results in a high degree of inflexibility, since the program is difficult to change. Once a particular series of items is programmed into an information network for the computer, any major changes in the information requirements necessitate a new program.

This very inflexibility can be a major advantage by eliminating haphazard information systems. The tendency in most information systems is for individuals to arrange for the collection of data that are relevant to their own function. Rarely is there a conscious effort to integrate this information into an overall system. The introduction of electronic data processing forces management to integrate such information and develop an overall information and communications network.

But electronic data processing is not the panacea for information-network weaknesses. Management must decide what information is required and how it is to be prepared and distributed. The design of an effective information network requires the participation of all levels of management, so that the information required by the first-line supervisor may somehow serve the needs of top management as well. At present, most firms have separate information networks that often collect similar information to supply the needs of varying levels of management.

An interesting development in scientific research—the information retrieval system—may prove to be of great use to management as well. In its scientific uses, the information retrieval system would permit the use of computers to retrieve information from memories containing raw data. For example, an article in a scientific journal may have references to a number of concepts. When the researcher in a totally different academic discipline is searching for concepts from other fields that may assist him in the development of scientific theories, the information retrieval system would recall the information from this particular article out of the raw data contained on its memory.

If information retrieval were applied to business data, all the basic information from inspection reports, accounts payable, and specifications would be stored either on punched cards or on computer memories. When management required some particular compilation of information to answer its planning and decision-making needs, the information retrieval system would cull the relevant material from the raw data to compile a report. Although this application may be far in the future, such a system would render obsolete the need for detailed information network programs and for manual record-keeping.

REDUCTION OF UNCERTAINTIES IN THE PLANNING PROCESS

The manager is continually faced with the need to predict the future and therefore to reduce uncertainties. Although he may obtain the most accurate and up-to-date information, such information relates only to the past, not to the future. He must rely upon the projections of others, especially staff specialists. From these projections and other data, he attempts to narrow his prediction down to a limited number of courses of action. He documents, perhaps not overtly, the basic premises or conditions necessary for a particular course of action. (This approach is similar to that in succeeding chapters on decision making, because plans are merely a series of coordinated or integrated decisions made in advance of the event.) This is an important consideration, since the success of his chosen course of action is dependent upon the basic environment's remaining constant. Changes in the premises invalidate the plans, and the manager must consider alternative courses of action if these environmental conditions do change.

Any manager is constrained by the amount of time he has available for the development of plans, but unless his planning is thorough, its chances of success are limited. A plan is only an attempt to predict the future and to marshal events in a structured manner. But the difficulties of prediction vary greatly from one level and one function of management to another. The prevalence of planning in manufacturing or production may very well result from the higher degree of certainty in that function of the business enterprise.

For the most part, production planning and control works with facts rather than uncertainties. Sales has given manufacturing a definite schedule of the number of items to be produced. Engineering has supplied specifications on the parts to be manufactured. Industrial engineering has provided standards indicating the amount of time required for manufacture. Manufacturing engineering has supplied the necessary processes and route sheets for the flow of the parts through manufacturing. The capacity of the shop has been established. Purchasing has indicated the delivery time for purchased parts. Production planning and control relates these factors to produce a plan of manufacture, often called a schedule. Little wonder that planning is an accepted tool in manufacturing, where the number of uncertainties is not nearly so great as in other parts of the organization.

The usual situation in business has greater uncertainty, with many more alternative courses of action open to the planner. With such uncertainties, the manager must plan for changes in the premises or environmental conditions. In order to compensate for uncertainty, the planner sets forth not only his detailed plan of action but also a series of alternative plans to come into force in the event of a change in the basic environmental conditions.

This kind of planning can be used, for example, in the introduction of a new product. A price policy may have been predicated on the premise that competition will leave prices unchanged. If the manager has formulated only the one plan on the basis of this premise, a change in the price policy of competitors will invalidate his plan. If the manager has anticipated this possibility he will have thought through in the planning stage the alternative courses of action open to him.

Cost Planning

After the manager has made his predictions and chosen a course of action, he must develop the plan itself. One of the first factors to consider is cost. In a business enterprise, all decisions and plans are related to expenditures and eventually to profit. Every manager, from the president down to the first-line supervisor, is constrained in the amount of expenditure he is permitted for a particular task. The impact of this cost limitation on management plans can clearly be seen in the illustration of planning for a new automobile model.

In the automobile industry, each firm sets the selling price of its cars as much as a year or two in advance of production. The design engineers, the production engineers, the manufacturing and assembly plants, the purchasing department, and other affected sections plan every element of the manufacture of the automobile within the cost limitations placed on them by top management.

With so many sections of the company affected by this cost limitation, the problem of coordination is immense. Yet somehow the plans of all sections must be meshed so that the factory cost of the automobile is the amount originally decided on by top management.

Timetables in Planning

Another major factor in developing maximum use of facilities and resources through planning is scheduling or setting timetables.

Time is often the crucial element in planning, either because of the difficulties involved in sequencing different parts of the plan or because of the need to introduce a new product ahead of competitors. In the manufacture or distribution of a product, each phase involves differing times for development or production. Furthermore, phases or processes may be interdependent, in that one phase cannot be started until another is completed. Rarely can this time lag be overcome, even with an attempt at concurrency or simultaneous development or manufacture, which is both expensive and prone to failure.

Planning begins with a delivery or due date and works backwards in time to include all the necessary phases. Each phase has a separate starting date; otherwise, there would be excess work-in-process inventory and consequently higher costs. The starting time of each element must mesh with the completion time of a prior element. (There is a central application here, with the determination of what is called the critical path and a separation of control procedures into critical and noncritical. This has led to PERT and similar planning and control systems.) But an additional element must be introduced in most organizations, since rarely can planning be unilateral. There must be a matching of the time demands with the availability of the resources. In other words, the time and deadline elements in each plan are matched against those of other plans to gauge the most economic time utilization of the resources. This is particularly the case where many projects or plans have common resources.

Timing is becoming increasingly important in the development and introduction of a new product or service or even in an advertising campaign. Innumerable cases illustrate the importance of timing, from the introduction of the hula hoop to the development of commercial jet airliners. Time and cost are closely related. It is possible in some instances to buy time, or to reduce it, through the use of overtime, duplication of facilities, or subcontracting, but such time reductions greatly increase costs. It is clear to see that good planning can reduce costs by eliminating the need to buy time.

One difficulty facing the operating manager is the unrealistic timetable forced on him by top management. The assessment of a competitive situation may lead top management to decide upon a crash program to meet competition. Time becomes a major factor, with increasing pressures from top management. The target is set and operating management is assigned the job of meeting it. When this happens, operating managers should develop their plans, *noting the time discrepancies*, to submit to top management at the outset of the program. Failure to take this step places operating managers in jeopardy, since meeting delivery dates has become their responsibility.

But top management realizes that the standard procedures in the firm contain countless safety margins. The assembly foreman's plans contain a period of time that is not required for assembly but is merely set as a safety margin against the failure of subassemblies to meet scheduled completion dates. Each manager in the process adds his safety margin. Through experience with this series of safety margins, which extend development or manufacturing time, top management may decide that the only way to cut the time required is to set arbitrary target dates.

PLANNING AND CONTROLS

An integral part of the development of a plan is the design of controls to insure that the plan is being carried out satisfactorily. Planning is but one of the skills of the manager and serves little purpose by itself. A plan is evolved that will coordinate resources to achieve a given task or objective. But the plan itself is ineffectual if it does not achieve the objective, and it is controls that permit the manager to know whether the plan is doing so.

Controls are often based not on a specific plan but on the day-to-day operation of the firm. Accounting collects cost information that is used for the preparation of financial statements relating to the general condition of the firm. Inspection reports are completed on all inspections, but are not necessarily related to a particular plan. These general controls may or may not assist the manager in assessing the performance of his plans.

For example, standard forms or control procedures already exist in production with move tickets, inspection reports, and the like. A production plan involving thousands of parts, each of which must go through multiple machining operations, presents a problem of great complexity, not only for planning but also for controlling the plan. Each part must be machined or formed according to a master plan, so that in final assembly each part is available in perfect condition.

It is possible to devise a control system to insure that parts are available when required by using the standard controls for inspection, movement of parts from one department to another, and the like. For example, a move ticket may be issued whenever a part goes from one department to another. The move ticket can perform a double function: (1) to dispatch parts from one department to another, and (2) to inform the planning section in production control on the progress of the manufacture of the part. The utilization of existing control systems to perform multiple control functions can give the operating manager the opportunity to control his plans without adding to administrative costs.

But whether such controls are currently available should not deter the manager from designing control systems to insure that his plans are working. The essential point is that the manager must receive information on the performance of his plans so that he can reformulate them if they are not working.

IMPLEMENTATION OF PLANS

Implementation is a critical phase of a plan. Up to this point, the manager has been utilizing conceptual skills and drawing heavily upon his technical competence. But the implementation stage requires that he use his leadership skills, which are often less well developed.

An important aid to the manager in the implementation phase is getting the participation of subordinates and delegating aspects of the planning to them. Participation by subordinates and others affected by the plan not only removes the emotional sting of being subjected to the will of others but may also eliminate technical and psychological difficulties. Participation may be severely limited either by the nature of the plan or by the qualifications of subordinates, but it is a useful technique to assist the manager in implementing his plan.

Delegation also aids implementation by providing the opportunity for the lowest levels of management to plan. The plan becomes identified as "our" plan rather than as "their" plan. Every effort will then be made to implement the plan. An additional advantage of delegation is that changes and improvisation of details of the plan will be made at the level where the information is first available and where such changes can be effected immediately. But such delegation must be clearly thought through and made in such a way that the entire plan will not be jeopardized by local action.

Pretesting of Plans

A relatively new technique in planning is the use of simulation techniques to test the plan in advance of its introduction. This technique has been used for many years in product design and development, through the building and testing of a prototype or scale model. Now computers and mathematical model building permit such pretesting through simulation.

Simulation involves the use of past operating data as input environmental conditions for a present plan. In other words, the new plan is tested by noting how it would have handled past situations. The simulated result with the new plan is compared with the actual results under the old system to see whether the one is more effective than the other. Another method for pretesting is the use of test areas for the introduction of new products. The experience in the test area will be analyzed by the marketing department to see whether the product merits national distribution.

Although there is a trend toward such techniques in planning, the cost and time factors have militated against their widespread use. Also, simulation techniques have not yet reached the stage where this tool is readily available to most managers or to most firms. Simulation for pretesting plans is utilized mostly by operations research technicians to determine or test their models. Most of these models are relatively simple in their relationships between dependent and independent variables. It could be said that such models are dealing with more or less known factors rather than with uncertainties. Where input factors are unknown, Monte Carlo techniques can use random numbers and probability to estimate or predetermine variables. A more detailed explanation of such techniques is given later in this book.

When the model has been constructed, it is tested to determine whether it is truly operational. This testing or evaluation is done by simulation. Data from previous experience are plugged into the model to determine what answers or decisions would have been forthcoming in the past, had this particular model or formula been used. These simulated results are compared with actual results to ascertain whether the model is more effective than the previous method.

In the future, the manager will automatically use simulation techniques to pretest plans. A major drawback at present is that most historical information is inadequate and perhaps inaccurate. But there is no reason why an information network cannot be planned to overcome the inadequacy of information. Another problem may be the amount of detail that must be developed in the planning model, but computers can easily handle this complexity of information. Future simulation models will have complex formulations that provide the opportunity to pretest plans and decisions so as to determine their effect on the profitability and total operation of the firm. If this research is successful, it will present a major breakthrough for planning.

Most plan pretesting is now mainly an intellectual process. The planner sorts out the premises on which he bases his plans and predetermines as far as possible what uncertainties will be involved during the operation of the plans. He uses his experience and judgment to decide which of these uncertainties are most likely to occur and which may be eliminated.

Pretesting, whether by simulation models or computers or by the mere process of elimination, serves to rule out unsatisfactory plans before they are implemented. A major difficulty with planning and decision making is that the failure of a plan or decision may be discovered too late. When satisfactory models and techniques are developed to permit more extensive use of simulation for pretesting, the probability of success will be greatly increased.

EVALUATION OF THE PLAN

Controls serve to inform the manager that the plan is proceeding satisfactorily. They indicate when corrective action is required and provide information for evaluation. Evaluation has two objectives.

The first is to improve the process of planning itself by identifying technical and other weaknesses in the plan. The second is to serve as a training vehicle for management development.

The pressures on operating management are often such that little or no evaluation takes place. Yet how can experience be gained and judgment sharpened except through evaluation? Evaluation is one of the most important roads to effective management. Learning takes place only when an individual recognizes either that a mistake was made or that there was something to be gained from a particular experience. It is true that only rarely will exactly the same situation present itself to management for action, yet there is a high degree of similarity among business problems.

Evaluation must not be undertaken vindictively. It is but part of the learning process for management development, providing a concrete example of what a manager has done to solve particular problems. What better example can be found than one in which there has been total involvement? But unless the evaluation is undertaken as a joint experience in learning, defense mechanisms on the part of the individual take over, and there is little learning.

It is particularly important that evaluation be based on factual information. The control system evolves reports or information that can be scrutinized as a means of evaluating the total plan. Unless evaluation is based on factual information, it will degenerate into a series of opinions, many of which are quite unrelated to facts. If the purpose of the evaluation process is learning, there should be little or no resistance to the presentation of what might be pertinent factual information.

The general tendency in industry, government—almost any-where—is to cover up mistakes. Usually this is because mistakes are held against the individual rather than considered part of the price of management development. The best teacher is experience, but it must be useful experience. The evaluation of plans can result in such useful experience.

SUMMARY

The objective of planning is effective management action. The organizational difficulties in attaining horizontal coordination, the need for clearcut statements of objectives, the recognition that participation and involvement are requirements for effective planning, the consideration of communication and its effect on planning, the conflict of objectives and suboptimization, and the need for controls are vitally related to the efficiency of planning. Yet even thorough understanding and recognition of the realities of the process do not necessarily insure effective planning and the resultant effective management action.

Planning is an attempt to predict and control future events. But future events necessarily are uncertain, and so innumerable factors not under the control of the individual manager may invalidate his plans. Since no one can predict the future absolutely, the plans themselves must be extremely flexible. Planning must be sufficiently detailed that, flexibility notwithstanding, it can be followed by those responsible for carrying through the plans.

How is it possible to build both flexibility and detail into a plan? This question can be answered quite simply. The manager must recognize his inability to prepare for every uncertainty. But he can set forth alternatives for coping with uncertainties and, once he has sorted them out, formulate his plans.

The appraisal of future uncertainties and alternative courses of action will lead to one particular plan of action. The manager makes a series of judgments on the alternatives and estimates their consequences. Then he documents his course of action in such a way that a detailed plan can be evolved that becomes *the* plan. By means of delegation and participation, the details become the responsibility of subordinates. This provides a degree of flexibility, since immediate revisions in the details can be made by the implementing manager.

Now, if the manager's prediction of the uncertainties is incorrect, his plan is obviously invalidated. Should this happen, alternative plans would come into force.

Another major part of planning is the determination of just what changes in the original parameters of the environment invalidate the plan. What is required is a set of guidelines for reevaluating the plan and reorienting it to the new situation.

It is not enough to put a detailed plan in writing. The premises on which the plan was constructed must also be detailed. Then, if these premises change as a result of unanticipated events, the manager will know that his plan is in fact invalid. It is imperative that a control system be designed, not only to insure that the plan is proceeding according to schedule, but also to determine whether the original conditions under which the plan was formulated still hold true.

Through evaluation, the manager can improve his planning while simultaneously developing his subordinates. But the climate for evaluation must not be punitive. When evaluation is used for the allocation of blame, hostility patterns are built up between the manager and his subordinates. But when evaluation is used as a training device, it creates a team spirit between the manager and the managed.

Decision making is closely related to planning. In fact, planning is merely the predetermination of a series of decisions. The advantage in planning lies in the orderly coordination of decisions well in advance of the actual need. But decision making is still really the core of planning, for decisions must be sound if a plan is to be effective. This subject of decision making is discussed in subsequent chapters to complete the examination of planning as a management task.

10

The Decision-making
Environment and Process

AN INDIVIDUAL DECISION has consequences far beyond what seems to be its limited sphere of action. Rarely can a decision be unilateral in one section of the organization; its ramifications will affect decisions and functions in other parts of the firm. There are also important behavioral consequences, since a decision may change important social and structural relationships. And the failure to coordinate and relate decisions may result in inconsistent acts by the organization as a whole.

Every decision is affected by organizational environment. The manager considers how the decision he is making is related to the hierarchy of management and the formal organization. What authority has he been granted to make this decision? What responsibilities does he have to others in the organization for the decision? What assistance will he receive to carry out his decision? The formal organization has as one of its objectives the coordination of the activities of all its members. Such coordination is in turn related to decision-making powers delegated to management in the organizational pyramid.

The organization is jealous of decision-making prerogatives and does not allow them to be delegated lightly. (The tendency of managers in large businesses today is not to usurp decision-making authority but rather to be unwilling to make decisions on their own.) Decisions are made within the formal hierarchy of organization. The practicing manager recognizes that the purpose of his decisions is to further the attainment of the organization's objectives and that they must therefore be closely related to these objectives. He recognizes that his decisions do have ramifications beyond his own area of responsibility and carefully considers their effect not only on his own suborganization but on the organization as a whole.

The manager in the lower levels of management may wonder whether his decisions are sufficiently important to merit careful attention to decision making. He may consider that his decisions are routine and rarely go beyond the confines of his own small part of the organization. But this is not so. The action of every part of the organization must be in concert if objectives are to be attained.

An illustration of this interrelation of decisions is the case of the foreman in a small manufacturing firm who was directly responsible for a major delay in the national defense effort. This man, who was foreman of a welding department, had great difficulty in reading the prints and specifications of a customer's drawings. As he examined the prints in detail, he had the feeling that they were incorrect in specifying the welding of a section onto the superstructure. He asked some of his highly skilled welders what they thought of the prints, but they were divided as to exactly how the section should be welded to the superstructure. The superstructure was part of the launching pad of a missile and had to meet extremely rigorous specifications tests for the military. The plant was a subcontractor to one of the major prime contractors for the missile. The foreman knew how important the project was both to his company and to the prime contractor. He could not decide what to do, since he knew that going to the prime contractor for verification of the prints would cause a long delay that his firm could ill afford. Finally, he decided to follow the prints exactly as they came from the prime contractor.

When the superstructure was finally secured to the other parts of the mechanism, the welded sections were found to be incorrectly placed. The missile was delayed; the national defense effort was delayed; and all because of the decision of a welding foreman in a subcontracting plant.

Thus the decisions made by even the first-line supervisor can have far-reaching effects on the conduct and success of the enterprise itself. It is debatable whether the foreman could truly be blamed for failing to exercise initiative, since he felt that the potential delays were critical. But his uncertainty should really have been shared with his superiors, which might have resulted in a verification check by the prime contractors and the creation of a small problem rather than a gigantic one.

DECISION AND OBJECTIVES

In the formulation of his decisions, the manager considers not only the formal organizational environment of authority and responsibility but also the informal organization. Although he may make a decision, there is no automatic guarantee that it will be carried through to a successful conclusion. The act of making a decision is only a conceptual exercise if it is not implemented. And implementation is dependent upon the cooperation of those responsible for it. The manager considers the effect of his decision on the attitude and the potential actions of those affected by the decision. Chester Barnard, in his penetrating study of the reality of executive decision making, noted that the manager should never give an order unless he is positive that it will be carried out. Since an order is merely the communication of a decision to a subordinate, Barnard's point applies equally to decisions.[1]

The manager considers the ramifications of his decisions not only on the organization but also on the objectives and ambitions of his subordinates. Every individual looks at every event in the company as it affects him personally, and even the most objective of individuals can never be truly objective about himself. Civilization and our culture have made us more aware of our obligations to our fellow man, but still each individual considers himself first. This is not to say that employees will not be loyal to the company or be willing to make sacrifices for the attainment of its objectives. What is being said is that each individual nevertheless looks at events in terms of their effect on him personally.

The manager is faced with relating the personal objectives of his subordinates to the objectives of the organization. This is a primary task. If the manager is to elicit the fullest cooperation of his subordinates for the attainment of the task, every decision made by the

[1] Chester I. Barnard, *The Functions of the Executive* (Cambridge, Mass.: Harvard University Press, 1958), passim.

executive must be related, not only to the objectives, but also to the satisfaction of the individuals in the organization.

Many practicing, successful executives would acknowledge that relating decisions to the objectives of subordinates is little considered in business today. They could go on to point out that decisions must be made quickly, and rarely is there time even to obtain the information needed for the formulation of the decision, let alone to consider all the possible ramifications of the decision, not only on the organization but also on the persons who constitute that organization.

No one will deny that the hustle and bustle of most organizations give the manager little time to think and no time to consider all the ramifications of the decisions he has to make. In many firms, it seems that the rule is to give the manager a great deal more work than he can handle, although this is usually not a conscious policy. Realistically, however, the success of the manager depends upon the effectiveness both of the decisions and of their implementation. The manager cannot afford to disregard the needs of his subordinates, since they are the ones who are instrumental in implementing decisions. Therefore, he must somehow find the time to predetermine the personal ramifications of his decisions.

Decisions do have far-reaching consequences that require careful consideration. The manager considers the effect of his decision not only on individuals but also on the groups that constitute his part of the organization. These groups may be formally organized with quite explicit rules of procedure. They may be informally organized, also with rules that govern the actions and attitudes of the members. The manager knows the rules of the formal groups because he is instrumental in setting them forth. But the rules of the informal group are not explicit; they develop over time to guarantee continued existence of the group. The manager may not be aware of the existence of such groups or of their rules of behavior. But it behooves him to learn these group rules if he is to elicit the cooperation of his subordinates.

DECISION-MAKING RESPONSIBILITIES

The effective manager recognizes his decision-making responsibilities. The hierarchy of management allocates to each manager separate and distinct areas of responsibility that involve him in making decisions relating to the management of his part of the organization. He is responsible for coordinating the resources placed under his jurisdiction, and such coordination requires choices among alternative uses of the resources.

Failure to accept decision-making responsibilities results in loss of the confidence not only of superiors but also of subordinates. For example, a manager of a major engineering project in a large company was highly qualified in engineering but poorly qualified in management. He was placed in charge of a project with an 18-month life and a budget of more than $1.5 million. His staff was chosen for him by the vice-president of engineering. The project demanded constant consultation with the customer as well as a heavy input both of electrical and mechanical engineering talent. Because the customer's engineering staff was limited in size and capability, a great deal of dependence was placed on the engineering project manager.

Shortly after the project had begun, a controversy arose between the mechanical and electrical engineers on a technical point. Eventually, the manager was called on to make a decision that would have a considerable effect on the design of the project. There was something to be said for both the mechanical and the electrical engineering viewpoints, with no clearcut technical consideration to incline the manager toward one decision or the other. He vacillated long enough to cause delays in other parts of the project.

The top mechanical and electrical engineers pleaded with the project manager to make a decision so that the entire program could be scheduled and integrated. When they were unable to get a definite decision from him, they went their own ways, each assuming that the other would somehow integrate the designs. Other engineers, who were responsible for coordinating their activities with those of the special mechanical-electrical group, were at a loss as to what to do, and finally they tried to accommodate both points of view.

At the weekly meeting between the president of the company and his staff, when progress was reported on the various projects, this engineering project manager always gave glowing reports of progress. As the delivery date approached for the project, the president began to hear rumors of trouble. When he finally made a thorough check on the project, he found that it would take over a year and almost a million dollars more to complete the design.

The subordinates could not be blamed for their actions. The alternatives open to them had been either to resign themselves to the indecisiveness of their superior or to make their own unilateral decisions. But the latter action on the part of a subordinate is always tantamount to disaster, since he will be blamed by his boss for mistakes but will receive little credit for good decisions.

The question might be asked: Why isn't indecisiveness noticed in the manager before major responsibilities are given to him? Unfortunately, many an executive covers up his indecisiveness with an attitude of careful attention to detail. He may very well have collected an impressive array of facts and figures about every situation and have impressed his superiors. Furthermore, he may actually have had little experience in decision making; perhaps his superiors have rarely delegated decision-making power to him. When placed in a position of considerable authority, he finds he has little or no experience to call upon.

DECISION RAMIFICATIONS

The cost of indecisiveness is high, but so is the cost of a poor decision. Each manager must recognize the limitations placed on his decision-making power by the organization structure. Certainly, he is at liberty to make decisions that affect only his own sphere of operations. But rarely can the executive make decisions that do not in some way affect other parts of the organization. No decision can be made in a vacuum.

The manager considers the effect of his decisions not only on other parts of the organization but also on previous and subsequent decisions affecting his own organization. Every action he takes has a reaction among his associates. A decision may have far-reaching consequences, even if it seems to be somewhat inconsequential and limited in scope.

Decisions also affect the manager's own previous decisions. But all too often the manager considers that the decision is going to affect only the particular circumstances facing him at the moment. He fails to recognize that the decision must be related to his previous plans and to the objectives of the total organization as well as to those of the suborganization that he heads. Furthermore, each decision sets a precedent in the light of which all subsequent decisions must be made. If he pays careful attention to this fact, his subordinates should be able to make similar decisions in the future without having to refer to him.

At a management seminar one speaker presented a skit to illustrate the importance of precedent in decision making. The skit opened with the manager sitting at a desk on which three telephones were ringing constantly. In addition, there were endless visits and interruptions by subordinates to ask the manager countless questions requiring decisions.

The speaker indicated after the skit that he was once in the position of making all the decisions in his organization. Then one day, after studying the decisions, he realized that he was making the same ones over and over again. As he examined his experience more closely, he came to the conclusion that his subordinates were not considering his decisions binding on similar, subsequent problems. He recognized that this was his fault, since he had encouraged his subordinates to bring their problems to him, thereby satisfying his ego and giving himself a feeling of importance.

The speaker developed the point that decisions must be made in such a way that they will be binding on all similar situations until circumstances change. He said it was a responsibility of every manager to train his subordinates to recognize that, except when circumstances were different, a decision once made by a superior sets a precedent and should be binding on all subsequent problems of the same kind.

The environment within which decisions are made will have far-reaching effects on their efficacy. The relationships of subparts of the organization, of subordinates and superiors, and of the informal groups and the manager must all be taken into account in reaching a decision. Routine decisions which have been provided for by the organization over time will undoubtedly have had this organizational environment predetermined, so the manager need spend little time in considering the ramifications of such routine decisions. But any decisions that are not routine—the ones that are normally the most critical to management effectiveness—must take into account this organizational environment.

The Decision-making Process

The decision-making process is identical whether mathematical or nonmathematical approaches are taken. These six steps are followed in most scientific and mathematical research:

1. Formulating the problem.
2. Constructing the model.
3. Testing the model.
4. Deriving a solution from the model.
5. Testing and controlling the solution.
6. Implementing the solution.[2]

These steps can be applied equally to the nonmathematical development of the decision-making process, but the emphasis placed on each of the phases will differ. There are, essentially, eight steps in this conceptual approach to the decision-making process:

1. Identification of the problem.
2. Coordination of the problem with previous plans and decisions.
3. Collection of factual information.
4. Determination of alternative courses of action.
5. Selection of one alternative (the decision).
6. Formulation of a plan of action to implement the solution.
7. Design of controls and implementation of the decision.
8. Evaluation of the decision after its implementation.

Identification of the Problem

Although it seems obvious that the first task facing any decision maker is to determine what problems require solution, in actual practice insufficient attention is paid to the identification of the problem. This is well recognized by executive development programs and graduate schools of business where the case method of instruction is used, forcing the student to identify the problem as his first step in solving a case.

---

[2] Russell L. Ackoff, Shiv K. Gupta, and J. Sayer Minas, *Scientific Method Optimizing Applied Research Decisions* (New York: John Wiley & Sons, Inc., 1962), p. 26.

Inability to grapple realistically with the identification of a problem is well illustrated by the case of one small company that decided to call in a consultant. In the first discussion with the president, the consultant wanted to know exactly what task he was to be assigned. The president was somewhat general and evasive in his answer, simply saying that "lots of things could be improved." The consultant was wary of such an assignment and asked the president to be more explicit. The president finally indicated that in his opinion the company should obtain a higher percentage of profit on net sales than it was then enjoying.

The consultant asked for more facts, but soon came to the conclusion that at most the president merely had a feeling that he should be making more profit. The president finally said he thought the major difficulty was in production. He felt that the production workers were not performing the way they should. When the consultant asked the president for his reasons, the president replied that he had observed them and thought they were not working hard enough.

The consultant made a thorough investigation of production and came to the conclusion that there had been little change in direct labor costs over previous years. Eventually, his investigation revealed that a number of separate circumstances were responsible for the decline in profits. Advertising expenditures had risen drastically, the prices of raw materials had increased without any increase in the price of the finished products, executives' salaries had been increased, and the markup permitted to retailers of the company's products had been increased several times without any upward adjustment in the retail price.

This president could easily have conducted the investigation himself if he had identified the problem or series of problems facing the company. The identification of the problem is not only the first task for the decision maker but also one of the most important.

COORDINATION WITH PREVIOUS PLANS

The executive is never faced with one decision; he must make a series of interrelated decisions. In driving an automobile, the decision to change gears or change direction does not stand by itself, but is related to the task of reaching a particular destination. Similarly, each decision made by a manager is related to other decisions, which in turn serve to permit the attainment of objectives.

The effective decision maker considers the objectives both of his own part of the organization and of the organization as a whole. Failure to consider objectives will cause erratic behavior on the part of the organization and perhaps even turn it in a direction quite unrelated to its final destination. Each manager must consider the relation of his decisions to objectives if he is to be effective in marshaling his resources for maximum gain.

Each manager is responsible for the formulation of plans to integrate his behavior with that of other parts of the organization and to permit him to make the most effective use of his resources. Planning requires decision making and in turn results in the predetermination of decisions. But not all decisions can be made in advance of an event. Sometimes the plans themselves are formulated to gather data for decision making. In other instances, the plans set forth alternative decisions that are to be considered at the appropriate time. It is most important for the manager to be conscious of the need for integrating his decisions with his previous planning and with the plans of others in the organization. Just as the bridge player must keep track of the bidding and of all the cards that have been played in all four suits, so must the manager keep track of all the decisions and plans that have been made before.

The pressures to make an immediate decision to solve a problem may force the manager to take short-range actions that invalidate his long-range plans. This was the case in a company whose sales manager was faced with deciding on the replacement of one of his salesmen. The sales manager had spent considerable time in formulating a long-range plan for the redistribution of sales territories. He had considered such factors as the long-term growth pattern of the industry, the changing nature of the market, and the effect of discount houses on retail sales. In addition, he had studied the selling patterns of his salesmen, including such factors as the number of calls per day, the relationship between sales expense and size of order, and the effect of territory distances on productivity. Although he was under pressure to reduce his distribution costs, he decided to keep his representation in the major metropolitan areas, even if this meant inadequate coverage of some less populated areas.

But when the salesman for the northern half of Ohio left the firm to go into business for himself, the sales manager decided not to replace him. Instead, he extended the three contiguous territories, in effect eliminating the separate northern Ohio territory. Obviously the pressure to reduce distribution costs resulted in a short-run decision that invalidated the long-range plans. Unless a manager is willing to integrate his current decisions with his previous plans, he is wasting his time in formulating such plans.

Collection of Factual Information

An integral part of the decision-making process is the planning of an information system to supply factual information for decision input. But such information must be planned in advance of its need for decision making. The collection of specialized information at the time of the decision is often impossible because the data in the company records are unavailable.

The information system also provides data for control. Such dual use of information both for decision making and for control permits the design of a sophisticated information system. In fact, since the exercise of control itself leads to decision making for corrective action, the major purpose of any information system must be to facilitate decision making.

The accounting system, which is the lifeblood of any information system, has been oriented in the past toward record-keeping for the preparation of historical documents. But because of the information technology revolution through computers and high-speed data processing, accounting itself is faced with a revolutionary reorientation of its systems. There is a trend now toward decision-oriented collection and combining of cost information. But this does not absolve the manager of the need to determine what types of information he requires for decision making. He cannot abdicate this responsibility to staff, since staff is necessarily specialized in some narrow discipline and does not have the manager's breadth of experience and judgment. The manager must plan an information system designed to make available the factual data necessary for effective decision making.

ALTERNATIVE COURSES OF ACTION

The determination of alternatives is an essential part of the decision-making process. The manager has the all-important task of identifying the variables affecting the decision. But often he is faced with so many variables that he has no alternative but to make value judgments and eliminate the variables that he thinks would not measurably affect the decision. Such a choice of variables is a decision in itself and has far-reaching effects on the alternative choices that are open to the decision maker.

Not only must the manager choose among variables; he must also rank these variables in the order of their importance to the choice of alternatives. In operations research, the executive quantifies the variables to accomplish this ordering or determination of priorities. Ideally, all variables entering into any decision should be quantified so that an arithmetic answer is available for each alternative. In practice, the task of quantification is not only difficult but in some instances misleading.

In time the experienced manager develops an intuitive ability to weed out or order the variables affecting the decision. He does not actually quantify these variables, but the effect is that of quantification. The manager's thought processes become so attuned to the decision-making process that he is himself almost unaware of his method in reaching the decision. If he consciously attempts to quantify and weight every variable, he is likely to spend a great deal of time and perhaps even make decisions that are less effective than they might be if he relied solely on his judgment.

This is not to say that the manager should not quantify and weight the variables that affect a decision. If this is the most effective way for him to make decisions, then this is what he should do. But the intuitive sense developed by an experienced manager often serves him as well as the quantification and weighting of variables.

It is at this point that the manager should consider participation. He has the task not only of making decisions but also of implementing them and coordinating the resources allocated to him to attain his objectives. No decision can be considered as something that stands alone; it is only one part of the total process of management. The manager must think equally about the implementation of the decision and its formulation.

To achieve implementation requires the cooperation of the subordinates who are to carry it through. And such cooperation is dependent upon whether the decision is acceptable to them. Chester Barnard sets forth four conditions for the acceptance of a decision by subordinates:

1. There is effective communication.
2. The decision is consistent with the organization objectives and purposes.
3. The decision is compatible with the subordinate's interests.
4. The subordinate is mentally and physically capable of carrying through the decision.[3]

There is considerable difference between passive and active acceptance. People who work in the industrial environment are conditioned to a high degree of passive acceptance, and few decisions are ever totally rejected by subordinates. The normal autocratic authority patterns in industry have established superior/subordinate relationships attuned to passive acceptance. It is a rare decision that infringes so greatly on the personal interests of the subordinate that he will totally reject it.

But often it is this insidious passive acceptance that dooms the decision to failure in the implementation stage. The view that "it wasn't my decision" can be deadlier than the more honest lack of cooperation. The key to success is to gain active acceptance through motivation. And one of the best possible motivators is participation. Participation not only acts as an effective motivator but also permits better decisions. Considerable controversy has raged about group decision making as compared with individual decision making. One school of thought [4] considers that group decision making is ineffectual and costly and results mostly in compromises instead of in good decisions. The other school, made up primarily of those who advocate the human-relations approach to management, advances the point of view that the total product of a group exceeds the sum of the products of the individuals constituting the group.

The major problem involves the locus of the decision-making

[3] Op. cit., pp. 165–166.
[4] William H. Whyte, Jr., *The Organization Man* (Garden City, N.Y.: Doubleday and Company, 1956).

power. The organizational hierarchy dictates that individuals should be responsible for decisions. If a group or committee is made responsible for decisions within the formal organization, there is great difficulty in allocating responsibility. Is the chairman of the committee responsible for the decision of the committee? Can individual members be charged with responsibility when any decision that is reached is made jointly? On the other hand, the complexity of business today makes it impossible for any one man to have the varied and extensive knowledge necessary to make important and effective decisions. The crux of the problem lies more in the actual responsibility and authority for the decision than in who might be involved in making the decision. The criticisms of joint decision making are leveled not against the use of expert opinion from the group but against the joint responsibility of the group for decisions.

The tendency in the modern corporation is to call a meeting whenever any problem arises. The larger and more complex the organization, the greater the number of conferences required. There can be little argument against the use of conferences or formal committees to appraise situations and discuss matters of common interest. The objection must come when the major purpose of the conference is to have the groups reach a decision that could and should be made by an individual. The members of the committee can consider what alternatives are open for solving the problem. They can consider the interrelationships that exist within the organization. They can supply specialized and expert opinion. But they should not jointly arrive at the decision!

There is not and cannot be democracy in an industrial organization. There is not and cannot be election of managers. There is not and cannot be a majority vote for decisions. The very nature of the organizational hierarchy demands that managers make decisions that are carried out by subordinates. The astute student of government might inquire at this point why, if democracy is so efficient for society as a whole, it does not work equally well in the subunits of society, such as the firm. But within a democracy, autocratic organizations are responsible for decisions and decision implementation. It is true that a congress or parliament makes decisions through democratic voting. But officials are elected to and form part of an autocratic organization not subject to the will of the people for a stated term of office. A major difference is that elected public officials must stand for reelection, which makes them subject to the will of the electorate.

From the president to the local dog-catcher, government is organized autocratically. In the United States, the president has the sole responsibility to sign acts of congress into law. The difference between government and the private firm is that citizenship is required for a vote in the former, ownership in the latter. In practice, ownership of a firm's common (voting) stock is so widespread that little or no control is exercised over the autocratic managerial hierarchy.

In a business enterprise the power to make decisions must be vested in the individual. The manager must be in a position to take decisive action quickly. In addition, there must be a firm and definite allocation of responsibility to the individual executive for decision making.

Although the individual executive has the responsibility for the decision, there is still a place for participation. Participation not only brings the expert opinion of subordinates to bear on a problem but also acts to motivate the subordinates to accept the decision. Every individual is interested in having some say in matters affecting his behavior. Although it might be expected that such actions would be highly subjective in nature, it is amazing how much objectivity an individual has when he is given some responsibility.

Through participation, the manager is in a position to gauge the reaction of his subordinates before actually making the decision. In this way he can avoid a course of action that his subordinates will resent. Although some decisions must be made in spite of the adverse reactions of subordinates, most business decisions are such that the needs of subordinates can be taken into account.

There is one firm rule regarding participation of subordinates in the decision-making process: that the prerequisites for participation must be ability and knowledge. Participation in decision making must be restricted to individuals with the ability to comprehend what is required and the knowledge to contribute to the decision.

When a manager has already made his decision, he should never ask his subordinates to participate. The subordinates will soon recognize that the executive has made the decision and is merely attempting to placate them by a discussion of alternatives. If he does not believe in participation, he should be autocratic in his behavior without giving lip service to some technique he distrusts. But participation can result not only in better decisions but also in better implementation. Subordinates will recognize the problems faced by the superior in making the decision and will do their utmost to implement the decision.

THE DECISION

The choice among alternatives is not an easy one, and rarely can it be completely relegated to a mechanical process. It is the central function of the decision-making process. Because of the many uncertainties inherent in predicting future events, the manager can never be absolutely sure that his decision is sound. But his chances of success will be much higher if he has faithfully performed all the steps in the decision-making process and tempered the results with good judgment.

The internal pressures in the firm, coupled with the dynamic nature of free enterprise markets, make it imperative that the executive reach his decision quickly. There is rarely time to seek further information or even to reconsider alternatives. Little wonder that decisiveness is one of the most important personality characteristics required of a manager.

PLAN OF ACTION

The choice of one alternative in making a decision is not the end of the decision-making process. Decisions are of little use and little note unless they are carried through successfully. The manager is judged not on his decisions but on their success, which depends upon how well he plans their implementation. Plans must be formulated, authority and responsibility must be delegated, and perhaps an organization must be set up to carry through the decision.

The decision of the allies in World War II to launch an invasion on the beaches of Normandy in June 1944 well illustrates this need for a plan of action. Obviously such a decision was not reached lightly, but was the end product of the decision-making process. The problem facing the allies was to establish a beachhead with port facilities that could be supplied from England. The problem itself was part of a greater objective of opening a second front that would force the Nazis to fight on two fronts. The integration of this problem with previous planning was a major operation on the part of the allied staff, since this particular action was merely part of the overall strategy of destroying Germany's war power.

A gigantic amount of factual information was assembled and a number of alternative courses of action were considered, including beachheads in Norway, Greece, and Southern France, as well as other parts of France, Holland, and Belgium. Although the decision itself was extremely difficult and complex, the most gigantic task was the construction of a plan of action to implement the decision. The construction of the Mulberry Floating Docks to be towed to the beachhead at Normandy for the establishment of a port, the assembly and deployment of hundreds of thousands of troops, the coordination of the military forces of a number of countries, and countless other major tasks all had to be formulated and coordinated as part of the plan of action.

Although the logistics involved in the average business decision obviously do not reach the magnitude of such an event as the invasion of Normandy, nevertheless the plan of action must be as well formulated if the decision is to be successfully implemented.

DESIGN OF CONTROLS

The manager is charged with the responsibility for successful action, which involves not only good decisions and adequate plans of action but also controls to insure that the decisions and plans are being carried through successfully. The manager cannot make a decision and then assume that it will necessarily work. He must design controls to tell him whether the plans are being carried through and whether the decision itself is satisfactory. There may be controls already built into the organizational hierarchy that will automatically keep the manager informed. But often the manager has to design special controls to provide him with information on the effectiveness of his decisions and plans.

DECISION EVALUATION

Exercise of the controls designed by the decision maker should carry the decision through to its successful completion. But the final stage in the decision-making process has not yet been completed.

There must be an evaluation and an appraisal of the decision and its implementation to complete the process.

The game of golf has much to teach the manager about decision evaluation. Every golfer keeps a score of the number of strokes he has taken to complete a hole. There is a standard of performance or par for each hole, against which the golfer may measure his own performance. The standard of excellence required for a par hole is beyond the average golfer and so spurs him on to greater achievement.

The manager may also learn a major lesson from the way in which the golfer approaches his game. He has learned certain rules on how he should address the ball, how he should place his feet, and which club he should use for which particular lie or distance. After the golfer has swung at the ball, he immediately proceeds with the evaluation. If the ball goes to the left or to the right or does not go sufficiently far, the golfer asks himself, "Did I keep my eye on the ball?" "Did I keep the correct grip on the club?" He may even stand aside and swing again at an imaginary ball in order to correct the mistakes he made in his previous swing.

Unfortunately, the pressures of business hardly give the manager sufficient time to make a decision correctly in the first place, let alone to assess the decision. But since the ability or skill to make good decisions is one of the paramount qualifications of an effective manager, time must be found for the evaluative process in order to develop more effective decision-making skills.

It is not possible to learn how to make good decisions from a textbook or even from the advice of fellow members of management. The ability is learned only through experience. But experience can be a good teacher only if the manager reconsiders and appraises the effect of his decisions to improve his decision-making skills.

Decision Making in Perspective

There is a great tendency to oversimplify the management process. To consider decision making as the major skill of the manager is just such an oversimplification. Certainly, the manager is responsible for making decisions, but decision making is only one of the skills required of him. An understanding of human behavior, or leadership skills, is as much a requirement for the manager as are decision-making skills. As he applies both leadership and decision-making skills, he may even take actions that could be considered irrational in order to compensate for shortcomings among the members of the organization.

A decision is effective only when it is carried through successfully. This requires a sound organization structure, well-formulated objectives, a recognition of the need for planning and control, and myriad other considerations. The enterprise should move as far as possible in the direction of automating all aspects of its organization, including the making of decisions. If the manager is relieved of repetitive tasks of any sort, he will be able to focus his attention on the more important parts of his job.

The effective manager understands the process of decision making and the need for developing decision-making skills. He utilizes every possible aid in making better decisions, recognizes the impact of his decisions on the organization and on his subordinates, and continually sharpens his decision-making skills.

The reader who wishes to pursue the subject of operations research in the context of decision making will find a special section on the subject in the Appendix.

11

Information Networks
for Decision Making

A PREREQUISITE for effective decision making is accurate and timely information. A decision based on false premises or inaccurate information obviously is destined to failure. But complete information is impossible in business. There is uncertainty in forecasting the economy, the actions of competitors, even future internal costs. In addition, time and cost factors seriously constrain the collection and dissemination of information. Data collection is both time-consuming and costly.

Decision making requires planning to insure that information is adequate and available when needed. The manager predetermines what decisions he expects to make. Next he considers what information he requires in order to make these decisions. Finally, he designs the network for the collection of the information.

The need to predetermine what information will be required is well exemplified by the firm in which the key executives were examining a quarterly profit and loss statement. The volume of sales has decreased over the comparable period in the previous year, and the executives were speculating about reasons for the sales decline. The production manager thought that a change in the product mix in the previous six months might have brought about an increase in the sale of low-priced items at the expense of the higher-priced items. The sales manager felt there had been a general decline in business, with a resulting decrease in sales of all products. The treasurer, who had just returned from a field trip, was of the opinion that the major decline in sales had been restricted to certain regions and was only temporary.

The president terminated the meeting, saying he wanted more facts and fewer guesses. He said it was impossible to take action when no one even knew the facts. It was deplorable that the company was not in a position to have such facts at hand and that it would take a special study of company records to collect them.

No decisions could be made here for counteracting the downward trend in sales simply because no one knew where the causes lay. Without information there could be no decision. But the collection of factual information takes time and planning. Usually it is not possible to assemble information at the time the decision is to be made. Many companies have never seriously considered what information is necessary for effective decision making. Often what is lacking is not information but the right information.

Accounting supplies the major portion of cost information, but accounting for record keeping and accounting for decision making are rarely the same. The decision maker thinks in terms of incremental or marginal costs, while accounting is oriented toward average costs. The accountant is interested in the cost of manufacturing or selling the product. He attempts to set forth some standard of performance in cost terms for pricing, costing, and control. To do this, he determines the standard cost or, alternatively, what might be considered the *average cost* of manufacturing or selling a product.

Accounting Systems and Decision Making

Both incremental and historical cost information are required in modern business. The accountant is forced by tradition and by tax regulations to use certain methods of cost determination. But the manager usually bases his decisions on incremental cost data, not on historical standard costs.

This dichotomy plagues most companies and most accountants. The progressive accountant may be interested in cost data for decision making, but he knows that he must satisfy the historical cost data requirements. The manager who formulates his decisions on historical cost data soon finds that his information is inaccurate for his purposes, although the accountant's traditional data often serve as the base for recalculations for decision making.

Throughout the history of corporation income taxes, legislative and regulatory agencies have evolved accounting reporting procedures to insure conformity of methods of reporting corporate income. These agencies codified the practices originated by the accounting profession many decades ago, which has resulted in imposing extremely rigid rules on accounting systems. At the same time, this codification of accounting practices by government fiat has established very strict qualifications, and written examinations must be taken for certification. The certified or chartered public accountant has become an established professional with considerable status and prestige.

ACCOUNTING AND TAXATION REGULATIONS

The strict procedural approach of tax authorities and of accountants themselves has resulted in an even greater accent on historical accounting methods. Not only are these methods unsuited to the needs of management for decision making; there is even some serious doubt whether they meet the need of government for accurate profit reporting for tax purposes.

The accounting profession is forced by law to continue unsatisfactory and outdated accounting practices. Specific limits on depreciation of assets frequently cause a corporation to carry an asset on its books with a life longer by law than it has in actual fact. Since the corporation is entitled to a capital loss on equipment sold at less than book value, arbitrary depreciation rules bring little tax advantage to the government in the long run. The profit shown by the firm is not realistic. Since it does not take into account management's educated estimate of the life of the asset, a realistic asset use cannot be charged against current profits.

Such practices as unrealistic depreciation regulations make accounting statements almost useless as the base of managerial decision making. To counteract this, a special branch of accounting has arisen called industrial accounting, or, in the universities, often called managerial accounting. But for the most part the present state of accounting information requires that the sophisticated and experienced manager rely heavily on recalculations and educated guesses in decision making.

Decisions Based on Tax Considerations

Many decisions are not necessarily best in the long run for either the corporation or the economy but are made for good tax reasons. One example is the sale of a fully depreciated plant on a sale-and-leaseback arrangement. The corporation pays capital gains tax on the sale of the building but deducts from current taxes the total rent paid under the leaseback arrangement. In some instances the only justification for this sale is to gain a tax advantage. There are other good managerial reasons for such a sale-and-leaseback arrangement. One of them is to achieve a higher return on invested capital than the rate of return on real estate holdings.

In some circumstances a corporation may make unwarranted expenditures merely because the government will in effect pay about half the cost through the reduction of taxable profits. Expenditures for research and development are a case in point. If a firm is in a good profit position, it may decide to make a much larger investment in research and development than it would otherwise, placing the charges against current income. As a result, two equally efficient companies could make the same profit before research and development expenditures, but one would pay a much lower tax than the other because of these expenditures.

It is all but impossible for governments to institute drastic changes in income tax laws and regulations. Indeed a case could be made that the cure might be worse than the disease. Countless thousands of decisions have been predicated on existing tax regulations. Drastic changes in these regulations would upset both personal and corporate decisions. Furthermore, it would be impossible to build in enough flexibility to meet the needs of all firms and all industries.

Exhibit 4

Example of Equipment-Replacement Decision

Factors	Old Machine	New Machine
Cost	$110,000	$150,000
Labor savings of new machine over old per year		$50,000
Scrap value	$10,000	$10,000
Age of equipment	Two years	New
Depreciation factor (straight line)	Ten years	Ten years
Book value	$90,000	
Current interest rate	6%	6%
Current corporate return on investment	12%	12%

Calculation A *Accounting Orientation*	Calculation B *Managerial Decision-making Orientation*
Cost of new machine $150,000	
Plus book value of old 80,000	
$230,000	

Depreciation increase

New machine

$$\frac{230,000-10,000}{10} = \$\ 22,000$$

Old machine

$$\frac{110,000-10,000}{10} = \$\ 10,000$$

Increase in annual depreciation	$ 12,000
Interest cost increase 6% × $40,000	$ 2,400

Annual savings		Annual savings	
Labor savings	$ 50,000	Labor savings	$ 50,000
Minus increase in depreciation and interest	14,400	Minus opportunity cost (12% of 150,000)	18,000
	$ 35,600		$ 32,000

Payoff period (not taking into account tax factors)

$$\frac{230,000}{35,600} = 6.5 \text{ years}$$

Payoff period (not taking into account tax factors)

$$\frac{150,000}{32,000} = 4.7 \text{ years}$$

THE PROFILE OF A DECISION

In order to serve both the decision information needs of management and the need for historical records for tax purposes, the accountant may be forced to work out a dual recording system. Decisions pertaining to equipment replacement afford an excellent illustration of the inadequacies of standard accounting information for decision making.

Accounting records provide data on the depreciation rate, the book value of the equipment, its estimated useful life as permitted by tax regulations and its estimated scrap value at the end of its useful life. But the decision maker needs data on the rate of obsolescence, the opportunity cost, and the economic advantages of the new equipment over the old, none of which are supplied by accounting records. Let us examine two different approaches to an equipment-replacement decision. (See Exhibit 4.)

Calculation A utilizes standardized accounting information to determine the number of years it would take the firm to recoup its costs in purchasing the new machine and scrapping the old. The major factor indicated by the accounting records is that the old machine carries a book value of $90,000, which by accounting rules would constitute a charge against the new machine (less $10,000 scrap value). In other words, if the new machine replaces the old it must absorb the loss or undepreciated value of the old equipment.

Accounting calculations would also consider the difference in the depreciation rate between the old and new equipment, since the increased depreciation would be a charge against annual profits. In addition, the accounting figures reflect the need to borrow additional funds in some form of chattel mortgage against the equipment, with the attendant interest charges. The difference in the depreciation rates and increased interest costs would be subtracted from the estimated labor savings of the new equipment over the old, and this figure would be divided into the cost of the new machine plus the book value of the old. This calculation would give a payoff period of approximately seven years. It must be noted at this point that this illustration is greatly oversimplified; it does not take into account tax considerations, amortization of the cost of the new equipment, and so on.

Calculation B illustrates a managerial decision-making approach to equipment replacement. The book value or "sunk cost" of the old equipment is considered merely an accounting entry required for income tax purposes and for reporting profits. The funds have been expended and need not interfere with the manager's concern over future plans. A major element in the equipment replacement decision is "opportunity cost," which may be defined as the alternative returns, or profit, if the funds were invested in other ways. Perhaps the best measure of opportunity cost is the rate of return on net worth. This would have a floor, however, of how much the funds could earn in any safe liquid investment such as a bank.

The reason for using opportunity cost in equipment replacement decisions is that the firm must be able to realize at least its average return on investment before it can consider further investment in equipment. If this is not possible, either the equipment replacement is not feasible or alternative decisions must be made in favor of other methods of manufacturing or subcontracting.

It matters little whether the firm uses its own funds or obtains loans to purchase equipment; the opportunity cost is the same. In strict accounting terms, if it were not necessary to borrow funds to purchase equipment, no interest charge would be leveled against the new equipment in the calculation of an equipment replacement decision.

In the managerial decision-making orientation, the simplified calculation is labor savings minus opportunity cost, which would give the net economic advantage annually of the new machine over the old. The calculation of the payoff would be cost of the new equipment divided by annual savings. Again, for purposes of simplification, in this example many important factors have been disregarded—for example, the tax advantage of the increased depreciation, the tax disadvantage of taxes on profits (since the entire $30,000 would not be available each year), and the like.[1]

Thus standard accounting procedures—such as providing information on reserve for depreciation, depreciation rate comparison, capital loss on sale of equipment—do not supply the information necessary for the calculation of such a managerial decision as equipment replacement. The kinds of information that are supplied by

---

[1] George Terbourgh, *Equipment Replacement Decisions* (New York: McGraw-Hill Book Company, 1952), presents a sophisticated account of the calculation of equipment replacement decisions.

other sources and that do enter into an equipment-replacement decision are the opportunity cost and the obsolescence factor (both arrived at through calculations made by management), the original
cost of equipment (from the supplier or the purchasing department),
and the competitive cost advantages of new equipment (from the
industrial engineering department).

ACCOUNTING AS A MANAGEMENT TOOL

Accounting is one of the most important tools available to management. But it must extend beyond its historical and average-cost
orientation to serve the decision-making and control needs of management. When the accounting staff fails to meet these needs, a
different agency has to do so. This was the case in one large firm
whose controller had risen through the accounting ranks. His manner was courteous but firm. He considered it his job to collect accurate and timely information that could be developed into financial
statements and accounting reports on such matters as budgets and
variances. He insisted that all members of his organization follow
his philosophy, which was that his department was to provide management with whatever information and services it required for its
operation.

In reality, what the controller meant was that he would provide
whatever accounting information the accounting department *thought*
management required. When individual managers asked for special
manipulations of accounting information, the controller always replied that the system was not set up to generate such information.
He noted the difficulties in collecting special information and the
incompatibility of cost information within the firm. After repeated
failures to obtain information for decision making, management
moved to set up a separate staff agency for the collection and dissemination of decision-oriented information. Though it was called
a computer center it was in fact a management information center.

The technological revolution in the processing of raw data by
computer has all too often been accepted only partially by accountants. For the most part, accountants consider computers to be
excellent devices for calculating payroll and the like, but not enough
have extended computer applications to develop a true manage-

ment information center. Yet this technological revolution is a means for accounting to take its all-important place at the right hand of management by supplying accurate and timely decision-oriented information.

Management itself is not blameless. There is a tendency among line managers to be too dependent on staff. The manager says, "Give me the tools and I will do the job." But how is staff to know what tools are required? Of course the job of the manager is becoming increasingly complex. Certainly he must depend upon staff for much of the help he needs to permit him to operate in a dynamic industrial environment. This does not absolve the line manager from any of his responsibilities, and one of these responsibilities is to determine what kinds of information are required for the most effective decision making. Then and then alone can staff perform its task in the design and operation of a control system and information network.

A plea must be made for the integration of control systems, accounting records, and managerial intelligence services into one system designed to facilitate the making of decisions. The modern corporation can ill afford the operation of three separate systems to achieve the one end. A case might be made for the multiple operation of systems where such an arrangement can guarantee the highest level of performance. But the existence of these three systems does not in itself guarantee a high level of performance. Each produces specialized information. Although all three may use the same basic data, each may combine the information in different ways to give conflicting results.

The integration of these three possibly different systems requires a central focal point: decision making. Compliance with standards of performance, or the collection of historical cost information, should be translated into information that enables the firm to reach its objectives through effective decision making. Once an objective is established for what may be termed the new control system, separate parts of the organization can integrate their activities to permit this.

Even with decision making as its focal point, the design and implementation of a control system is not easy. There will be many errors in any firm before definitive accomplishments result from this integration of systems. Undoubtedly both line and staff will need to be reeducated, but such a start is long overdue. Management cannot expect miracles overnight. Although there will be much frustration, management has no alternative but to carry forth this research if it is to keep pace with the accelerating technological and sociological changes that are complicating the task. Management requires sophistication in its methods to carry through its responsibilities of coordinating resources to satisfy the needs of society. One of the major innovations lies within this information network of decision making.

INFORMATION NETWORKS IN REVIEW

A decision is only as good as its input. Often it is not possible to know what information will be required for a decision, yet at the time of the decision either facts must be available or estimates will have to be made on the basis of the decision maker's experience.

This sort of intuitive reasoning places the manager and the organization in jeopardy, because the decision will be based on one man's perception of conditions, which may be colored by his organizational role or experience. For example, a marketing manager may be quite optimistic about past sales, but the facts show spotty performance in some territories or in the sales of particular products. He will project this feeling into his decisions if factual information is not available. The consequences for the organization may be disastrous.

Accounting is the major source of factual information in a firm, and the accounting profession has always prided itself on professional competence and conservatism in reporting financial information. But now the accountant is faced with an information technology revolution coupled with increasingly sophisticated management, which is demanding digestible decision-oriented information. The time is ripe for the accountant to reevaluate his role vis-à-vis managerial intelligence. By broadening his function, he enchances his value.

12

Control Philosophy

A FIRM must generate profits to encourage investment. It is at this point that the concept of control comes into play. The investors charge the management of the company with the responsibility of insuring that there is in fact a generation of profit. Management in turn utilizes controls to insure that the firm does make a profit to satisfy the needs of investors. Control in this sense is an internal guard against overzealousness by investors or managers in generating the profits required for survival.

The Western democracies have assigned the responsibility for the effective allocation of resources to private enterprise. The mainstay of the private enterprise system is investment by individuals in companies to turn these resources into goods and services. But there must be some incentive for the individual to invest his savings through the stock market in private companies. This incentive is profit. Management has the responsibility and trust to control the company in such a way as to satisfy society's needs for efficiency in the production of goods and services and the investor's desire for profit.

Control in some sense pervades all aspects of life. Yet there is an attendant danger, whether in society at large or in the business firm as part of society. This danger is inflexibility. Progress requires change, yet change would be difficult or impossible should control be overemphasized.[1]

In any effective control system less emphasis must be placed upon compliance than upon stimulating imagination. The art of the skillful manager lies in knowing what does not require control as much as what does. Expressed differently: Managers must learn that preventing mistakes is less important than catching them before they become significant. One of the tricks in living with change and in keeping a system of management control open-ended is the ability to tolerate a certain amount of imperfection in order to achieve maximum profits in the longer run.

CONTROL AND THE ORGANIZATION ENTITY

Conformity is a necessity if there is to be effective coordination of the parts of an organization. But such conformity must not stifle initiative in the process of providing a high predictability of behavior. The organization cannot *assume* conformity and predictability of behavior. Perhaps communication has broken down; perhaps there has been a misunderstanding; perhaps there is an inability to perform to standard. Some form of control or managerial intelligence is required to keep management informed on progress.

It is not the mark of a police state that a control system exists to insure that the parts of an organization are carrying out their assignments so that the total can achieve the objective. Control connotes compliance, however, and presumes some formal understanding of requirements to permit a comparison of actual with planned performance.

The crux of the problem lies in whether standards of performance have been established. There can be no measurement unless there are standards against which performance is to be measured. In many instances the major fault lies with the standards, not the control system. Unfortunately, the only standards in many firms are those established by time studies or by quotas that are based on past performance.

---

[1] This concept is developed in considerable depth in William Travers Jerome III, *Executive Control—The Catalyst* (New York: John Wiley & Sons, Inc., 1961), p. 6.

The lack of adequate standards is not the only problem besetting controls; another is in the very role of control itself. If control is to effect corrective action, how is this action brought about? Information systems in most firms are the responsibility of staff rather than line personnel. One of the most important information systems in any organization is designed for control. Often even the design of the system is made the responsibility of staff. The question then arises whether the information collected by the staff agency and used to inform the line manager that corrective action must be taken is control, or whether control is the corrective action taken by the manager.

STAFF AND CONTROLS

This controversy has occupied a great deal of attention in management literature, with particular focus on whether staff exercises command in the operation of a control system. If collecting the information is in fact control, it could be argued that staff is no longer in an advisory capacity but in a command capacity. If staff exercises command, much of the philosophy underlying the line and staff concept is invalidated.

Although it may be drawing a fine line, the collection of information and the design of the information system are the proper responsibility of staff and do not invalidate its role. Corrective action is the province of line management; whether information precipitating such action comes from staff through the information system is incidental. The ancillary function of operating the information network is properly the role of staff.

Although the two functions of collecting control information and applying corrective action can be delineated in theory, to do so may be difficult in practice. The preparation of a budget is an excellent illustration of this difficulty. Large firms have a budget director who works for the controller or in the accounting division. His role is therefore defined as staff. The organization charges the budget director with the responsibility of preparing and implementing budgets. He exercises this responsibility by coordinating the activities of line managers responsible for the input information.

As each section of the firm presents the information required for the budget, it is coordinated and detailed. The budget forecasts a surplus of revenue over expenditures, which usually requires the paring of expenses. Who is to decide which department is to have its expenditures curtailed? There may be a budget committee composed of line managers with a sprinkling of staff to assist in preparing the budget. But, realistically, knowledge is power. The budget director is the one best qualified to prepare the budget, so he has a major say in its preparation.

The preparation of the budget and a profit forecast is not the end but the beginning of the budgetary task. A control system must be engineered to collect information on whether the budget is being adhered to or not. In the event that the budget is not being followed, normally the control system flags deviations. Since the budget director is responsible for insuring that the budget is followed, he informs the delinquent manager of any budget variances. Although the budget director is merely passing along information and only the line manager can take corrective action, it is difficult to distinguish advice from command in this case.

Control connotes appraisal of individual performance. It is difficult to sort out the manager as a person from the manager as a manager. When the budget director tells a manager he is over budget, a criticism of the manager's performance is implied. The tendency is for the manager to devise his own control systems to *avoid* appraisal. This control avoidance takes many forms, one of which is to overestimate expenditures so as to insure a good performance rating. Sometimes in government such overstatements are so common that it is the practice to cut all budget requests automatically by some predetermined figure. It then becomes a battle between budget directors and operating managers to guess what amount will be forthcoming this year. One common approach is for the line manager to devise an information system to confound the control system—perhaps to the point of doctoring or misstating figures in such a way that the control system does not catch their inadequacies.

Information and control systems are often misunderstood and looked on as a form of secret police which has as its purpose not the achievement of objectives but some insidious function such as singling out individual managers for punishment. Rarely is the system accepted by the individual manager even when he is responsible for implementing the corrective action. It is in this atmosphere of suspicion and intrigue that somehow the manager must operate effectively and the firm must attain its objectives. It is no easy task in the present state of control theory and practice for the manager to be effective.

CONTROLS DEFINED

Controls are essentially a pool of information on the progress of a plan. But a great danger is that the control system may enforce compliance to a plan that is itself inadequate. The paramount consideration must be achievement of the objective, not adherence to the plan. It is at this point that most control systems break down. This was the case in one firm with a control system but no sure knowledge that its overall plans could achieve the corporate objectives—one of which was to obtain a larger share of the market. Top management was dominated by engineers who felt that the best route to a larger share of the market lay in building a superbly engineered product. Since the product involved potentially high maintenance costs for consumers, this strategy seemed quite logical.

A plan was formulated to increase the time spent in designing and insuring greater reliability of the product through quality control, and controls were set up to insure that the plan was adhered to. Over the next few years the firm found its market share shrinking rather than expanding. A thorough investigation revealed that the consumers were not as interested in the product's reliability as they were in its general appearance. Competitors had devoted their energies to designing a better-looking product, which, although inferior in performance, appealed more to the consumers than the superbly engineered product. The controls in this illustration worked well in insuring that the plan was carried through but failed completely in determining whether the firm was going to increase its market share.

Though every plan must include controls to insure its effective implementation, the fallibility of both plan and controls must be recognized. If the manager relies too much on his control system, he may become complacent when the controls indicate that the plan is being followed. Assuming these limitations are correct, control cannot be defined in the usual sense of action to correct deviations from standards. Rather, it must focus on eliciting behavior patterns which will permit attainment of the objectives. It is imperative that any definition of control emphasize not adherence to standards solely but the most effective allocation of resources to attain the objectives. In a competitive economy this effective allocation of resources is evaluated in terms of profit. Under competitive conditions the firm that most effectively allocates its resources will best be able to sell its product in the marketplace.

ORGANIZATION FOR CONTROL

This philosophy that line should command and staff should advise is particularly applicable in control systems. This is not to deny that major problems still exist in the delineation of line and staff in any organization. But there are particular dangers in utilizing staff in control systems. In many organizations the president depends upon a controller, often the chief financial or accounting officer, to insure that the firm is "in control." If the sanctity of line and staff is to be retained, the concept of a controller as one who takes action to insure compliance with plans is inappropriate. Acceptance of this philosophy requires a realignment of top management responsibilities and functions so controls can be exercised by line managers and not by staff.

Again the problem of defining control rears its head. There must be a differentiation between collecting information through control systems and exercising corrective action. The former rightfully is a staff function but the latter must be reserved for line. If strict adherence to this concept requires a major realignment of executive activities, this may be all to the good. The often cited but little practiced concept of commensurate authority and responsibility seems to be cast aside when control is mentioned. The old adage, "trust a man and he will be trustworthy," is particularly applicable in control systems. Most people both in and out of management want to perform well, but assigning responsibilities to staff militates against this concept. This is not to say that controls need be abandoned; rather, responsibility must be realigned.

It bears repetition that control has as its objective the patterning of behavior to achieve the firm's objectives and must therefore be exercised by those whose behavior is critical to the attainment of the objectives. The design of control systems and the collection and evaluation of information may rightfully be assigned to staff. But the actual control—the action-oriented aspect of the system—must be exercised by line. It could be argued that a controller performs truly staff functions and that the president exercises corrective action. It is also true that the very possession of information gives an action orientation to staff. Such a de facto assignment of power is reinforced by the importance given to control staff in the managerial hierarchy. To effect a true delineation of staff and line in control requires a reorganization of the control function in the average firm.

To elicit behavior which will insure attainment of objectives, control must assist the line manager in coordinating the resources allocated to him, not in insuring compliance through punitive action of some sort. What is required is a control system that provides the individual manager with information to facilitate intelligent decision making.

The punitive connotations of control with overtones of constant evaluation must be replaced with the positive concept of better performance. The dictates of organization hold both the superior and the subordinate responsible for accomplishing a delegated task. The superior obviously is vitally interested in insuring that the task is being accomplished satisfactorily. This seems to dictate that the purpose of control is to keep the superior informed on the performance of the subordinate. But this cannot be the major function of control.

The typical control system does not fulfill the true function of control: to initiate corrective action. When responsibility is delegated, it is the subordinate who must take corrective action as required. If the superior takes the action he should not have delegated it in the first instance. Furthermore the connotation in the superior's taking action is that the control system is more or less a spy organization. Certainly this will not build a sense of responsibility in the subordinate for self-discipline and self-corrective action.

CONTROLS IN ACTION

The type of control exercised through a programmed system on a computer can apply equally well in the nonprogrammed system. The system receives inputs from the superior (the controller), the subordinates (the controlled), and the control staff agency (the system operator). The control system monitors operations and pinpoints deviations from the plan. In the fully automated system the feedback would set self-correcting devices into operation to correct the deviation.

The same principles can apply to the nonautomated control system, with the staff control agency performing the same function as the computer in monitoring the plan. Some form of reporting device informs the staff agency of any deviation from plan. The agency in turn reports to the individual best able to take corrective action—the manager or subordinate responsible for operating the plan. It is not necessary to report the deviation at this point since the objective of the control system is to pattern the subordinate's behavior.

The subordinate knows that he can take corrective action without in any way involving his superior. Furthermore, he knows that the deviation will not be communicated to his superior if corrective action is taken. This obviously aligns the objectives of the control system with those of the subordinate: effective performance according to plan. He has all the necessary current information as well as the necessary discretion to take action. If he finds that corrective action cannot be taken according to the plan, he is at liberty to take this up directly with his superior. The relationship of the two is now that the subordinate is taking a problem to the superior; it is not the superior checking on the subordinate's failure.

If the subordinate fails to take the requisite action the semiautomated control system swings into action to elicit behavior elsewhere which will permit attainment of the objectives. Failure of the subordinate to act is reported to the superior as a last resort. It might be argued that the time lag in this system could have dire consequences. The answer to this criticism is that the time factor must be built into any control system. When time is a critical factor, the system would limit the time permitted the subordinate.

DECENTRALIZATION AND THE DESIGN OF THE CONTROL SYSTEM

The problem of control is magnified in the large decentralized organization. As organizations become unwieldy or establish widely separated facilities, centralized decision making is increasingly difficult. Much of this difficulty stems from the lack of factual, timely information about local conditions. One solution in increasing use is the organization of autonomous or semi-autonomous units within the corporate structure. This is a logical extension of delegation. But decision-making advantages are accompanied by the intensification of the problems of control.

A review of the decisions and control problems in General Dynamics which led to a tremendous corporate loss in 1961 well illustrates the magnitude of the control problems facing the decentralized firm. The development and sale of the 880 and 990 jet aircraft by Convair is a classic case where the desire to give autonomy and discretionary powers to a division endangered the very existence of the total corporation.

In 1956 Convair, the major division of General Dynamics, accounted for 75 percent of the corporation's total sales. Convair had been a successful producer of propeller-driven aircraft; it took its first step into the jet age when it undertook to design jet transports for Trans World Airlines. Two designs were submitted. Six months later, Boeing had an Air Force contract for 707s and Douglas had preliminary designs for the DC-8; Convair and TWA had conferences but no decisions.

The division was assailed by blow after blow after it finally settled on a design (the 880) and went on from there. For example, although some members of top management considered the 880 to be underpriced from the start, not till parts were ordered was it discovered that the cost of the components of the aircraft (normally 70 percent of the total cost) exceeded the selling price of the delivered aircraft. Moreover, because the TWA contract restricted sales of the 880 to TWA and Delta Airlines until the spring of 1957, Convair was the loser when United Air Lines ordered 30 of Boeing's new 720s.

It was obvious that the 880 was a disaster. The corporate response was to promise delivery of the 990 to American Airlines on a fixed date although the new plane was not yet designed and was to be built without a prototype or advance model. The 990 was delivered late and failed to live up to its specifications; American canceled the contract in favor of Boeing; and Convair and American negotiated a new contract for fewer planes at a considerably reduced price.

The final blow came in 1959 when TWA refused delivery on the first 880s. Convair decided to pull the planes off the assembly line rather than finish them, deliver them, and then sue. When work was eventually resumed, each plane (all in different stages of production) had to be individually completed on the field.

By the end of 1961 General Dynamics had had to write off $425 million—a staggering loss even for a $2 billion corporation.

Obviously, even with decentralization there must be control—but not enough to destroy the environment which permits discretion for decision making and the exercise of initiative by lower management. When survival is paramount, control may receive a higher priority than decentralized decision making. For most firms the issue is not survival but improved performance and profits, which might best be accomplished through decentralization. Although many firms are moving toward decentralization, there are as many tending toward a high degree of centralization, utilizing more sophisticated information networks with high-speed processing through computers.

Centralization fails to take into account the ego needs of employees. It does not recognize many of the findings of the behavioral sciences, which indicate a deterioration of personal motivations when there is no opportunity to exercise initiative. Thus, regardless of the sophistication of information networks and data processing systems, there must be a continuing decentralization of authority if employee commitment to the organization is not to be permanently weakened.

One way to satisfy both the human need for self-realization and the organizational need for closer control is to use automated control that emphasizes the concept of influencing behavior to attain objectives and abandoning punitive control. Just as the policeman should not be feared by the law-abiding citizen but should instead be looked on as an official whose responsibility is to help and protect the populace, so the control system should be treated as an aid to better management rather than as a check on performance. It cannot be denied that the policeman will always be feared by the lawbreaker. Nor can it be denied that continued failure to adhere to corporate plans will result in the manager's removal. But this is not the primary objective of a control system.

CORPORATE DESIGN OF CONTROL SYSTEMS

Once divisional and corporate management have accepted the need for control systems and the philosophy that such systems do not

have as their purpose the constant evaluation of short-run performance, the stage is set for the design of the corporate controls. When
corporate staff designs controls over divisional managers, this leads
to antagonism and conflict.

Rather than the superimposition of controls on the division or
other subpart of the organization, there must be an integration of
control systems to facilitate management action. Acceptance of this
doctrine will result in a changing relationship between corporate and
divisional management. Corporate staff will become facilitators
rather than controllers, which will satisfy the needs of both divisional
and corporate managers.

The corporate design of control systems requires as its first step
an acceptance of the need for master planning. Master planning
leads to the full-scale meshing of all plans, but it must be preceded
by long-range planning and the establishment of objectives acceptable at all levels in the organization. Many firms operate with
master plans converted to dollars and cents through budgets. But
budgets are related to annual costs, revenues, and profit planning;
they are rarely related to specific plans. (There are major exceptions
in industries where funding is obtained through contracts for projects which operate under separate budgets.) Furthermore the major
budgetary control agency is accounting, which usually collects information related to some form of standard costs, budgets, or financial statements. Accounting does not necessarily collect other information pertaining to the fulfillment of plans. The other control
agencies have very specific assignments. Quality control and its enforcement agency, inspection, collect information pertaining solely
to quality; inventory control, to inventory; production control, to
production. And these controls are not necessarily coordinated with
each other or with accounting.

Although control and planning may go on throughout a firm,
there may not be what could be called a total systems approach to
either function. And as there cannot be controls without standards
of performance, which on the managerial level must be supplied by
plans, any corporate control system must also be a corporate planning system. The master plan and its ancillary parts supply the standards of performance; controls measure performance against these
standards.

To achieve a master plan and standards of performance requires a high degree of standardization. The plans of all parts of the organization must mesh, which means they must be in essentially the the same form and the same language. But a standard format need not stifle initiative. In fact, standardization of planning permits greater attention to content and less to form. Staff can be of great assistance in facilitating this standardization, but line management must be involved. The line manager cannot abdicate his responsibility to staff if the system is to achieve what the manager requires of it. Certainly standardization requires considerable time of line management. But the rewards are well worth the investment. Once standardization is accomplished, computers can take over much of the drudgery now handled by individual managers. Furthermore, computers can be an impersonal aid that removes the stigma of evaluation and punitive action.

Without planning, control systems become meaningless. Arbitrary standards of performance and control through these standards may endanger the very survival of the firm, as was the case in a corporation whose management wanted to decentralize authority but retain some control over the autonomous divisions. The president decided that each division should be run essentially as a separate business with divisional profit and loss statements. The ratio of net profit to net assets was to be the gauge of each division's effectiveness.

One division that performed consistently better than all the others over a ten-year period was always held up to the others as an example. At the end of ten years the director of this division retired and was replaced by a bright young man from another firm in the same industry. At the end of the first year under the new divisional director the ratio of net profit to net assets had fallen far below that of the other divisions. When the president of the corporation investigated, he found that his control system had not been nearly as effective as he had thought.

The previous director had consistently made decisions which, although they enhanced the ratio of net profit to net assets and the standing of his division, seriously endangered its long-run future. He had failed to replenish assets, with the result that his equipment was antiquated and run down; and he had failed to cultivate new customers and had discontinued divisional products which did not make an immediate major contribution to profits.

These short-run decisions made this division's ratio of profit to net assets the highest in the industry. But the long-range effect of this strategy was to set back the growth of the firm considerably and to force it to incur large expenditures over the next five years to regain its position in the industry. It could be argued that gross assets (excluding depreciation) should have been used in the ratio calculations instead of net assets, but the previous division manager would no doubt have optimized the ratio rather than future profits.

The control system in this firm resulted in behavior which focused on meeting standards rather than attaining long-run objectives. The use of arbitrary standards such as net return on investment will not necessarily achieve the required results. This is why it is necessary to set forth master plans on the corporate level with the involvement of divisions and of lower management; these can be examined before the fact to ascertain whether they will permit the firm to attain its objectives. Once the master plans are complete the control system can be instituted. Here again it must be understood what the controls are and what they are to accomplish.

What information is needed by each level of management to institute corrective action? What time factors are involved? Since the plans will already have been correlated and approved, the controls are operative solely to insure compliance of actual events with plans. There is no censoring or evaluation by the staff control agency.

The corporate decentralized control system utilizes the same principles as the more simplified automated self-regulating control system. But since the relationship between the divisions and the corporate headquarters is far more complex than that between subparts of the organization, progress reports are required to supplement the system. These reports could have been specified in the design of the control system and would serve both corporate and divisional management. If the entire planning and control system could be programmed and computerized, the computer would store these progress reports on its memory drum and issue reports only when progress was not according to plan.

If a problem on the divisional level has resulted in corrective action by the divisional director, such information need not be communicated to the corporate control agency. This is the case because the purpose of the control system is to influence behavior, not to evaluate the interim decisions of operating management. Only when interim decisions do not conform to the plan is operating management informed. But the control system does not report these deviations to the next higher level of management as in most control systems. To do so would encourage operating managers to confound the control system. But if the system is designed to help operating managers fulfill their functions, cooperation will increase.

Master planning and decentralized control centers permit the decentralization of authority without loss of control. This end result is well worth the major investment required to standardize the planning process and design the decentralized control system.

13

Performance Standards
and Control Systems

THERE IS a tendency to rely too much on controls. When elaborate standards of performance have been met, management becomes complacent and considers performance to these standards as a green light. Only when such standards of performance are not met is an adequate investigation initiated. Yet major dangers may not be indicated by a control system that uses return on investment as a performance standard.

A control system may operate well internally but fail to record major environmental shifts. Many firms have been lulled into complacency because their control systems do not initiate corrective action. The steel industry did not consider aluminum or prestressed concrete as serious competitors until its market share slipped. Some soap firms failed to consider detergents a serious threat. Countless control systems do not alert management to future crises. A control system may register that current return on investment is meeting all performance standards. But rarely does it consider the action of competitors or correlate current performance with such indexes as gross national product. Although the problem seems to be lack of foresight on the part of the system, in fact the blame must be allocated to management.

It is not enough to design a control system. Management must be alert to conditions not anticipated when the system was designed. Complacency is a luxury no manager can afford. Recognition of the fallibility of controls is implicit in the trend toward decentralization of authority. Coordinating and controlling a far-flung industrial empire are not within the abilities of any one man or, for that matter, any group of men. As one man becomes overburdened with detail he may assign some of his work to others. Although this cuts down on the detail in the manager's task, it also multiplies his coordination and control problems. Not only is there a new relationship between superior and subordinate but there is also a multiplicity of relationships among subordinates which further complicates the task of coordination.

One solution to this problem is to set up an elaborate control system with very explicit standards of performance. But such a system itself is essentially static, whereas the process it controls is dynamic. The control system must be rigid because of its need for definitive standards. But this very rigidity leads to unsatisfactory total performance in the dynamic sense, although it may very well adhere to the static standards. In other words, the static standards may force management behavior into a predetermined pattern without permitting the latitude required to cope with dynamic, fast-changing business conditions.

Designing a control system to permit the exercise of initiative and yet control performance absolutely is further complicated by the human factor. Human beings are ambivalent toward controls. On the one hand people prefer order to disorder. But on the other hand they do not like to be constrained. This ambivalence, this simultaneously seeking controls and damning their existence, makes predictability of reaction to controls particularly difficult. Controls result all too often in frustration. Individuals may accept intellectually and logically the need for controls, but this rarely makes controls more palatable.

A firm will normally recruit people for or promote them to important managerial posts on the basis of their intelligence, their experience, their knowledge, and above all their drive and initiative in getting things done. When such an individual is fettered by controls designed by others, he is unable to exercise that very initiative the company so badly requires. Over time, many major corporations have met this challenge by decentralizing operations. The concept is essentially a simple one. The man who is to captain a decentralized operation has already proved himself in battle by his past managerial successes. When he is given the discretion to run his operation as if he were the president of his own corporation, the firm is in a position to gain every advantage from his ability and experience. But this does not solve the problem of control. In fact, it further complicates the process.

When decentralization and delegation of authority are carried to the point of giving managers full discretion, how is the corporation to control the actions and destinies of its parts? Logically it would seem that centralized action (even if only with regard to information) and decentralized authority (with its connotation of divorcing the actions of the parts from those of the whole) are necessarily incompatible. Does this mean that the corporation must abandon one of its divisions to the vagaries of an individual's whim?

How can the corporation be protected against these vagaries when discretionary authority is delegated so widely? The answer is that the separate parts of the corporation must be judged and controlled just as the corporation itself is. One way to control decentralized operations is to set up profit centers. If the division is large enough it may be appropriate to have a completely separate accounting system with divisional financial statements. A further step may be to set up the various parts of the main corporation as subsidiary corporations, which would permit the use of boards of directors and identical standards for the parts and for the whole. But it must be recognized that profit centers and separate financial statements are essentially after-the-fact controls. To make financial statements useful requires accurate systems of reporting information, sophisticated analysis, and an awareness of actual conditions during the period under review. Yet even with adequately prepared and thoroughly understood financial statements, the information is too late for effective control.

A MANAGERIAL INTELLIGENCE SYSTEM

It might be said, then, that the best control is no control. Until far more sophisticated control systems are designed and more is known about behavior patterns in management, it seems more practical to depend upon experienced, qualified managers than on inadequate controls. But this should not eliminate what might be termed a managerial intelligence system, which would keep top management at both the corporate and the divisional levels abreast of current trends and conditions. Such a system should not transcend the authority relationships set up in the decentralized organization.

The relationship between the total corporation and its divisions or subsidiaries should be akin to the relationship between top management and the board of directors. The board has the power to set policies or guides which top management must adhere to, and it has the power to remove the president. But members of the board have no individual power to interfere with the operation of the firm. Furthermore, the board is strictly prohibited from interfering in day-to-day operations. The factor of review remains a board prerogative, and it must remain the prerogative of top management in monitoring the actions of decentralized operating management.

A managerial intelligence system must not be considered a control system requiring rigid adherence to predetermined standards. The relationship between corporate top management and divisional operating management must not resolve itself into power politics. Division managers cannot be given a task without the authority to carry it through.

Two questions might be asked at this point: Why is such a managerial intelligence system necessary? If management is to be trusted, what will be achieved by such a system? To answer these questions requires an understanding of the relationship between any superior and subordinate in an industrial environment. The manager cannot abdicate his responsibility to his subordinates. He must provide leadership. And he must train and evaluate his subordinates. Even at the highest levels these managerial responsibilities do not change particularly except in degree. No effective manager at any level interferes in the subordinate's handling of a task once the task has been formally delegated. But this does not mean that any manager should be ignorant of what his subordinates are doing.

Just as the president of a corporation must answer to the board of directors and to the stockholders for the survival and success of the corporation, so managers at all levels are responsible for the success and survival of their sections of the organization. Even when there is complete confidence in the individual manager and complete delegation of authority through decentralization, survival of the firm must be the paramount issue. But the accent must be on information, not on control. (The General Dynamics case illustrates this need for a managerial intelligence system to keep corporate management informed independently of the progress of divisions.)

Managers of subsidiaries in a decentralized organization should not have to ask permission or clear decisions with corporate management. To require this would make a farce of decentralization. But this does not absolve management at the corporate level of its responsibility to know what is happening at other levels. The concept of delegation demands that corporate management take no action except when the firm's survival is at stake. It should be noted that corporate action to override divisional decisions in a decentralized organization will lead to the replacement of the divisional management. Even then, the power exercised at the top in relieving subordinates of command will seriously damage the decentralization effort. There will always be a residual fear that it is only a matter of time before such power is again exercised.

LONG-RUN VERSUS SHORT-RUN CONTROLS

One of the principal shortcomings of controls is the accent on the short run. Eventually all performance standards relate to profitability. But sophisticated control systems can eliminate many of the special difficulties of measures relating directly to profit. For example, using a ratio of net profit to invested capital or net assets has the major limitation that decreasing the investment itself can improve the ratio.

It is only natural that the control system's measurement of performance will encourage behavior patterns to achieve these standards. It is very difficult for the manager to take the long view when his rewards come from short-term performance. Despite this tendency to judge performance on a short-term basis, many managers continue to take the long view. But even this has dangers. From a manager's limited point of reference within the organization he is really unable to ascertain whether such action is best for the firm. Countless individual managers have taken action which they considered best for the company but which in fact prevented top management from attaining objectives.

This problem of long run versus short run plagues not only operating management but also top management. The president or managing director, who should be the one individual who can take the long view, is also often forced into short-run practices to satisfy the board of directors or even the stockholders. Some observers of the business scene have decried the end of effective control over professional managers by the stockholders or owners of the company. They have felt that this would lead to a self-perpetuation of professional management which might not necessarily be in the best interests of either the company or the economy. But here is an instance where the ability of professional managers to make decisions unfettered by the shorter-term demands of stockholders may be best both for the corporation and for the economy. This does not necessarily hold in all instances, of course, and the dangers of a professional management dynasty are still present.

PERFORMANCE STANDARDS

A study of one major firm which has wrestled with the problem of measurement and the resulting behavior patterns should serve as an excellent take-off point for considering the problem of how to attain control without sacrifice of the long term. Over a number of years the General Electric Company evolved eight key result areas for the evaluation of managerial performance. To assist in the development of these eight areas, the following philosophy and control objectives were evolved.

1. The measurements within the scope of the Project are designed to measure the performance of *organizational components,* not of *individuals.*

2. The Project is concerned with the formulating of *indexes* of performance but is not concerned with the developing of *standards* of performance. For example, rate of return on investment is an *index* common to all businesses but the *standard* in terms of this index might be 10 percent for one product business, 20 percent for another and 30 percent for a third.

3. Measurements are designed to supplement, not supplant, judgment. Measurements provide a valuable tool to help management make decisions based on a greater amount of factual knowledge, but they cannot be substituted for judgment.

4. Measurements must be so constructed as to be useful in appraising both current results and future projections in order that a proper balance may be maintained between immediate results and long-term objectives.

5. Measurements must be kept to a minimum at each level of the organizational structure.[1]

It is worthy of note that this philosophy of control and measurement at General Electric emphasizes the need for these measurements as guides to action, not strict controls on individual action. In addition there is an emphasis on both the long and the short term. The accent in this philosophy of control is that measurements should avoid personal identification and focus on organizational performance.

An examination of the eight key result areas used for control in General Electric reveals a sophisticated awareness of the shortcomings of many of the more standard performance measurements in industry today.

1. *Profitability.* General Electric recognizes the weakness of the rate-of-return index in stating

> that the acid test of an index should be its effectiveness in guiding decentralized management in making decisions in the best interests of the company overall, since operating managers' efforts naturally will be to improve the performance of their businesses in terms of the index used for evaluation. . . . This weakness is the tendency to encourage concentration on improvement of the ratios rather than on improvement in dollar *profits*. Specifically, the business with the better results in terms of the ratios will tend to make decisions based on the effect the decisions will have on the particular business's current *ratios* without consideration of the *dollar* profits involved.[2]

To solve these problems in measuring profitability General Electric uses an index of the dollars of residual income or net income less the capital charge. This is an attempt to recognize capital contribu-

---

[1] Robert W. Lewis, *Planning, Managing, and Measuring the Business: A Case Study of Management Planning and Control at General Electric Company* (New York: Controllership Foundation, Inc., 1955), pp. 29–41.

[2] Ibid., p. 32.

tion, individual effort, organizational needs and objectives, and the need for the exercise of managerial initiative. But with these all-inclusive objectives on profitability, General Electric's measure still accents short-run goals. Of course, profitability is not the sole measure of the performance of the organization or its parts.

2. *Market position.* The inclusion of market position as one of the key result areas provides a broader measurement of performance than the profitability ratio. In essence the market position is the ratio of sales of General Electric products to the total market for such products. Considerable thought is given to how to measure this market to provide realistic and meaningful figures. Within the market position classification is included the rather nebulous concept of customer satisfaction. General Electric sets no internal standards for customer satisfaction; rather, this evaluation is done by consumer attitude surveys. The current share of the market provides a measure of goal attainment. Although GE does not explicitly state that this area is coordinated with organizational objectives, it may provide one of the most useful measures of whether separate parts of the organization are attaining their objectives. It is hoped that this measurement will be directly related to objective formulation by the divisions or organizational sections as well as the corporation.

3. *Productivity.* The measurement of productivity is designed to test the degree to which management has coordinated and marshaled resources efficiently. Essentially, it is a comparison of the output to the input which measures the contribution of management in the more effective use of resources and the increase in output through more efficient use of labor and capital. The actual construction of the index has been somewhat difficult. Output has been tentatively defined in terms of value added or contributed, which would reflect the elimination of costs of goods and services purchased from other suppliers. Input utilizes payroll dollars plus depreciation dollars to reflect the employment of capital. The final figures have to be adjusted for price level changes in order to have a constant base for comparison.

A scientific measurement of productivity will indicate the contribution of management in improving the coordination of resources even when the profit and loss statement does not reflect such a contribution. Heavy competitive pressure on prices, services, and quality without increased effort and effectiveness on the part of management would result in a lower net profit. But extra effort and efficiency would go unnoticed in the profit and loss statement under these conditions unless such a measurement as productivity were included in the control system. Undoubtedly this measurement can serve well to document and reward efforts.

4. *Product leadership.* Product leadership is another gauge of overall progress. However, at this point the problems of quantitative measurement become insurmountable. General Electric decided not to go the route of an elaborate weighted numerical evaluation system. Instead, it recognized that product leadership had to be measured qualitatively.

In place of a numerical ratio or index General Electric evolved what might be called a product review and analysis system. This annual product review compared GE's products with those of competitors, determined whether truly new concepts were first introduced by General Electric or by its competitors, and correlated these results with the research activities carried on in the firm. This annual product review permitted the inclusion of research activities with the key result areas to be examined by top management. This rightfully placed emphasis on research activities. The key to the future in many industries is a well-defined research program. But to give proper emphasis to research requires effective evaluation of research activities by top management. General Electric's inclusion of this factor as one of its eight key result areas emphasizes the importance of research in the firm.

5. *Personnel development.* General Electric has always stressed employee education; at one time it had more than 15,000 courses available for employees. It was only natural that General Electric would want to include personnel development as one of its key result areas. But measurement in this area posed difficult problems. Indexes on turnover, promotion, and the like had to be tempered with information on expansion, general business conditions, and individual differences. To arrive at a measurement General Electric inventoried managers and functional specialists and tried to correlate their training background with their progress in the firm so as to gauge the effectiveness of the training program. Another measurement it used was to study the progress of individuals who had completed in-house training programs. But it still is not easy to correlate personnel development with individual manager performance. It is difficult to compare the contribution of training with the contri-

bution of development through counseling and job assignments. Undoubtedly these difficulties limited the emphasis on this key result area.

6. *Employee attitudes.* The measurement of employee attitudes was two-pronged. The first checked objective factors such as labor turnover, absenteeism, safety, and suggestions. The collection of statistics over time permitted the establishment of a norm which in turn could be compared with the norms of other firms in the same industry or in the same area. Variations in the statistics from these established norms were interpreted as a reflection of employee attitudes. The second utilized employee attitude surveys to identify inadequacies in management practices to permit corrective action. Many firms measure employee attitudes. But their inclusion as a major measurement of managerial performance was something of a departure.

7. *Public responsibility.* The inclusion of public responsibility as one of the key result areas is related to one General Electric objective: "to conduct its affairs in a manner becoming a good citizen." In this context General Electric defines the public as shareholders, customers, employees, vendors, the plant community, the business community, educational institutions, and all areas of government. In attempting to measure its action in meeting its public responsibility the company has made shareowners, educational institutions, and government overall corporate responsibilities. The operating divisions—or, as General Electric calls them, the individual product businesses— are assigned the other responsibilities. In the area of responsibilities to employees it is possible to measure such factors as stability of employment, improvement in standard of living, job opportunities, and family security, all of which can be directly measured. In regard to vendors, the plant community, and the overall business community, measurement can best be accomplished through attitude surveys.

The measurement of public responsibility must necessarily be nebulous. No one measure can be applied to this factor realistically. Nevertheless the way in which management carries out its public responsibilities is an important factor in overall managerial performance. Its inclusion as one of the key result areas emphasizes its importance and permits management to take action to meet this objective even at the expense of another objective.

8. *Balance between short-range and long-range goals.* This fac-

tor has to be a key result area if short-term considerations are not to overrule the longer term. General Electric did not set forth direct indexes or measurements in this area, but included the concept to emphasize that evaluation of management in the other seven areas must take into account both long-range and short-range goals. For example, performance is appraised in product leadership not only on this year's results but also on current research programs whose results will be felt over the next five- or ten-year period. In this way, there will be no undue influence on operating management for short-range results.

General Electric's attempt to spell out criteria other than immediate profit or return on investment for measuring managerial performance was an important step forward. High-sounding objectives are ineffective in influencing management action unless there is some way in which performance can be evaluated. The use of multiple standards or reference points for evaluation permits the exercise of individual initiative at the same time that it allows top management to measure overall performance. However, the inability to quantify many of these measurements may result in overemphasizing immediate profit or return on investment. The inclination is to judge the manager on as objective a measure as possible so as to avoid subjective feelings. Although it may seem overambitious, the consolidation of the measures into one index number may serve to emphasize the interrelationships of all these key result areas. Such an index number has a great danger common to averages and also might diminish emphasis on short-term profitability.[3]

BUDGETS AND PERFORMANCE STANDARDS

The use of budgets has been hailed as a major step toward effectiveness and greater control. Although budgets serve as an excellent control system, they also have limitations.

In its simplest terms a budget consists of a forecast of expenditures and revenues, with an excess of revenue providing a planned

[3] William Travers Jerome III provides a detailed analysis of General Electric's key result areas in his text on *Executive Control—The Catalyst* (New York: John Wiley & Sons, Inc., 1961), pp. 217–240. Professor Jerome also discusses in considerable detail the approaches of Du Pont and Koppers in his section on "Studies in Control."

profit. It must be emphasized that the budget is dependent upon the accuracy of the forecast. The forecast of revenues is based upon a forecast of sales. But sales are influenced by many factors—the state of the economy, the action of competitors, the general demand for the industry's products, the quality of the product, the effectiveness of the sales force, and the price. Even with sophisticated measures it is all but impossible to make a completely accurate sales forecast. Large firms sell their products in many markets, each of which has different characteristics. The determination of the actions of competitors is at best an educated guess. Many firms place greater reliance on past performance than on a sales forecast for future performance, with the result that some percentage increase or decrease from last year's sales is the estimate of this year's sales.

A budgeting refinement to compensate for this difficulty in estimating sales is called the variable budget, which provides differing levels of sales and commensurate levels of expenses. In the event that the sales forecast proves to be incorrect, the variable budget permits the firm to redetermine its principal expenditures.

The sales forecast is converted into a production budget utilizing dollar costs for direct labor and direct materials. Usually there is a high degree of accuracy in the calculation of these figures because the firm ordinarily has some form of standard cost figures or refined estimates of manufacturing costs. The third factor involved in costing, overhead, is determined by preparing separate departmental budgets for the indirect costs of producing and selling goods and services. Estimates are prepared for administrative expenses, sales expenses, and factory expenses—usually through a comparison of the previous year's expenditures with those required to achieve the current year's sales volume. It is indeed rare that a calculation is made from the beginning to determine what administrative costs will actually be required. Rarely is a special study made of the expenditure items included in the budget.

The budget requirements for each department are coordinated by a budget director to ascertain the total expenditure required to meet the projected sales volume. It is at this point that the departmental budgets are carefully scrutinized to insure they project a profit figure. The aggregate of these indirect departmental budget items constitutes the overhead, which should include the projected profit figure. This overhead is spread over the cost of individual products by a number of methods, including direct labor hour and direct labor dollar. Adding the overhead (including profit) to the direct labor and direct materials costs yields the price to be charged for the individual product.

This description of the budget process is of course oversimplified. But it does emphasize that the budget is at best a collection of educated guesses. Its success depends upon a number of variables, many of which are not under direct management control. While it is true that strict adherence to the budget will produce the planned profit, this does not mean that there has necessarily been effective performance. Luck may have played an important part in achieving the budgeted projections, or there may have been major errors by competition or unexpected economic growth.

For the most part, budget projections are based on results from previous years, tempered by the judgment of experienced managers and the infusion of relevant data concerning present and future conditions. Rarely is the preparation of a budget accompanied by a thorough audit to determine what manpower and equipment are needed to achieve the projected sales volume. The budget is more a crystallization of past performance, good or bad. That is why strict adherence to it does not necessarily indicate a high level of performance or effectiveness.

PRICING AND BUDGETS

There is an obvious relationship between the budget and the price charged for goods and services. Translating sales volume into sales revenue requires multiplying sales of individual items by the price for these items. So both the budget and the price variable require management decisions. Although some firms ostensibly price their products and services on the basis of full cost, marginal pricing methods may be utilized to temper these price decisions.

Full-cost pricing involves determining the amount of overhead, direct labor cost, and materials cost which must be charged against each product. This allocation serves to differentiate between full-cost and marginal pricing. To illustrate these two pricing methods, let us assume the following budgeting figures:

Selling price per unit $10.00
Sales forecast   1 million units

Overhead $5 million
Direct labor hours   1 million
Direct labor average wage $2 per hour
Direct materials cost per unit $2.50
Planned profit $500,000

Given these budgetary figures, we calculate overhead per direct labor hour by dividing the total overhead by the total direct labor hours. Thus:

$$\frac{\text{Overhead per}}{\text{Direct Labor Hour}} = \frac{\text{Total Overhead}}{\text{Total Direct Labor Hours}} = \frac{\$5,000,000}{1,000,000} = \$5.00$$

The full-cost pricing method of finding the selling price calls for adding direct labor and materials costs, profit, and overhead. Given the same budget, this is the result:

Direct labor	$ 2.00
Direct materials	2.50
Overhead (excluding profit)	5.00
Profit	.50
Selling price	$10.00

If the sales volume should fall below the predicted level of a million units, the firm would not make a profit of $500,000 even if all costs were exactly as predicted in the budget. Alternatively, where sales exceeded the forecast the full-cost pricing formula would result in the firm's earning a larger profit, but not as large as it would have been had a marginal pricing formula been used.

Using the same budget, consider what happens when sales are actually 1.1 million units.

$$\text{Profit} = \$0.50 \times 1,100,000 = \$550,000$$

But profit actually is as follows:

Sales revenue	1,100,000 × $10.00	$11,000,000
Direct labor	1,100,000 × $ 2.00 $2,200,000	
Direct materials	1,100,000 × $ 2.50 2,750,000	
Overhead (assume unchanged)	5,000,000	
Total costs		9,950,000
Profit		$ 1,050,000

But the moot question is this: If the firm had resorted to marginal pricing and charged a lower price, would its sales have reached 1.5 million units?

Marginal pricing begins with the sum of the fixed direct labor and direct materials costs, to which is added a variable overhead figure. Thus:

Direct labor	$2.00
Direct materials	2.50
Contribution to overhead	?
Selling price	?

The firm would then vary its selling price anywhere above the range of its direct costs of $4.50, depending upon its executives' judgment of the relationship between price and sales volume. If a selling price per unit of $9 resulted in a sales volume of 1.5 million units, this is what would happen to profits:

Sales revenue	1,500,000 × $9.00		$13,500,000
Direct labor	1,500,000 × $2.00	$3,000,000	
Direct materials	1,500,000 × $2.50	3,750,000	
Overhead (assume unchanged)		5,000,000	
Total costs			11,750,000
Profit			$ 1,750,000

The breakeven chart shown in Exhibit 5 indicates that fixed and variable costs are in direct linear relationship, whereas in fact they are undoubtedly discrete or discontinuous. It also hides the effect of the prices of various items in indicating that there is only one price. In this greatly simplified form the chart illustrates the effect of changing price, costs, or sales volume on profit and shows the major components of a budget. As noted earlier, the variable costs include the direct labor and direct materials costs, which can usually be predicted with a relatively high degree of accuracy. The fixed cost—overhead minus profit—is normally based on projections of past costs and rarely subject to scientific scrutiny. The sales revenue is exactly the same as total sales revenue in the budget. Obviously, varying the price charged for the firm's products will change the slope of the sales revenue curve. This pushes the breakeven point to the right or, in other words, increases the volume of goods and services the firm must sell before it can make a profit. But as the demand for most products is elastic (as prices go down, more is sold), lowering the price should increase the sales volume.

In making price decisions, management must be in a position to determine whether such actions as increasing or decreasing price will decrease or increase the volume of sales. In order to do this it must take into account not only the demand curve for its products and those of its competitors, but also the action its competitors will take to counter these price changes. Price is not the only variable. A change in either variable or fixed costs will have an appreciable

Exhibit 5

Breakeven Chart Analysis

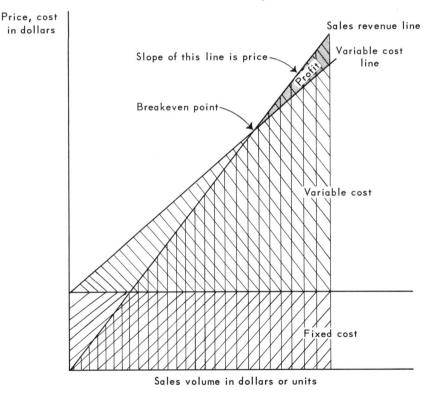

Legend

Fixed Cost   Variable Cost   Sales Revenue   Profit

effect on the breakeven point and on the accruing profit. If a firm is in a highly cyclical industry the position of its breakeven point may be of greater importance than the lowering of its total costs. The firm could shift a number of its fixed costs into variable costs by eliminating such facilities as manufacturing or even sales. Manufacturing could be eliminated by subcontracting it to other firms. To lower or eliminate fixed sales costs the firm could discontinue its own sales force and utilize manufacturers' representatives on a commission basis, which would turn the fixed sales cost into a variable commission cost. These actions may give the total cost curve a steeper slope but will lower the breakeven point in terms of sales volume.

Exhibit 6

Lowering the Breakeven Point

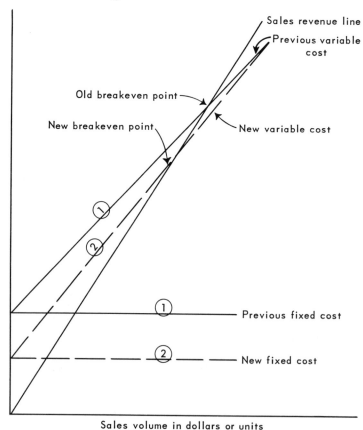

As Exhibit 6 illustrates, a firm decreases its fixed costs at the expense of having a higher total cost through increased variable costs. The firm would now be in a position to have a lower breakeven point; but, in the event of greatly increased sales volume, there would be less profit under the new cost arrangement than there was when fixed costs were higher. (In the cyclical automobile industry, lower-volume firms like Chrysler and American Motors have reduced their breakeven point by reducing fixed manufacturing costs.) By utilizing the budget and its graphic counterpart, the breakeven chart, management is in a position to quantify the result of changes in variable factors affecting the firm's profit position.

The Budget as a Constraining Control

Where the budget is used to obtain rigid conformity, it serves not only a limited function but also a dangerous one. The budget is based upon projections about an uncertain future. When the future becomes the present, management is fettered by its earlier judgments. Generally the budget is made for a year in advance and is rarely revised during the year except when the firm operates on a variable budget. Under these circumstances the budget is an overrated control. It is controlling present behavior on the basis of a potentially inaccurate projection of the future. But the budget can serve as an excellent control device with certain modifications.

Through the use of simulation techniques on computers, budget projections could be programmed against any of a number of different circumstances. The entire breakeven chart analysis could be programmed to show the effect on profit of price changes, volume changes, and the like. In this way next year's budget could be tested by simulating last year's results or projecting future probable results. This concept is not particularly novel, as simulation techniques are constantly being used in decision making. A far more important by-product of this simulation would be the opportunity for management initiative within budgetary constraints.

The budget should become a guide to management action, not a constraint on its initiative. Operating management should be given the prerogative of determining what actions are required to meet both short- and long-term objectives. Management should not be straitjacketed for an entire year by its estimates about an uncertain future. But the use of budget as a tool to control expenditures and generate a planned profit need not be lost. The solution is to recalculate budget estimates on the basis of accurate current data.

Management action through budgets could run something like this. A sales manager in the firm has based his projections of sales revenue on the probable action of competitors. A major competitor has made a decision on product innovation which is currently unacceptable to the market. Now is an excellent time for the firm to increase its share of the market at the expense of the erring competitor, but this requires some major changes in strategy.

The sales manager believes the firm must differentiate its services and products if it is to capture this essentially new market. This will require increased expenditures in warehousing as well as increased sales cost for additional salesmen. But the sales manager is of the opinion that a much larger increase in sales volume will generate a profit over the increased expenditures.

Under the narrower concept of budgets it certainly would be possible to persuade top management that the increased expenditure is justified. But such action is normally considered an exception to the budgeted figures and in effect the budget is scrapped. All too often the projections of the sales manager are accepted without qualification or a thorough examination of the effect on the budget and on preplanned profits. Alternatively, some firms hold the budget sacrosanct and would not permit the sales manager to take any action not projected in the current budget. But through the use of simulation techniques and the automatic budget revision resulting from such techniques the budget could still serve as a control device. In addition there would be a scientific testing of the sales manager's premises and projections. In this way the budget would become a tool for management action and decision making as well as for control.

Budgets are not a panacea and cannot substitute for managerial judgment. On paper a budget seems to have a high degree of precision and exactitude, but it is no better than management's projection of uncertainty. Undue reliance on the budget may result in attaining the projected profit, but it also may result in failure to attain a much larger profit. Furthermore, the budget may destroy initiative by making managers adhere to it strictly instead of taking effective management action.

To become a thoroughly effective tool of management, the budget must continue to exercise its control function, but such control must be interpreted more liberally. When a budget is made truly flexible by means of simulation techniques, it can become one of the most effective tools for decision making and for control.

THE CRITICAL ITEM OF CONCEPT CONTROL

Management is constantly striving to achieve greater precision in its practices and to improve its managerial skills. The trend toward the utilization of such techniques as operations research and PERT is testimony to management's interest in greater quantification of information. Accounting has been a moving force in this quest for greater accuracy. The accountant has always been oriented toward specific verifiable information. It is only natural that management should turn to the only common denominator available for quantification in a business enterprise: the dollar (or franc, mark, lira, or pound). The translation of business data into the appropriate currency units permits comparison both within the firm and between firms. The concept of the dollar is readily grasped not only by accountants and others who commonly use dollar figures but also by engineers and technicians who commonly use other measures. The dollar is also the final standard by which the firm is judged through analysis of its profit and loss statement.

With the accolades paid to the dollar as a standard, it would seem that little criticism is in order. But dollar comparisons also have their limitations—including the very great possibility that averages will hide variances in critical items. Often it is the comparison not of total results but of critical items which will best serve as a control.

An example of overdependence on dollar comparisons for controls was the case of a small company with a good profit record. At the annual board of directors meeting one director was devastating in his criticism of the president and operating management. His remarks were unanticipated, as the firm had shown a higher profit and a higher return on investment in the past year than in any preceding year. Furthermore, the president painted a glowing picture for the coming year. Both the balance sheet and the profit and loss statement reflected no special problems for the firm.

The director's account made little reference to these dollar figures. Rather, his quarrel was with the firm's apparent overdependence on a few major customers. This man served on the board of directors of a firm in the industry supplied by this company. It was because of his knowledge of the industry as well as his general competence that he had been named to the board of this company. He said the firm's increase in sales was the result of greatly increased purchases by one customer in the television industry. Furthermore, these sales had included not only finished products but special dies which would permit the television firm to manufacture its own products.

The president replied to this criticism that it was normal practice in the industry to supply duplicate sets of dies to a customer. The director said he knew this was the practice, but he also knew that the customer was now in the process of purchasing a supplier plant to manufacture this very product. Further, he noted that this criticism was not of the actions of management in providing these dies or even in increasing its sales to this account. His criticism was that in doing so the company had failed to keep abreast of its other business, which had in fact declined considerably over this same period. His conclusion was that when the television firm did begin making its own products, this firm's future would be in jeopardy.

In this illustration the dollar figures themselves did not provide adequate control. It could be argued that the control system itself was inadequate, but not the dollar figures. But this is begging the issue. The point is that dollar controls themselves are subject to major errors because they can hide significant information. Management must make an analysis and a critique of whatever information it has before drawing conclusions and taking action.

Dollars express absolutes. But comparisons and evaluations are best made in relative terms. The modern trend in the presentation of financial statements is to express all expenses and profits as a percentage of sales and a comparison of balance sheet items between one year and another. This does not lessen the importance of dollar equivalents, but percentage figures facilitate further analysis. Even with percentage comparisons of dollar figures, a major problem remains: that the human mind cannot assimilate infinite amounts of data. This very mass of the data makes it difficult for the manager to sort out the important from the unimportant. What is required is an isolation and recording of critical items.

CRITICAL ITEM CONTROLS

The concept of using critical items for control is not new. The securities market makes extensive use of Dow Jones and similar market averages as critical indicators. Individual firms are inclined to rely on profit as the critical indicator. Although individual managers must devise their own critical indicators, generally there is no standardization of such indicators within the firm. The tendency is for control systems to collect as much information as possible without adequate censoring or filtering of such data. The ability of computers to amass more and more information makes the use of critical indicators a necessity.

Management is being pulled in two directions simultaneously in this concept of control. On the one hand electronic data processing and computers make the collection and digestion of masses of raw data relatively simple. On the other hand management is becoming ever more aware of the need for critical items control. This is evidenced by the PERT system, which emphasizes the concept of the critical path for the manufacture and development of individual products and projects. It is also evidenced by such innovations as the ABC system of inventory control, which considers that only the major items entering into the cost pattern of the firm should be closely controlled, with much less control being exercised over the noncritical items. The ABC system utilizes a value analysis of the firm's inventory, taking into account frequency of use and total cost. The usual pattern found by the value analysis of inventory is something like this:

Classification	Percent of total items in inventory	Percent of annual value of inventory (cost × annual usage)
A	5	50
B	15	30
C	80	20

Such an analysis indicates that 80 percent of the items in inventory constitute only 20 percent of the total investment and that 5 percent of the items constitute 50 percent of the total value. The next step would be to calculate the cost of maintaining control over the large number of items which constitute a small percentage of the total cost. The end result may be that these items are controlled very loosely and ordered for a year in advance to reduce purchasing and record-keeping costs.

The critical items are then controlled very closely, with considerable attention to their ordering and to their use. Most firms adopting an ABC system of inventory control soon find that their total investment in inventory is greatly reduced, as are their costs in ordering and maintaining the inventory.

The critical item concept must become part of the total management information system to permit the effective incorporation of large masses of data into a control system. The introduction of the critical item concept into managerial control systems will have the twofold result of (1) focusing management's attention on the major factors entering into managerial effectiveness and (2) reducing the cost of the control system. It would also seem possible to introduce random sampling into the collection of information. No one knows the total cost of control in American and European industry, but conservative estimates place it in the hundreds of millions of dollars. Much of the increase in the number of indirect workers has been caused by the increasing use of control systems in industry. (Random sampling techniques could be used as well in the collection of control information as in the inspection of production work in the plant. Accountants now use these techniques for the auditing of accounts, which should serve as an excellent recommendation.)

If dollar controls are carried to their ultimate use, dollar information will be provided to all levels of management. But since most dollar information is accounting data, distribution of such information can create more problems than it solves.

The provision of accounting information to first-line supervisors and foremen often has an adverse effect on their morale. What the foreman receives is information on direct materials costs, direct labor costs, indirect labor costs, and overhead. In turn, overhead may be translated into a total cost per dollar of product being processed in the department or may be set up as a charge per direct labor hour. These figures are likely to seem astronomical to the foreman. As a matter of standard practice, the direct labor hour of production carries the total administrative and overhead costs of all other parts of the operation, so this figure may well exceed the direct labor dollar costs. The foreman thus is made to feel that he is carrying the rest of the organization.

This may result in the foreman's having a negative attitude toward the whole system of control, particularly when he is blamed for failing to control costs. His attitude is that his part is so infinitesimal in the total operation that there is little he can do to improve total profits.

The solution is to divide costs into controllable and noncontrollable items. In addition there must be a program to teach the foreman how costs are calculated. He has to recognize that other costs are involved in the operation of the firm and that it takes more than production to make a profit. But it is also important that the control system hold the foreman responsible only for items under his control. The accounting profession has evolved a special system for this very purpose called responsibility accounting. This concept is that each and every manager should be charged with responsibility for the items over which he has control, but that the system will break down if any foreman or other manager is held responsible for items beyond his control.

Yet another problem in overdependence on dollar controls is the intangible or nonquantifiable item. Although all items can be quantified, if not in a cardinal sense (dollar value) then in an ordinal sense (ranking in order of importance), it may be that the cost of a control system must be measured against the savings it can generate. The apparent accuracy and preciseness of dollar controls can easily lead the manager into a pattern of overdependence on such information. Dollar controls alone, like any other management tool, are not a substitute for management analysis and decision making. An understanding of their limitations and judicious use of their advantages can make dollar controls one of the most useful tools in the managerial toolbox. But it requires experience and common sense to make this or any other tool useful in action.

AUTOMATED CONTROLS AND CORRECTIVE ACTION

A whole series of controls through organization could be enumerated at this point. Policies, assignment of responsibilities, committees, procedures, the organization structure itself—all serve in some measure as control devices. These various aspects of control might be called preventive rather than corrective control systems.

A difficulty is anticipated in advance and measures are taken to forestall its occurrence. Preventive control can be a most useful and effective control device.

One particular preventive control deserves to be singled out for special comment. This is the concept of internal control, advocated and practiced at the insistence of accountants. Internal control was originated to minimize the opportunities for embezzlement. If one man has control of the records as well as physical control of the items, it is relatively simple for him to steal from the firm and doctor the records to hide the theft. Internal control separates the physical function from the record-keeping function to make it impossible for one man to steal or make false entries without being checked by another. This is often carried one step further to involve a third person in some form of audit or check on the other two.

Internal control is accomplished by placing such functions as purchasing, receiving, and accounts payable in three separate hierarchies within the organization. Purchasing places a purchase order with a vendor but cannot conspire with the vendor on delivery since it is the task of receiving to match incoming shipments against the purchase order—thus also preventing collusion between purchasing and receiving. Accounts payable checks the invoice against the receiving report and the purchase order to insure that all three match. Internal control through organization is one of the easiest ways to practice preventive control.

Preventive control cannot serve all the control needs of the firm; there is still a need for automatic controls, which can be considered as self-correcting action. The ultimate program for control through computers is what is called the closed-loop system, which has built-in self-correcting mechanisms so that deviations from plan will be corrected automatically. Such self-adjusting control systems are common in the electronics field and the petroleum industry.

This closed-loop concept obviously can be utilized in many control systems. For example, a computerized inventory control system would automatically initiate corrective action to rectify inventory overages or deficiencies. This self-correcting mechanism requires a sufficiently sophisticated program to incorporate judgmental factors so as to adjust for changes in price levels, sales forecasts, and manufacturing cost schedules. The self-correcting adjustments must take all possible variables into account if the need for individual management decisions is to be eliminated. Ideally, the inventory control system would be part of a larger system which would incorporate such factors as overall consumer demand changes, working capital requirement changes, return on invested capital performance levels, and others which have a direct bearing on inventory levels.

Current practices have not advanced to the stage of this inventory control model. A fantastic amount of research is required on management control systems through simulation techniques as well as on exactly what takes place in the mind of the manager in making decisions. The complexity of interrelationships both of a technical and of an interpersonal nature further complicates this problem.

Two separate research activities in the building of a model of a business firm have been conducted in the United States. Professor Jay Forrester of the Massachusetts Institute of Technology evolved a model which is discrete in its simulation of the interrelationships of the various parts of the business firm and published the results of his research in *Industrial Dynamics* (Cambridge, Mass.: The M.I.T. Press, 1961). The other research was carried out at the Systems Development Corporation in Santa Monica, California. Preliminary findings from this research were presented in *Management Control Systems*, edited by Donald G. Malcolm and Alan J. Rowe (New York: John Wiley & Sons, Inc., 1960).

Future management research may result in the ability to change various inputs so as to determine the effect of these changes on profit, investment, and other factors. The programming of the interrelationships among different parts of the firm is a necessary prerequisite to designing a general system for decision making and control. There will have to be many pioneering projects of this sort before control systems can be completely automated.

Although automated control systems lie in the distant future, many of their basic concepts can be applied to current management control systems. The charting of the interrelationships among functions through procedure audit and analysis will lead to a better understanding of system design. This charting should lead also to work simplification by eliminating duplicative and obsolete control mechanisms. But the major lesson to be learned from research into a general systems approach to managerial decision making and control is the self-regulating or automatic corrective action of such a system.

Wherever possible a control system should be self-regulating and self-correcting. Corrective action should be an automatic byproduct of the system without involving higher levels of management. This does not remove the responsibility for corrective action from the line manager but merely delegates it directly to the individual able to effect such action. It will still be necessary for the system to insure that the action was in fact taken, but this should be done only as a last resort. Management could well sharpen its current approach to control systems by studying some of the general systems research.

PERFORMANCE EVALUATION AND CORRECTIVE ACTION

Performance evaluation is directly related to control systems. In developing the individual as well as in perfecting the overall performance of the firm, it is necessary to evaluate the performance of individual managers and workers. Most people can be guided by counseling and advice into performing more effectively. A man must be made aware of his weaknesses as well as his strengths so that through training and work experience he may overcome the weaknesses. But it is necessary to evaluate both individuals and the organization itself.

Performance evaluation is generally an after-the-fact device. The control system, on the other hand, should operate concurrently with the action being controlled. The accent in the control system is on helping managers to take corrective action to insure that the plan is being carried through successfully. The accent in performance evaluation is on the efficacy of the plan itself and of the managers responsible for carrying it through. The control system may provide the necessary data, but the performance evaluation must be conducted as a separate investigation.

Performance evaluation is not designed to be punitive in nature. Its objective is education so that management action will become more effective. This point bears repeating. Both in the control system itself and in the performance evaluation growing out of the system, the accent must be on corrective action. This relates back to the definition of control as the patterning of behavior to achieve the objectives of the organization. Punitive control will not channel behavior patterns toward the achievement of the objectives. Instead it will channel the behavior of managers into protecting themselves against the control system. Because performance evaluation relates more directly to the individual than even the control system, it is imperative that the accent be on sharpening future performance rather than condemning past performance.

Although it may sound redundant, performance evaluation must place emphasis on performance, as a look at some of the more common methods of evaluation will confirm. Yet many of the techniques used in industry do not in fact measure performance. Instead, these systems measure personality characteristics or potential performance rather than actual performance. The accent must be on measurable performance. Concrete examples are needed to insure that the individual can profit from his past mistakes and experience. Furthermore, it may be found that the mistakes of the individual are attributable less to his own performance than to the performance of the organization within which he works.

An example of the failure of performance evaluation to examine structural and organizational defects was evident in the evaluation of a production control supervisor who was held responsible for setting production schedules for the manufacturing section of a firm. Manufacturing was plagued by both late deliveries and ineffective utilization of its facilities. This firm used a performance evaluation system which within two years had led to the transfer or separation of at least three production control supervisors because of ineffectual performance. The current supervisor received a similar unsatisfactory rating because of his inability to set and meet production schedules.

Subsequent to this last unsatisfactory rating an independent agency was called in to investigate the scheduling of production in manufacturing so as to determine whether such scheduling could be programmed on a computer. It found that each subsection of the manufacturing division planned its production schedules independently. The production control supervisor's schedules applied only to departments which serviced these other essentially autonomous subsections of the manufacturing division. But this supervisor could get no adequate information or schedules from the other managers. The independent agency recommended reorganizing the manufacturing division to give complete scheduling authority to one central agency. Only then would there be any chance for the successful programming of production scheduling through computers.

In this instance the production control managers were being given poor ratings although their performance was poor because of an unsatisfactory organization structure. Basing the evaluation on measurable standards and concrete evidence might in this case have identified the organizational shortcomings and forestalled the allocation of blame to the production control manager.

Although the accent in performance evaluation must be on developing better workers and managers, rewards and penalties have a part to play. A major difficulty arises in deciding how to use a performance evaluation system to bring about more effective future action while at the same time rewarding good past performance. If the evaluation is used as a control device, it will lead to transfers, demotions, and dismissals as well as rewards. But when the negative aspects come into play, it is difficult to stress the positive considerations of individual development.

It is a reality of organizational life that employees at every level must perform effectively. Sometimes the organization cannot afford to continue investing in an individual who is ineffective at his task. To protect the organization, some managers and workers must be replaced. But such a decision must be based on facts, not on hearsay or emotions.

It is common practice to give pay increases to employees annually or semiannually. If these increases are granted indiscriminately the system fails to reward superior performance. Through effective performance evaluation, rewards for above-average performance would replace automatic pay increases.

This accent on performance rather than on personal factors as the basis for promotion and pay increases relieves the manager of one of his major difficulties in evaluating his subordinates. When the problem is further complicated by the interpersonal factors which often form the basis for evaluation, the manager's all-important task of developing and promoting the best men is doubly hard. It would of course be naïve to expect that any performance evaluation system will eliminate the personal factor in pay increases and promotions. Personality defects or strengths will continue to play an important part in rewards and penalties, but they will be minimized by the system.

An employee with a personality problem may be effective in his job if his personality defects do not affect his performance. But if he were promoted to a higher position these personality defects might make it impossible for him to perform satisfactorily. The judgment of the individual manager must come into play here. Overdependence on performance evaluation, no matter how effective, will lead the manager into major errors. But overdependence on personal factors will have even worse results. The accent in any system must be on assisting the manager in exercising judgment, not replacing his judgment.

*   *   *

No manager can abdicate his responsibilities for control either to staff agencies or to the control system itself. It is the task of the manager to coordinate the resources allocated to him to achieve the organizational objective. Controls and such preliminaries as formulating objectives, planning, and decision making are useful and important tools. But they cannot substitute for management action. The manager is paid a high salary because management is one process that cannot be automated.

Although management cannot be replaced by systems it certainly can be greatly aided by them. In the use of any tool its limitations as well as its strengths must be recognized. There is a tendency to undue dependence on many accounting and dollar controls. The effective manager recognizes the limitations of these apparently precise control measures. Furthermore the side effects of unwanted behavior patterns through the exercise of controls must be well recognized in the design and implementation of the control system.

14

Designing the Management Control System

THE DESIGN of the management control system is critical to the success of both the individual manager and the firm as a whole. Organization structure, objectives, planning, and decision making are all dependent upon the existence of an effective control system to develop the critical feedback loop of information and evaluation.

A great difficulty in control systems is to provide timely information to managers responsible for corrective action. The very lifeblood of modern industry is speed of decision making and action. Before the days of electronic data processing and the computer considerable manual posting and preparation were required for a control system, which made it difficult to obtain timely information. So managers had to make decisions, many of them vital to the survival and success of the firm, on the basis of inadequate information. But this should be a thing of the past. Today's high-speed computers digest an unbelievable volume of raw data with amazing speed and accuracy. The computer revolution should result in a control revolution which in turn will have as its product more effective decisions.

Although the computer has made it possible to utilize far more elaborate control systems, there are important limitations on information collection. One limiting factor is computer language. Punched cards or perforated tape require special coding to permit direct input into the computer. For example, if an inspection report is to be an integral control of the information system, the report form must be prerecorded, keypunched in advance, or translated by a keypunch operator into a form that can be used by the computer. This is an obvious limitation on the operation of an automatic control system. A technological breakthrough is now being made available in this area, with the computer being able to scan and digest raw data without the preliminary step of translation—as in the case of a post office letter sorter.

Even with the high speed of a computer, the collection of information must not be too complex. The technical difficulties in collecting and preparing information for control systems are compounded by the dangers inherent in the wholesale collection of raw data. Careful selection of information will improve the results from the control system. But there is an inherent tendency to go on doing things in the same old way rather than to look at the objectives of the control system itself. What are the critical events to be controlled? What information is required to exercise this control? What are the sources of the information? Can control of the whole be achieved through control of the part? These are the kinds of questions the manager must ask himself in designing his control system if he is to obtain information quickly.

INFORMATION IN DIGESTIBLE FORM

Too often, control systems overwhelm managers with data. The result is that managers pay scant attention to the information, contenting themselves with picking out a few critical bits and pieces to use in formulating decisions. This is a disservice by the control system. The system should be designed in such a way as to pattern the behavior of individuals toward the attainment of objectives. The simpler the presentation of control information the greater the likelihood that the manager will pay attention to it. If the information is to be digestible, it cannot be in too great detail. Yet it is not detail alone that will invalidate the system. The very design of the report form is of great importance. Wherever possible, all statistical manipulations should have been performed before the information goes to the manager. But these manipulations must not hide the original information because most managers wish to consider figure analysis both in absolute and relative terms.

The managers must know whether action is required, whether action has been taken by the subordinate, or whether special consultation is required. Any steps that can relieve him of the need to keep his own records and set up his own control system should be incorporated into reports. This does not remove any management prerogatives. It does not mollycoddle the manager but rather facilitates his job. In view of the fantastic time pressures on today's manager, any system that can simplify his job should be instituted. Control information can be made more digestible merely by the appropriate design of the forms or reports—even to so simple a thing as using different colors for different types of action requirements.

EASY ACCESS TO CONTROL INFORMATION

As periodic control reports are issued, the manager has to fit them together in some way to permit thorough evaluation of the total project and not only of the part covered in the report. Wherever possible, the matching of reports or posting of information should be eliminated as part of the manager's job. Ideally, control reports should incorporate information from earlier reports so that no filing or cross-posting is needed. Although this may seem relatively expensive, in fact the contrary is true. The cost of keeping duplicate records in various parts of an organization is much greater than is generally recognized. One objective of any control system should be the elimination of duplicate records. There should be one master file, which itself could eventually be destroyed if the information is not required for legal reasons. The memory drum of the computer can be the file, replacing separate pieces of paper.

EXERCISING CONTROLS

Control actions should be exercised by the manager and not by staff. It is a legitimate function of staff to design and operate a con trol system, which is essentially an information-gathering service. But the exercise of decision and of command must rest with the line manager. Many firms separate the job of the manager into two functions: action and paperwork. The paperwork is often delegated to an administrative assistant. If the administrative assistant is a staff man charged with designing and operating the informational aspects of the control system, there can be no quarrel with this function. But when the administrative assistant exercises command functions, exception must be taken. Under these circumstances it is much better to subdivide the task of the manager by appointing an assistant line manager.

No control system should be so complex that the manager cannot understand it, digest it, and act on it without help. If a special administrative assistant must be hired merely to digest the control information and advise the manager of what action is required, the system itself is in need of a drastic overhaul.

CORRECTIVE ACTION BY SUBORDINATES

Controls must be readily apparent to the subordinate so that he can take corrective action wthout involving his superior. This concept can be designed into any control system. If possible, the subordinate himself should design the controls that are to monitor his operations. Of course, these controls must be correlated with those of his superior and of the total organization so that there can be total control and not partial control. A plea has already been made for the development of a control philosophy that the subordinate responsible for action receive control information requiring his action before his superior receives it and that only in the event that the subordinate fails to carry through his assigned task should the superior be involved. There is no reason why the individual manager cannot implement this philosophy regardless of the total control system in the firm.

In the design of his control system the manager should remember that controls have no raison d'être except to insure that plans are being carried out. There is a tendency at all levels in an organization to institute or continue controls without ascertaining their worth in influencing appropriate behavior and attaining objectives. One firm that questioned the usefulness of some if its controls was Marks and Spencer, a chain department store in the United Kingdom somewhat similar to J. C. Penney's in the United States. After critically examining its control systems, Marks and Spencer did away with the requirement that salesclerks punch a time clock every morning and every evening. Since salesclerks were paid a weekly salary, not an hourly wage, little was being done with the information collected on time cards. Furthermore, the supervisors of salesclerks were considered better able to control the activities of their subordinates than the central control system could, so time clocks were eliminated.

Marks and Spencer went even further in eliminating antiquated controls. An elaborate inventory control system had compiled statistics from sales slips and entered issue data on inventory cards whenever stock was taken out of a stockroom. Examination of inventory control practices revealed that a visual control system in the stockrooms would permit the ordering and control of inventory without the high cost of keeping elaborate records. Although it was recognized that this might result in more thefts, the management of Marks and Spencer was of the opinion that individual supervisors could control this better than the elaborate paper inventory control system did.

Every attempt should be made to simplify control. One of the best ways to do so is to charge individual managers with eliminating unnecessary controls. Every manager should be reminded that controls must serve management and not be served by management. The accent must be on inducing the appropriate behavior patterns in those responsible for action, not merely on collecting information for the records.

A TOTAL SYSTEMS APPROACH

A reorientation of control concepts and systems is long overdue in industry. Management has all too often abdicated its control responsibilities to such staff organizations as accounting. Control is an integral part of the management process. It cannot be divorced from the other tasks of management because in many ways it is the vehicle for attaining objectives.

To date, control systems have rarely utilized what might be

called a total systems approach. Controls are likely to be haphazard in design and operation to satisfy a particular need rather than the overall needs for control within the firm. This has resulted in overlays of controls one on top of the other, each to satisfy a special need. What is required is a complete redesign of control systems and information networks rather than mere rehabilitation of some existing controls.

An example of a start toward a total systems approach is the case of the Librascope Division of General Precision, Inc., which originated what it calls the Librascope Operations Control System (LOCS) in an attempt to integrate many existing controls into one operational system. In the preliminary investigation at Librascope, industrial engineers discovered that basic data, part numbers, schedule dates, and so on were being manually duplicated as many as 30 or 40 times. Not only was this expensive in operation, but it multiplied the chance for human error greatly.

Librascope solved the problem of translating raw data into computer language by collecting the data in a form that could be fed directly into the computer. This was accomplished by preparing punched cards for all the data required for the control system from the original preparation of a production or sales order. When an activity being controlled was completed, the prepunched card for that activity was fed into the computer, thus eliminating the need to keypunch the data onto cards or tape at this stage.

In order to eliminate the many logs or separate records commonly found in the average firm, Librascope initiated a real-time, on-line control system, in which data are recorded as the event occurs rather than waiting to be processed with a lot of other information at a later time. The information is transmitted immediately to an on-line computer and is thereafter readily available for reports or display. Librascope also utilizes random access, which permits the computer to stop a program and search its memory for information required immediately for control purposes. This eliminates the need for separate records.

In addition to the record-keeping function, LOCS is programmed to permit the simulation of events that would occur should schedules be changed, and so on. This serves as an excellent aid to managerial decision making when changes are necessitated by breakdowns, market demand, or whatever.

The operation of the manufacturing control aspects of LOCS provides some insights into the automation of a control system. The standard procedures for providing engineering specifications, blueprints, test criteria, and parts lists to the production planning department were followed. The production planning department correlated production schedules with the parts lists and, utilizing other pertinent information, arrived at a make-or-buy decision. If the decision was to buy a part, purchase requisitions were forwarded to the purchasing department. It was at this point that the computerized control system went into effect. The typist produced not only a purchase order but also a punched tape for feeding directly into the computer and punched cards for materials follow-up and for receiving.

When the goods arrived, the receiver card was inserted in a receiving department data transmitter which transmitted the information to the computer. The receiver card and the parts were dispatched to receiving inspection, where the results of the inspection were sent to the computer center by inserting the receiver card in the data transmitter. This same process was repeated when the items were received in stock.

With the basic raw data now stored on the memory drum of the computer, a number of programs generated control reports such as a comparison of purchase requirements and purchase orders actually issued; a comparison of purchase order due dates and actual receipt dates (to evaluate vendors); and a comparison of incomplete and outstanding purchase orders (to generate cash flow information).

If the parts were to be manufactured within the plant rather than purchased, the methods department prepared operation sheets and instructions as well as a punched tape for the computer. This system provided material and tool withdrawal cards as well as work tickets. As materials were withdrawn from stock the previously prepared withdrawal cards were transmitted to the computer, which automatically kept a running inventory balance. Similarly, work tickets provided check through the computer on work in progress throughout the plant.

This system eliminated the need to keep separate control information in various parts of the company. The memory drum's stock of raw data could be used for numerous analyses and reports on any detail of the operation as well as overall reports on status, costs, inventory, manpower distribution, scheduling, and the rest.

Such reports not only permitted decisions to be made regarding the current operation but also provided feedback to permit the scheduling of future work to be based on an accurate picture of the current workload.

The Librascope Operations Control System is only a start in the automation of controls. The effective use of computers with a complete overhaul of control systems will save countless millions of dollars not only in manufacturing but also in distribution and in the provision of services.

The function of controls must be to facilitate, not to hinder the work of the manager. If controls are properly designed and used they will be welcomed by operating management. To accomplish this will require a completely new orientation toward controls and control systems. But without such a reorientation in control philosophy there cannot be truly effective management controls.

The Design of the Control System

There are four distinct steps in the design of a control system: (1) determine objectives; (2) develop standards of performance; (3) design the information network; and (4) evaluate whether the system meets the criteria of an adequate control system.

The objectives of a control system are closely related to corporate objectives but require more specific and concrete bench marks to permit measurement. The objective of growth or profit or stability does not automatically provide these bench marks. Instead there must be shorter-term objectives which can be quantified, such as the capture of a certain share of the market. To accomplish this objective requires a blueprint or plan indicating what actions are to be taken over a period of time and what results are to be expected from these actions. An integral part of this blueprint is the design of a control system to monitor achievement by collecting information on such things as gross national product, industry figures, and competitors. In addition to monitoring these environmental factors, it is necessary also to monitor or control the internal specialized strategies or plans.

Top management may decide that the best strategy to achieve increased penetration of the market is to increase the size and strength of its sales force. Its plans may call for setting up new territories, establishing special trade discounts for suppliers, setting quotas for new accounts, and changing the compensation plan to reflect the new emphasis. The necessary controls would be set up simultaneously to show whether the plan is being implemented correctly.

But even if the plan is carried through successfully, it may fail to achieve the objective. Though the new accounts are being cultivated, the change in the salesmen's compensation plan is in effect, and so on, increased penetration of the market may not have been achieved. When this happens, the plan was not the correct one for attaining the objective. Competition may have taken steps that have invalidated the plan. Or perhaps the emphasis should have been placed on product development or on cutting manufacturing costs.

This hypothetical case illustrates the need to set objectives for the control system. If the objectives are narrowly defined to monitor only internal compliance such as number of calls per salesman, then the only guarantee the system can give is that all salesmen had met their quotas of calls. In this case if competition had evolved an effective defensive strategy or had introduced new products, the meeting of sales quotas would have contributed little to increasing the market penetration. More broadly stated control system objectives would have monitored the critical environmental factors as well. This would have provided management with the timely and critical information needed for appropriate corrective action.

DEVELOPING STANDARDS OF PERFORMANCE

It is almost axiomatic that controls must measure deviations from standards. Exhibit 7 shows a typical control chart used for controlling a semiautomatic process such as a screw machine. The machine is set up to turn out simple screw stock from bars of metal fed automatically into the equipment. A setup man initially places the cutting tools in the correct position and then starts the machine. The setup man who attends a large number of machines without any machine operators makes periodic checks on the output of each machine and records his findings on the control chart. The control chart shows the trend of adherence to standard, which must lie between the permissible tolerance limits on the chart. When the chart indicates that a machine is going out of control the setup man stops the machine and resets it, starting the process all over again.

Exhibit 7

A Typical Control Chart

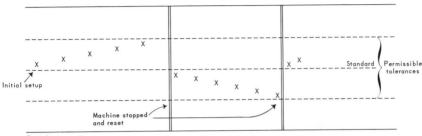

If all controls could be as simple as this, the job of management would be eminently simplified. It is an easy step to the next stage of development—which general systems theory calls the closed-loop system—to have the machine shut itself off automatically and reset its own tools. But controls are rarely this simple. The standards for the screw turned out by the machine can be determined with a high degree of precision. The machine itself is a known quantity. The metal ingredients are highly standardized. All this adds up to an extremely high degree of probability that this simple control system will turn out an acceptable screw.

Management controls are far more difficult because the degree of predictability drops precipitously. Although the person doing a repetitive task can be expected to do it in the same way time after time, the manager doing nonrepetitive tasks is nowhere near as predictable. Much as this factor complicates control systems, a far more serious difficulty lies in the establishment of standards.

Although standards and control are important aspects of planning, neither is arrived at automatically. In planning, the manager realistically appraises resources, time and cost. To permit control, time and cost must be quantified and correlated at every stage. For example, a production plan may call for the manufacture of certain products over a period of time. The control cannot operate solely on the completion time of the end product but must also act upon the manufacture of the components which make up the final product to insure that the completion date is met. This requires the detailing of the entire plan in such a way that the necessary control will be facilitated.

Standards have many shortcomings. How much work can one man do? What standard should be set for an engineer at a drawing board? How much work and of what kind should a manager do? How long should it take personnel to hire a single new employee? What is a standard for the overall performance of the firm? This difficulty of setting standards affects all industries in one way or another. One of the most enduring of the standard-setting devices, time study, is itself beset with shortcomings. Countless millions of dollars are paid to wage earners whose tasks are set by time study or some of its offshoots, such as work measurement and methods-time measurement (MTM). What are the elements in the typical time study?

The objective of time study is not to study a man but to study a job. The study of the man is merely the means by which the job itself is studied in order to set the standard. The first phase is to pick the time study subject—an operator typical in his abilities and methods. The second phase is to observe the operator on the job and try to identify the elements or parts of the job that should be timed individually. The third phase is to use a stopwatch to time the actions of the operator as he goes through the various elements of his work cycle. Some 10 to 20 work cycles are timed and recorded. The fourth phase is to eliminate any observations that seem too extreme. Then an arithmetic average of the observations gives the average time to complete one cycle.

Up to this point the time study has been somewhat scientific in its application. But there are basic questions. The choice of subject could invalidate the entire study. The elimination of the extreme observations is doubtful statistically. Statisticians might question the use of the arithmetic mean. The stopwatch itself is not truly accurate because of the human factor in its operation. Yet other aspects of time study are even less scientific.

The time study technician now has to equate the operator with the job because the study is of the job, not of the man. He "levels" his observations by ranking each operator in such categories as speed and skill, rating each on his deviation from the judged performance of the average operator. This is done solely by judgment. Nor is this the end of the adjustments. Allowances must be made for such factors as personal needs, fatigue, and delays—known among time study men as PF&D. These adjustments are usually percentages determined not by study but by standard practice or negotiation between the trade union and the company.

The setting of standards through time study thus involves judgments. A number of studies have shown that the judgment of time study technicians is relatively constant even from firm to firm. But this does not make the setting of standards any more scientific.

Except for what might be called engineering standards or standards not involving people, time study standards are considered among the most accurate for control purposes. Yet much of the judgment on which standards are based is not scientific but intuitive. Some techniques developed out of time study, such as ratio delay or work sampling, can be used to check the standards set by judgment. Ratio delay or work sampling can replace perhaps the poorest control in management today: haphazard observations.

A useful lesson in the ineffectiveness of casual or haphazard observation can be found in a restaurant. The new waitress who rushes around making separate trips for water, silverware, butter, bread, and condiments can be contrasted with the efficient waitress. The experienced waitress seems to be slow moving. To the casual observer she does not seem to be nearly as busy or hardworking as the inexperienced waitress. But a quick comparison of the number of patrons served by the two would soon reveal the efficiency of the experienced waitress.

DESIGNING THE INFORMATION NETWORK

An effective control system requires a detailed flow of information to and from all parts of the organization. This information takes many forms: oral instructions from a superior to a subordinate, written memorandums directing parts of the organization to perform certain tasks, sales orders, purchase orders, tool orders, move tickets on work in process, progress reports, accounting reports, and scrap reports. This great flow of spoken and written communication constitutes the information network.[1]

The growth of information networks is in most cases haphazard. As information is required, it is supplied. There is rarely any conscious design of the network to accomplish any integration of materials or economy of time and reports. The accent is on solving today's problems—which may have arisen through failure to plan the information network in the first instance. When time is not taken to plan carefully, the information network and the controls themselves will be makeshift. The tendency is to erect an information network independently of the planning and operating process and superimpose it on the existing management task. Much of management's frustrations can be traced to this haphazard approach to the design of the information network.

The processes leading up to a management luncheon meeting in one large firm illustrate this haphazard approach. Starting on Monday and concluding on Tuesday a bright young administrative assistant to the vice-president of manufacturing collected information on the status of manufacturing orders in different parts of the plant. On Wednesday morning he checked on the progress of the purchase requisitions and purchase orders as well as on inspection progress. During Wednesday afternoon and Thursday morning he utilized the services of another member of the vice-president's staff to prepare elaborate graphs documenting the progress of work in the shop. The resulting reports were 10 to 15 pages in length.

It is fortunate for the administrative assistant that he did not attend the Thursday luncheon meetings. The report occupied barely ten minutes and was used solely to decide whether overtime work should be authorized for the weekend.

Undoubtedly at some time in the past this company had had a serious problem in meeting delivery dates. Instead of conducting an investigation to get to the heart of the matter, someone instituted a system of progress reports to control variations from schedule. This superimposed information network served only as a substitute for

---

[1] An excellent sourcebook on designing information networks is Preston P. Le Breton, *Administrative Intelligence—Information Systems* (Boston, Mass.: Houghton Mifflin Company, 1969).

appropriate corrective action. Countless information networks of this type are superimposed on existing systems, not to cure the disease but merely to ease the pain.

Recent moves to automate information networks through electronic data processing tend toward integrating information networks and control systems. But in most instances such automation is married to the existing systems rather than taking a completely new approach.

The volume of paperwork generated in the average firm is almost beyond imagination. There is serious doubt that much of this paper need be generated or that it serves much purpose. What is required in most organizations is a complete overhaul and reexamination of the information networks and control systems. One approach which might be used in such a thorough investigation is to list the levels of management and itemize for each the information needed for action, information needed for control, and information needed to keep informed.

The objectives of examining the information network are economy of effort, accuracy, timeliness, and appropriateness of information. Analysts who study the minutiae of information networks often find records duplicated, logbooks kept unnecessarily, and reports incorrectly designed and distributed. Normally analysts must work with an existing system and attempt to refine it rather than redesign it in total. What is recommended here is a complete re-examination and redesign of the entire system. Each level of management—and eventually each manager—should be examined to learn (1) what information is required for action at this level; (2) what information is required for advice on the actions of others; and (3) what information is required for control at the next higher and the next lower levels. Such examination should be preceded by the standardization of the planning process and the controls needed to implement it. This will simplify the design of the information network and control system.

The information network and control system really require one set of information, not three separate sets. The sales order, for example, not only informs the sales department that it must arrange for the manufacture or shipment of products but also serves as the raw material for an analysis of sales information. Recording the internal sales order on a punched tape prepares the information for a computer program. A similar treatment in the integration of the various information flows throughout the organization permits the generation of all the necessary control reports automatically.

A total systems approach makes it possible to store the plan, including sales, on a computer memory drum. As sales orders are received the information is fed into the computer and matched against anticipated or planned sales. Where there is substantial agreement between the original plan and the results, no reports need be issued. In other words, the entire system works on the exception rule. There is no need to generate reports that merely confirm the plan. While it is true that some special reports must be generated even if the plan is being met, reporting only deviations from plans would result in major time and cost savings. Managers would no longer have to read countless reports that things are proceeding satisfactorily. Separate posting, compilation of separate reports by managers, and great masses of paperwork could thus be eliminated.

EVALUATION OF THE CONTROL SYSTEM

The control system and its related information network's effectiveness should be measured against four criteria.

1. *Objectives.* What is the purpose of the controls? Are they necessary? Do they duplicate other control systems? What information is required for the implementation of the plan? What information do subordinates need to carry through their tasks? What information do superiors need to evaluate performance?

2. *Standards of performance.* Effective management controls require a plan and standards of performance in terms of time, task, and dollars. Satisfactory performance in any part of the organization requires a plan of action that integrates each manager's plans with those of his superiors as well as his subordinates. But it is not enough to have a plan; also necessary are standards of performance against which actual performance can be measured during the implementation stage. Where possible, these standards should be set by means of ratio delay studies, time study, and the like. Even when these more objective methods cannot be used, the manager is not absolved from setting standards. What he must do is consult with the individuals concerned and then make realistic estimates that are broken down into segments small enough to be measured easily.

3. *Correlation of planning and control.* The plan itself must be developed in such a way that adequate performance on each segment will permit adequate performance on the succeeding segments. It is important that the integration of plans be done in advance if the controls are to be useful. The controls themselves must be built into the plan as an integral part, and both controls and standards of performance should be understood by the individuals responsible for performance before they start the job. These controls will inform the individual of his progress on the job and will thus become a useful tool for all concerned.

4. *Relationship to organization structure.* Effective management controls require that the assignment of tasks and the delegation of authority and responsibility be clear and specific. The manager should initially have designed his organization in such a way that these would not have to be done anew for every new task. But over time every organization is molded by its members into a working organization which may have little resemblance to the original structure. It behooves the manager to recognize what this structure now represents so that his assignments will not contravene the actual practice of management in the organization.

Even with a stable organization it may be necessary to redefine tasks and to correlate authority for a particular plan. Even an all-purpose organization structure may fail to provide sufficient flexibility to cope with special circumstances.

❈   ❈   ❈

Designing the control system and information network is a critical managerial skill that may call on such diverse knowledge as a recognition of the effect of controls on human behavior and the limitations and advantages of computers. And without control the other managerial skills cannot be effective.

An important adjunct to the inventory of managerial skills set forth in these pages is the examination of a manager in his organizational setting. What differentiates him from an employee? What are his prerogatives? What is the challenge of a managerial career? And what are his organizational responsibilities? These subjects, which constitute the final chapter, set the stage for the manager to apply his managerial skills.

15

A Management Philosophy

THE MANAGER has a multitude of responsibilities: to society, to his company, to his boss, to his subordinates, and to himself. To balance these myriad responsibilities, each manager needs to develop a personal managerial philosophy.

To be truly effective, a manager must develop his own philosophy of management to guide his actions. He cannot merely accept a philosophy promulgated by his organization or even by society. *The Organization Man* decried the frequent acceptance of a stereotyped philosophy and code of ethics.[1] *The Lonely Crowd* noted the trend toward the "other-directed" person who willingly accepts and even seeks a philosophy identified with that of the multitude rather than evolving a philosophy for himself.[2] While every individual should be guided by the tenets of society, as a reasoning human being he must develop his own philosophy rather than merely accept that of others.

MANAGEMENT AND THE ORGANIZATIONAL ENTITY

To develop a management philosophy one must study management objectively as an institution or organizational entity. Manage-

[1] William H. Whyte, Jr. (Garden City, N. Y.: Doubleday and Company, 1957).
[2] David Riesman, Nathan Glazer, and Revel Denney (Garden City, N. Y.: Doubleday Anchor, 1953).

ment and the business enterprise of which it is a part are generally considered synonymous by the general public and by the employees. The actions of top management are the actions of the corporation, since it is management that gives life and action to the inanimate body of the corporation. There neither is nor can be a separation of the two.

There is a tendency on the part of middle and lower managers in particular to fail to identify themselves or their actions with the enterprise. They are inclined to look on the organization as an entity which inflicts its will on its members. They see their actions as dictated by the corporation and not subject to their own will. Often this attitude results in the failure of lower and middle managers to assume their full responsibilities.

CONFORMITY AND THE MANAGER

To become a member of management requires acceptance of the overriding purpose of the organization. The price that must be paid is conformity—not conformity in manners, personal mores, and dress, but the more meaningful sublimation of some personal goals to further those needs of the whole organization that can be met only by coordination.

An organization could be represented as a series of pyramids within pyramids. The area within each pyramid defines the operations of the manager in charge of that section of the organization. In order to permit each manager to coordinate the activities of subordinates within a particular pyramid, his actions must be known to other managers, both on the same level and higher. This task of communication would be impossible if each manager were allowed to decide on actions that affect the operations of other managers within their own pyramids. Because of this problem of communication and coordination, managers cannot take unilateral action which affects pyramids other than their own.

The organization demands conformity to permit the meshing of its parts. This does not mean that the individual manager is forbidden to exercise initiative. But without prior approval he must exercise such initiative only within his own sphere of action. Whenever his action affects the performance of others not under his direct supervision, he must conform to the tenets of the organization by obedience to its rules, policies, and procedures.

The very term conformity raises spectres of George Orwell's *1984.* Even a democracy requires that we obey certain laws which limit some of our freedom while insuring all of us as much freedom as possible. In many ways conformity in an organization is analogous to democracy in the state. In an organization, failure to conform would result in chaos because of the lack of coordination in the actions of managers and workers. In a democracy, failure to adhere to restrictions on freedom would result in anarchy, with each individual doing as he pleased regardless of the consequences for his neighbor.

Conformity and Organizational Design

The demand for conformity in organization places a particularly heavy burden on the top managers charged with designing the organization structure. The top executives must design the organization so as to permit coordination at all levels, which in turn demands that behavior be predictable where it affects the actions of other managers. To attain a high degree of effectiveness and to utilize the special talents of every member of management, the individual manager must be permitted maximum latitude. Decisions can be made best at the point where the information is most current and most accessible. The task for top management, then, is to decentralize authority and responsibility and yet coordinate all activity to achieve the organizational goals.

Many large firms follow a policy of centralization of authority to the ultimate degree in order to achieve maximum coordination. Such centralization requires rules, regulations, policies, procedures, and the like—often characterized as red tape. If top management is overzealous, it may forget that coordination depends upon the cooperation of those being coordinated. This cooperation in turn depends upon an understanding of the rationale for orders and organization, which is difficult when little latitude is permitted the individual manager. Centralization will not elicit cooperation unless each manager can feel that he is making a personal contribution to his job and to his company.

The organization too must pay a price. Its members demand what all reasoning human beings must demand: human dignity and the right to make decisions affecting their own behavior. When the proper balance is achieved between the organization's demand for conformity and the individual's need for freedom of action, there can be coordination of all concerned without loss of initiative or effectiveness.

MANAGEMENT PREROGATIVES

Management no longer has any prerogatives. The prerogatives to set standards, lay off workers, and deal with unions are subject to negotiation between labor and management. The concept of the divine right of kings became obsolete with the French Revolution. The concept of management prerogatives became obsolete with the public policy of full employment and the rise of unions.

In history the divine right of kings was given to a leader in order to protect the people. During the Industrial Revolution the prerogatives of management were granted to protect the investors. Absolute monarchy failed because it did not consider the rights and demands of the people. Management prerogatives failed because, although the concept considered the rights of investors, it did not recognize that organizations must fulfill other responsibilities in society. Adam Smith well recognized that in a free enterprise resources would be allocated to further the financial interests of investors. But with an ever rising level of education and affluence among workers, and with the growing interest of central governments in economic policy, countervailing power has been brought to bear on corporate actions. Free enterprise has become regulated private enterprise. As the power of government grows and unions are able to secure economic and social advantages for their members, managerial prerogatives begin to atrophy. Do managers need these prerogatives, these rights to order or demand action? If the function of management is to coordinate resources to achieve an objective, what must be done to insure this coordination? To obtain full cooperation from the human resources requires persuasion and motivation, not coercion.

Managerial Privileges

If management has given up many of its prerogatives, it has retained certain privileges not accorded employees. Along with such
obvious privileges as not punching a time clock, having private of-
fices, and being given greater freedom of personal action are such
things as expense accounts, relaxation of supervision, and higher pay.
In today's equalitarian society there is considerable implied criticism
of such special privileges. Yet society has always rewarded those
with special ability or special responsibilities.

The military has for centuries differentiated between the private
soldier and the officer, not because the officer is a superior being but
because he has to be motivated with rewards to accept the heavy
responsibilities of management. The Soviet Union, for all its accent
on a classless society, soon recognized the need to grant special
privileges to certain classes. If anything, the Soviet officer has many
more rights and privileges than his counterparts in the Western
world. And the Soviet manager is particularly privileged, with superior housing and automobiles not available to others.

Some of the manager's rewards are far more important than the
carpeted office, though they may be less obvious. He has opportunities
for self-determination, for putting his own ideas into effect, and for
making decisions affecting not only his own behavior but also that of
others. He can exercise initiative, develop the abilities of others,
build an organization for the future. He has the chance to be creative
and contribute to the world in some small measure, even if only
through the manufacture of can openers.

The consuming desire of people to be of use to the world is too
often ignored in organizations. Frederick Winslow Taylor and the
scientific management movement considered that there must be a
separation of the worker's manual effort from the manager's mental
effort. The job of the manager, they said, was to observe and define
the job of the worker to the point where the worker's actions were
automatic. In other words, the latitude permitted the worker was
reduced to a minimum so that he could perform much like a machine.

While it is true that many mass production operations require
rote actions and may not be changed except by replacing people
with machines, on countless other jobs workers could have greater

latitude to make a personal contribution. The job enlargement experiments of IBM and AT&T [3] to permit production workers to enlarge the scope of their jobs is a step in the right direction. Frederick Herzberg develops the concept of job enrichment as a major means to employee motivation and satisfaction.[4]

MANAGERIAL RESPONSIBILITIES

When a man accepts a managerial position he considers such factors as higher pay, the opportunity to get ahead, and the feeling of stature and status among his fellow employees. What he really is accepting is a completely new way of life. No longer can he think only of how some action of the organization is going to affect him personally. Now he must consider the actions and reactions of his subordinates, his superiors, and his peers. Often he finds himself faced with responsibilities of a sort that he may never have considered before.

Each manager is confronted with the need to balance four major responsibilities: (1) to the department and the firm; (2) to his subordinates; (3) to his superiors; and (4) to himself and his future managerial career.

RESPONSIBILITY TO THE ORGANIZATION

The hourly paid employee's responsibility to the organization is often taken lightly. But a manager's responsibility cannot be taken lightly. Membership in the management hierarchy means identification with the organization, since the manager's acts are now the acts of the organization.

Though a manager's first responsibility must be to the organization, this does not mean he is expected to condone illegal or immoral acts on its part. Rather, it means that he must decide before he becomes a manager whether he can accept the organization's objectives. Once he has assumed a managerial position he must honestly

[3] Robert N. Ford, *Motivation Through the Work Itself* (AMA, 1969).
[4] "One More Time: How Do You Motivate Employees?" *Harvard Business Review* (January–February 1968), pp. 53–62.

align his personal objectives with those of the organization. And if one organization cannot satisfy his personal objectives, he must find another that can.

There are countless frustrated and unhappy people in the ranks of management who look on their jobs as a way to make money enough to maintain their standard of living. These people have failed because they have never really spelled out their personal objectives or, for that matter, assessed their capabilities. They do not consider their jobs as challenges or as opportunities to contribute to society. They are merely eking out an existence, perhaps satisfying their creativity needs through some hobby or outside activity. True, many organizations fail to provide opportunities for their employees to be creative. But the major blame must be placed on the individual who has not sought out an organization which demands that he be a reasoning, creative human being.

Once a man has accepted the concept that as a manager he must honestly align his personal objectives with those of the organization, he assumes some rather weighty responsibilities. He must advance his ideas to his superiors, *regardless of opposition,* if he is of the opinion that this is best for the organization. To many an experienced manager this concept is nothing short of heretical. Such a man would consider it suicidal to advance an unpopular idea or show up his superior by being cleverer than he. All this may be true, but it is assumed here that the individual manager is mature and sophisticated and knows how to achieve results without alienating those he must work with.

To be effective, the manager must have a sense of loyalty to the organization to the point where its objectives have absolute priority. Does this mean that when a superior stands in the way of attaining the objectives he is to be brushed aside? Does it mean that the subordinate must resign when his superior vetoes his suggestions? The answer is obviously no; what must be remembered is that the attainment of objectives is paramount in either case.

When there is controversy, it is all too often over means and not ends or objectives. Compromise in means is the mark of a successful and sophisticated manager. Lack of compromise in means is the mark of the immature and inexperienced manager. It is only when ends are compromised that we have the mark of the unprincipled individual.

There are a number of dangers both for the organization and for the individual when one man advances ideas and concepts, regardless of opposition, because they are deemed necessary for organizational survival and effectiveness. One major danger is that the individual's limited point of view may prevent him from understanding the totality of the problem. More information or experience would broaden the manager's point of view and permit him to judge whether he is advancing the right or only course of action. If he blindly continues to advance a poor solution, he is doing a disservice to the organization.

A limited point of view at lower echelons was evident in a major university whose faculty opposed an administrative decision to expand despite the prospect of a doubling of enrollment in the next decade. The university was in a sprawling industrial-residential complex where land cost was high, but it was situated across a river from a slum area where land cost was low. After considerable research and investigation the administration advanced a plan to create a new university complex on the opposite bank of the river where there was unlimited room for expansion at much lower cost than was possible on the university side of the river. The plan was to move schools and colleges that had the minimum sunk cost in equipment in the present buildings.

The reaction of the faculty whose schools were to be moved was to use every possible means including political action to block the move. The faculty's opposition was based not on personal motives but on what it thought was best for the university as a whole, considering duplication of dormitory facilities, eating facilities, library facilities, and the like. What the faculty members failed to see was the broader view of the administration, which considered parking facilities, lower costs, and the opportunity to create a unified architecture on the new campus.

How is the young executive to judge whether his ideas or concepts are valid, considering his limited experience at this point of his development? The organization must recognize the responsibility of the superior to broaden the subordinate's point of view. The subordinate should discuss his concepts and ideas with his superior, who in turn should advance any valid idea and discuss in depth the flaws in any idea that is not suitable.

A further danger facing the manager who has ideas is that he may find the superior unreceptive or even discriminating against him for advancing an idea. The subordinate should consider this a stroke of fortune since it compels him to reassess his future in the organization. Assuming that the manager is wise enough to recognize the need to achieve organizational aims without alienating a good superior, he must now assess the courses of action open to him. If his idea means the profitability or survival of the firm, he must continue to advance it even at the risk of displeasing his superior. Will the organization consider the formal hierarchy sacred and therefore turn the manager down regardless of the worth of the idea? It is this sort of information that will permit the manager to assess whether he can attain his personal objectives while also realizing those of the organization.

A noteworthy historical incident of overriding responsibility to an organization took place in the period following the Spanish-American War when a young American naval subaltern in the China Seas station met a British naval captain who had perfected an apparatus permitting much greater accuracy in firing naval guns by compensating for the roll of the ship. The subaltern, named Sims, tried this device on his own ship and was so impressed with the increased accuracy of his gunners that he advanced the idea to his superiors in the China Sea station as a way of making the U.S. Navy much more effective in the event of war. On the advice of naval experts, Sims' superior dismissed the idea as impractical. Sims brooded over the idea and, after further testing, decided to advance it directly to the Office of Naval Gunnery in Washington. As a result of this unprecedented action, Sims was transferred to the Panama station—a punishment deemed appropriate for the brash young subaltern who bypassed the usual channels of communication and incurred the disapproval of his superior.

Sims did not rest at this point; he decided that this compensating device for naval guns was essential to the well-being of the Navy and the survival of the country. He communicated the idea directly to President Theodore Roosevelt, who took a characteristically Rooseveltian action and appointed Sims to the Office of Naval Gunnery so that the country would not lose this important advance in gunnery techniques. (Sims was eventually promoted to admiral and was the presiding officer at the court-martial of Billy Mitchell, who risked his career to do for air power what Sims had done for naval gunnery two decades previously. Admiral Sims voted for the acquittal of Mitchell.)

When the individual accepts a managerial position, he assumes a responsibility to the organization that must be carried out with minimal conflict and without jeopardizing the objectives of the organization. When adherence to the principle advocated here results in conflict, all parties to the conflict lose, whether they are right or wrong. Conflict is not in itself unhealthy. The hazard lies not in conflict but in the aggressive acts often associated with it. A major cause of these aggressive acts is to be found in the confusion of personal and institutional objectives in an organization. It is only natural for people to seek recognition for their ideas or their work, but they must not do so at the expense of their organizational responsibilities. The manager who aligns personal and institutional objectives can have a sense of accomplishment when the institution's objectives are achieved.

RESPONSIBILITIES TO SUBORDINATES

Taking on a management position means accepting responsibilities to subordinates whose lives and prospects for the future are primarily in the manager's hands. This responsibility is not to be taken lightly. Whether a person derives any satisfaction from his work depends on the organizational environment and to a particular degree on his manager. The manager represents the company to the subordinates—putting its policies into effect, enforcing its regulations, applying its sanctions. But he cannot blame the organization if his subordinates are unproductive. He has accepted responsibility for their effectiveness, and his failure to carry out his responsibilities to his subordinates will usually mean his own ultimate failure.

One company with a large research and development staff had found it difficult not only to recruit professional engineers but also to keep them. The firm conducted exit interviews with departing employees and an analysis of these interviews revealed that some engineering supervisors had very little turnover of personnel whereas others had a very high turnover rate. A particular effort was made in the exit interviews to learn whether the supervisor was the reason for a man's leaving the company. Most of the engineers were reluctant to give this reason for leaving. But the evidence indicated that the major factor was the actions of the individual supervisor who failed to motivate, take an interest in, or generally discharge his responsibilities to his subordinates.

The newly promoted manager must be practical about his responsibilities to his subordinates, because failure to exercise them will determine whether he succeeds as a manager. His job is to coordinate the performance of a task, not to perform the task himself. His effectiveness depends equally on how well he plans and how well he persuades subordinates to carry out these plans. In other words, his success depends upon the cooperation of his subordinates, which in turn depends upon how well he carries out his responsibilities to them.

The manager's ability to coordinate depends upon this cooperation of the subordinates. To elicit cooperation requires a knowledge of human motivations. Chester I. Barnard [5] emphasized this when he noted that each individual has a "zone of indifference" in which orders will be obeyed with little question because they involve rights established by organizational tradition. Outside this zone of indifference the employee must be convinced that an order or a decision is in accord with his own personal interests or not contrary to the organization's best interests. In an industrial organization it is not a matter of mutiny when an employee fails to carry out an order. Instead of open conflict there is likely to be apathy—which foreshadows failure.

One responsibility the manager must not overlook is the development of the people who report to him. But he should act as a mentor, not as a sculptor; freedom of action and freedom of choice must be left to the employee and not preempted by the manager.

The dean of a major university failed to provide freedom of choice when he evolved far-reaching plans to make his school the leading institution of its kind in the nation. No school can be great without a great faculty. So the dean launched a program to develop individual faculty members in the particular skills he felt were necessary for his plans. He secured foundation support for his program to provide the faculty with specialized training, announced the plans, began to appoint faculty to the program—and encountered considerable resistance. When he discussed this matter frankly with some of

[5] *The Functions of the Executive* (Cambridge, Mass.: Harvard University Press, 1958), pp. 167–171.

the faculty members, he learned that they had their own development plans, which were different from those of the dean.

This dean was carrying out his responsibilities for the development of his subordinates, but without providing sufficient freedom of choice. Because he failed to counsel with the faculty and insure freedom of choice, he failed to achieve his own objective of upgrading faculty skills.

It has often been said that the only truly great executives are self-made men. Certainly it is true that the highly motivated individual will develop himself no matter what the quality of his superior's help. But most men are not highly motivated toward self-development and many are not even aware of developmental opportunities within the organizational framework. It is the manager's responsibility to provide motivation and to contribute to the development of subordinates.

Insurance companies and banks had great difficulty in attracting young college graduates in the years following World War II. Low starting salaries were one reason, but not the major one. College graduates were—and are—vitally interested in what would happen to them in their jobs, what future there was with a firm, what opportunities there would be for promotion and development, what types of jobs were available. And they gave insurance companies and banks low ratings on all these counts. One insurance company recognized this felt need of college graduates, and after considerable preparation it set up a management training program, provided for job rotations and merit increases, and furnished its trainees with outlines of the executive positions open in the firm. Whereas previously the firm had had little success in recruiting college graduates, it now had its pick of the crop without markedly increasing its starting salaries.

College graduates are highly motivated, yet they want to work for companies that take an interest in their development. Managers should consider well the lesson of the insurance firm and take considerable pains in developing their subordinates.

RESPONSIBILITIES TO A SUPERIOR

In the order of priority set forth earlier, the manager's responsibilities to the organization and to his subordinates were placed higher than those to his superior. Experienced managers may quarrel with this ordering of priorities on the grounds that it is organizational suicide to place responsibility to subordinates before responsibility to a superior, that the superior can make or break a manager, that loyalty to superiors is demanded in a hierarchy, and that success depends upon promotion, which depends on the relationship a man establishes with his superior. All these points are valid. Yet lack of cooperation on the part of subordinates can make it impossible for a manager to be effective.

The ordering of priority is not so absolute that it must be adhered to exactly. Rather, it should be used as a guide. The manager must not fail to consider all his responsibilities—to the organization, to his subordinates, to his superiors, and to himself. But he should keep in mind that many successful executives have used such an ordering as their guide or philosophy of management.

Managers low in an organization have tunnel vision of a sort. They know a great deal about their own operations but little about the organization as a whole. So their perspective is narrow and they may have little understanding of the corporate entity. Conversely, higher managerial levels have limited detail about the job activities of subordinates and therefore have a far different outlook. Every subordinate should recognize that a breakdown in understanding may be caused by his superior's lack of detailed information. But he must also recognize that his own narrow perspective may be the limiting factor.

No one can be altogether objective about his own shortcomings. Lack of objectivity and differences in point of view can combine to cause tension, conflict, misunderstanding, breakdowns in communication. It requires the concerted efforts of subordinate and superior managers to surmount these obstacles and work together effectively.

There are three major reasons why the subordinate must carry out his responsibilities to his superior. The first is that, by doing so, he is fulfilling his responsibilities to the organization. The second is that the superior usually has the authority and power to help or hinder his subordinate in fulfilling his obligations to his own subordinates. Within the constraints of the organizational hierarchy, each manager must fight for his subordinates and their needs, always remembering that the organization demands conformity so that it can remain a coordinated entity.

The third reason for fulfilling responsibilities toward the superior is self-interest. The superior's actions are a major limiting factor on the effectiveness of the manager. If the superior is himself an effective manager he can insure that the subordinate has freedom of action. Since each manager is in some measure dependent upon the other for effectiveness, each must do everything he can to make the other a better manager because in the process he makes himself a better manager. What is more, showing one's superior up in a good light not only improves one's relations with him but also improves one's own chances for promotion.

The Manager's Responsibility to Himself

Every individual has social responsibilities to his family, to his community, to his nation—perhaps to the world. Certainly the manager must recognize and carry out such responsibilities. In addition, he has two responsibilities within the framework of his company of which he must be aware. The first responsibility is to develop his own supervisory skills. For this, experience can be an excellent teacher. Every day the manager makes decisions, plans, controls, and coordinates the work of others. How effective are these actions? Analyzing both successes and failures will help him recognize his limitations and his strengths; then he will be able to minimize his limitations and capitalize on his strengths for maximum effectiveness.

There are also countless opportunities to develop management awareness through courses and reading. Some courses offered by university night schools, professional societies, vocational schools, management associations, and schools of business are open only to company employees, but many are open to the manager on his own time. The countless journals in general management and in specialized fields contain a wealth of information. Each manager should work out his own development program, if possible in cooperation with his superior, to overcome his shortcomings through training.

The second responsibility of the manager is to examine his role and his future in his present organizational environment. If conditions in his company or on his job cannot be changed, the manager may have to disassociate himself from the organization. As noted earlier, every manager must align his personal objectives with those of the organization if he is to be productive in an executive position. When he can no longer make such an alignment, he should either change his personal objectives or change his organizational ties to permit such a merging of objectives.

The decision to leave an organization should not be made out of spite or resignation; like all decisions, it must be made objectively. The manager must ascertain whether he is at fault, whether the job has insufficient challenge, whether it is a dead-end job, whether he has exhausted all possibilities in the present organization, and so on. Once he has made such an objective analysis he should not hesitate to act. It is the rare organization that does not have its share of disillusioned managers in their fifties who recognized the shortcomings in their positions but failed to take action to remedy them.

When a manager assesses himself and his situation, he may come to the conclusion that he is not happy in the management ranks. Many well-qualified technical men have taken management positions in order to make more money, gain more prestige, or contribute more to the world. When such men become managers they are often frustrated by administrative processes, by the necessity to please many people, both subordinates and superiors, and by a feeling of lack of accomplishment.

Unfortunately, many firms consider that the management ladder has no permanent resting place and that the only direction one can be permitted to move in is up. In such firms technical man cum manager is not free to return to the design bench or the experimental laboratory. He must continue to wrestle with management problems or fail as a manager and leave. A number of scientific organizations have faced this issue by creating technical positions with pay and prestige equivalent to upper levels of management for the brilliant scientist or engineer.

The transition from employee to manager calls for the formulation of a completely new philosophy or outlook of life. Just as the doctor must take the Hippocratic oath with its obligations to serve mankind, so the manager must privately take his oath of service to his organization, to his subordinates, to his superiors, and to himself as a member of the organization. If he is unwilling to accept such responsibilities he should not consider a management position.

The Organization and Its Social Responsibilities

Any organization, whether it be a corporation or a church club, is a part of society. Over the years, many of the difficulties between management and labor, and between labor and the general public, have resulted because neither business nor organized labor was considered by its leaders to be subject to the laws and mores of society. In democratic nations society imposes its will on business and labor by legislative regulation. Had such organizations recognized their debt to society and observed its rules, perhaps such legislation would have been unnecessary.

As part of society, the business enterprise is subject not only to written but to unwritten laws. The manager, as an integral part of the business's decision-making body, must be cognizant of its social responsibilities—not merely contributions to the United Fund or service in business clubs but recognition of the rights of other groups and possibly even economic sacrifices.

A case in point is water pollution. The major streams and rivers of the industrialized world are becoming clogged with industrial waste; fish are dying; water sources for our cities are becoming polluted. Complicated questions of political jurisdiction have made it almost impossible for local authorities in many areas to control the firms responsible for such pollution. When companies are asked to end pollution voluntarily, the answer often is that it is uneconomic to do so since other firms in the same industry would gain a competitive cost advantage. Here is a clear case of management unwillingness to fulfill its social responsibilities. But management has other responsibilities. It must remain competitive so its shareholders can make a profit. It must keep the corporation economically healthy to provide its employees with steady employment. And it must provide its customers the highest quality of products and services at lowest cost. In the case just cited can the firms cease polluting the rivers and also fulfill their other responsibilities? Dilemmas such as this have made many businesses insensitive to their social responsibilities.

It is when an organization fails to meet its responsibilities that society enacts laws and provides sanction to insure fulfillment of obligations. Private enterprise is part of the social structure because it fulfills the needs of society. When it fails to do so it may be replaced with state enterprise, with all the attendant inefficiencies.

The rights of individuals must be protected not only in society at large but in the subculture that is an organization. No man sells his rights as an individual or as a human being when be becomes an employee or a manager. The same rights to human dignity and freedom of action apply in the organizational environment as in the community, the church, and the family. Failure to insure such rights of individuals makes employees passive and unproductive or drives them to the point of resignation.

Managers generally deplore employees' lack of motivation and interest in the company and in their work. Many men and women turn their excess energies and talents to hobbies and merely tolerate their jobs as ways of earning a living, so they can afford to meet the challenge of life in leisure-time activities. It is not leisure as a pursuit but work as a drudgery that is to be condemned. Countless repetitive, monotonous, and uninteresting jobs can be made more palatable if management recognizes the rights of individuals; countless others have the elements of challenge and interest in them destroyed by management's failure to recognize human needs and motivations.

MANAGEMENT AS A POSITION OF TRUST

Management carries with it attendant responsibilities to the organization and to employees as well as to society as a whole. In essence management is charged with marshaling and allocating resources for the common good. To fill this position of trust a manager must recognize his responsibilities and balance them in a way acceptable to all concerned. He cannot serve one master at the expense of another, lest countervailing pressures lead to censure or even failure. Investors look to the manager to make their investment profitable; customers seek quality and integrity at the lowest possible cost; employees need human dignity and security; superiors demand loyalty and service; subordinates ask for understanding and development; the community requires public service as well as public responsibility; citizens in the community ask a warrant that the organization's power will not be misused; and society insists that its interests not be subverted to the interests of the organization.

Few people give much thought to these responsibilities when they become managers. And the typical manager is plagued with more day-to-day operating problems than he can handle, which leaves him little time to ponder some of the more abstract demands on his energies. But immersion in day-to-day operating problems should not blind him to his greater responsibilities to the organization and to society. Failure to consider them puts the private enterprise system itself in jeopardy.

THE MANAGER AND HIS JOB

The job of the manager is not an easy one. At first glance the carpeted office, the form-fitting swivel chair, the modern decorator desk seem to be the marks of leisure and give no hint of tension, urgency, or responsibility. The rewards are great but the demands on the executive are equally great. That each manager is held accountable for his decisions is exemplified by the case of the president of a large manufacturer of cleaning products when he was informed by his staff of the introduction of detergents. The president asked his market research director to make a thorough study of the acceptance of this new product by consumers to see whether his firm should invest in plant and equipment to manufacture it.

The market research director reported that after intensive study he was of the opinion that detergents would have a limited effect on the market. The president accepted the findings of his research staff and decided not to schedule the necessary facilities. Within one year detergents had captured 25 percent of the soap market, and the board of directors shortly thereafter asked for the president's resignation.

This executive's error and its consequences are evidence of a fundamental principle in business: The organizational hierarchy will not permit the shifting of responsibility from line to staff even though line decisions may be based on staff recommendations. It is the line executive who is charged with decision making, and he must suffer the consequences of incorrect decisions even if the fault lay with the advice he received from staff.

The manager may be paid on the basis of a 40-hour week but his responsibilities are measured on task accomplishment, not on the amount of time he spends in doing his job. There are inequities in job assignments in every company, with one executive bearing a disproportionate share of work without extra pay. Furthermore, the organization often makes demands on the manager that exceed the specifications for the job. Research on the distribution of executive time has established that executives rarely work only 40 hours per week, with the norm closer to 50 or 60 hours. Furthermore, the demands of the executive's job are not the only demands on his time and energies. A corporation often requires that its executives be active in community affairs as its representatives.

Yet another demand on executive time is for conferences. Coordination is often so complex in the larger firm that innumerable conferences and committee meetings must be held to resolve potential conflicts. Often such conferences are held not so much to provide answers to specific questions as to elicit the cooperation of other departments when utilizing the formal chain of command would be time-consuming and ineffective. An example of this use of conferences is found in a large research and development firm which was organized functionally into three separate areas: research and development, production, and customer service. This company had a number of separate product divisions using common facilities, and each reported to the president. But a functional organization emphasizes vertical coordination at the expense of horizontal coordination. In order for third-level managers from the three functions to work out problems they shared in common, they had to go up the chain of command to the president and then back down to the directors of the functions.

As an alternative to this formal, ponderous, up-the-chain-and-down-again communication, the third-level managers found it better to resolve their problems in weekly conferences of the product teams from each of the three functions. These conferences took considerable time, but they ironed out jurisdictional questions, settled disputes, and saw to the assignment of authority and responsibility. Short of changing the company's organizational structure—which might have created as many problems as it solved—these conferences answered a pressing need.

Every manager must also devote considerable time and effort to human relations. Not only must he establish rapport with individuals reporting to him, but he also has to resolve conflicts as they arise so as to insure that his subordinates work together effectively as a team.

The Creativity of Management

To most people there is little glamour in management—except perhaps as the top man with the top salary. Creativity and service to mankind are seen as the prerogatives of the scientist, the architect, the professor, the medical doctor. For the most part, business is considered a necessary evil and management is seen as a mundane pursuit for those who cannot attain greatness or who lack creative genius.

This picture of the business world has dissuaded many a capable young person from pursuing a career in industry. But is it a true picture? The business enterprise and its management are responsible for the production of goods and services in sufficient quantity to allow society the leisure time and resources to pursue cultural activities. Is this not creativity? Is not the very act of managing creative?

The manager rarely knows the satisfaction of the artisan because his task is to set the stage and coordinate the action, not to be the actor. His creativity must come from making it possible for others to produce. In the factory the manager arranges for raw materials at the workplace, for the necessary tools and fixtures, for the power, for the distribution of the product, but it is the workman who makes the product. Yet the workman could not have created the product without the coordinating acts of the manager. Was the manager less creative than the worker?

Administrative practices can be taught, and men and women can be trained to improve their administrative skills, but executives with exceptional administrative ability are limited in number. So much specialized administrative talent is required to manage the large, multiplant, multinational firm that organizations have placed large premiums indeed on executives with such abilities. For some years General Motors has paid an annual salary and bonus to its chief executive exceeding half a million dollars. Such high salaries are paid for creativity and imagination, not for routine administration.

Although the very job of managing is a creative activity, it is a strange paradox that business requires imagination from top management but demands a high degree of conformity from the lower echelons of management. This was made clear in the comments of one company's campus recruiter when asked whether his firm would hire a brilliant nonconformist student. The student was not a personality problem but had a questioning mind and rarely accepted things until he had examined them for himself, as the recruiter had already discerned.

The recruiter noted that his company would spend ten years indoctrinating a young man into its methods and ways, rarely permitting him to ask why it operated as it did. Then it would ask him to be creative, exercise his imagination, come up with new ideas—and he would probably fail. The years of conforming to company practices without giving play to his creativity and imaginativeness would have ingrained such habits into the man that, given the chance to exercise his talents, he would be unable to do so. The recruiter deplored this situation but said that, since the organizational environment could not permit creativity in the earlier stages of an executive's career, he had no alternative but to turn down the nonconformist.

A business's environment can encourage rather than stifle creativity at all levels. But first, top management must act to create a permissive, challenging atmosphere and allow enough latitude so the young, as yet untried man can exercise what creative ability he possesses. Superiors must take time with their subordinates to temper the exuberance of youth with the judgment of experience and maturity. Management must not stifle creativity but must provide a climate that encourages it. The business firm must provide more challenge for young people and not impose on them outmoded standards of a bygone era.

Management as a Career

The rewards of management can be great. Managers command high salaries and considerable prestige. Administrative talents are highly valued and, like any scarce commodity, they command a high price. The apprenticeship period is relatively long and highly competitive among those in training for executive positions. The opportunities for advancement are unlimited and yet limited.

If a young executive has limited scope because of the particular job assignment, then his chance to excel is also limited—and he may stagnate. On the other hand, vacancies for higher management positions constantly open up, either through retirement of incumbents or company expansion.

There are dilemmas both for the firm and for the individual manager in the need for an organizational hierarchy—which in many ways defeats its own purpose. The hierarchy is so designed that responsibility can be assigned along with commensurate authority. This arrangement automatically places every individual under the command of another. The organizational hierarchy must depend upon extensive communication in all directions to be cognizant of any one individual's particular abilities. The move toward decentralization of authority to let divisional or subsidiary top managers exercise more initiative also means greater departmentalization and separation.

This decentralization may severely limit the organization's ability to pinpoint the younger executives best qualified for promotion. Usually the individual suffers by having less scope for his talents because fewer parts of the organization are open to him, and the organization suffers because the more aggressive and highly motivated younger executives are driven to seek opportunities elsewhere. One solution is to circulate throughout the organization a list of job openings and the qualifications required for promotion to them so that recommendations can come from every section of the company. But few large firms really examine all their managerial talent in making promotions below the top management ranks.

Management as a career may make greater demands on the individual than other professions do. In a business enterprise there is always pressure to reduce costs. The manager is buffeted by superiors demanding lower costs, subordinates demanding higher wages, customers demanding special service. He must fight jurisdictional disputes with his fellow managers to obtain facilities and service. The organizational hierarchy makes demands on him for budget preparation, cost estimates, job specifications, and the like. He must plan his operations, set up and exercise controls, and spend considerable time in training and evaluating his subordinates.

The work of the manager is measured not in terms of time but in terms of results. The organization does not own the executive body and soul, but it demands that he perform the assigned tasks. Nor can the manager delegate this task responsibility to others. He can assign specific tasks to his subordinates, but the responsibility for task achievement remains his and his alone.

Management as a career requires more than a university education. It requires experience on the firing line as a company employee. Entry into the ranks of management is possible for anyone showing administrative ability regardless of his academic background. True, schools of business administration provide preparatory training that should give the potential young executive an understanding of business and the management process. But such training is neither a guarantee of executive ability nor a prerequisite for an executive post.

The business school graduate has an advantage in understanding the relationships between the functions of a business, but he may also be at a disadvantage in regard to qualifications for his first job. University training is not oriented to technical preparation in some specialized function—except for such fields as accounting. Although most business schools permit some specialization, this is necessarily limited if the student is to have training in all the functions of a business. So the qualifications of the graduate for his first job are generally less specific than those of the technical graduate.

The recent trend in education is toward less specialization on the undergraduate level both in engineering and in business administration. There is a strong movement afoot to give undergraduates broad training and a more liberal education. The philosophy behind this movement is that rarely does the young man or woman take the specialized job for which he was trained. The universities have to provide training not of a vocational nature but of professional caliber. They must train the managers of tomorrow, not the clerks of today.

In the academic field there is a secondary trend toward having undergraduates prepare for a liberal arts or engineering degree and focusing professional education for business at the graduate level. Such programs, normally leading to the Master of Business Administration degree, also emphasize more general training through a coverage of the functional fields of business, the social responsibilities of businessmen, quantitative tools analysis, and applied behavioral sciences. These programs more nearly satisfy the need for training in the managerial skills to prepare the individual for a management position on graduation. Yet one important element is missing: experience. The graduating engineer often can immediately assume an engineering position; the graduating business administrator must go through some form of apprenticeship in the business enterprise.

It is important for the young person contemplating a management career to recognize that there is a fairly long probationary period before he can assume management positions of authority and responsibility. The effective manager must be schooled not only in managerial skills but also in the technical requirements of his job. Often the individual who has no schooling in business administration is well trained in the technical requirements of his job but lacks knowledge about the process of management. Rarely can the neophyte manager satisfy both these requirements.

A Personal Philosophy for the Manager

Every individual must develop a personal philosophy and code of ethics regardless of whether he plans a career in management or in any other field of endeavor. The manager, however, has particular need for a personal philosophy since his actions can affect countless people, from his superiors and subordinates to the customers and the general public. He is custodian of a great number of resources, both physical and human.

Unfortunately, the ranks of management are filled with individuals who have failed to evolve a personal philosophy and consider their responsibilities as managers. Management has a reservoir of talent unmatched by any other group, as various presidents of the United States have recognized in their appointments to high government posts. Most of the top managers of the nation's largest corporations are dedicated individuals who, having developed their own personal philosophies, have been able to make great contributions to society. Countless other managers have failed to make this transition from self-interest to dedicated service to mankind.

Man is a gregarious creature, constantly seeking approval from society for his actions. He cannot live in isolation. To be truly happy and effective he must contribute to society. The manger's potential power to do so is considerable. But until he relates his work as a manager to his function as a member of society he cannot do so effectively.

APPENDIX

Decision Theory
and Operations Research

T HE MANAGER must decide how best to deploy the resources available to him to achieve the greatest success or profit. In order to make optimum use of his resources, he must anticipate and forecast the effect each combination of resources will have on profit. Such an activity requires decisions which in turn require the utilization of the sophisticated skills of operations research and other aids to decision making.

Planning and decision making are closely related and are in fact almost indistinguishable. The steps involved in decision making apply equally to planning. The major differences concern time, scope, and implementation. A decision can demand immediate action or future action; a plan, although it may demand immediate action, normally is made for the solution of longer-range tasks. The scope of a decision is most often limited to the determination and solution of a specific problem; a plan encompasses a number of decisions to solve a series of problems. A decision is usually a choice among alternatives to determine a particular course of action. The implementation of the decision may be considered either as a

259

separate function to be completed by the executive making the decision or as a responsibility that may be assigned to subordinates.

Planning, on the other hand, is concerned with implementation of decisions and cannot be considered complete unless the implementation phase is thoroughly detailed. But planning and decision making must go hand in hand, for plans are no more than a series of decisions made in advance of the actual events requiring such decisions.

With this relationship in mind, it is not important in actual practice to differentiate between the planning and decision-making processes. Such a differentiation would accomplish little, since the manager is charged with responsibility for both decision making and planning. The interrelationship of the two is such that one must naturally lead to the other. Planning can provide the right environment for decision making. Decision making requires planning for effective implementation.

THE THEORY OF DECISION MAKING

Contributions to decision theory have been made by a number of academic disciplines. Unfortunately the theory at the present time is highly abstract and difficult to apply to the business scene. For example, considerable discussion has taken place on the rationality of business decisions, which although of interest to the manager, provides him with little concrete assistance in learning how to make effective decisions.

Decision theory deals with decision making under uncertainty where future events cannot be predicted through probability. It assumes that the decision maker not only possesses all the information necessary to make the decision but also is able to anticipate the possible outcome in terms of the payoff resulting from particular combinations of strategies. In addition the decision maker is cognizant of his attitude toward taking chances.[1]

Decision theory has developed a series of decision rules that depend in their application upon two major factors, namely psychological makeup and pecuniary circumstances, which naturally

---

[1] The interested reader should refer to William J. Baumol, *Economic Theory and Operations Analysis* (Englewood Cliffs, N. J.: Prentice-Hall, Inc., 1961), pp. 368–386, on which this section is heavily dependent.

vary from decision maker to decision maker. The following five decision rules are typical:

1. *The maximin criterion.* The decision maker conservatively
determines the worst result of strategy combinations and chooses
the one that is least disastrous.

2. *The maximax criterion.* The decision maker determines the
most attractive combination regardless of the consequences of the
other combinations.

3. *The Hurwicz criterion.* This is based on a weighted average of
the minimum and maximum payoffs for each strategy.

4. *The Bayes (Laplace) criterion.* This accepts the ignorance
about the probability of certain events affecting the strategy and
therefore assigns equal probability to each. For example, the decision
maker may have narrowed his choices or strategies to investing in
government bonds or common stocks. The major uncertainties are a
recession and a boom. The Bayes decision criterion would accept the
impossibility of predicting recession or boom and therefore assign
equal probabilities to their occurrence.

5. *The minimax regret criterion.* This calculates the cost of the
incorrect decision in terms of lost opportunities. The decision is then
made to accept the strategy that minimizes the extent of the loss.

Another decision rule is promulgated for mixed strategies in
which the decision maker uses a random device such as a coin to
make his choice. Then the consequences of various strategies are
calculated.

These are merely the more esoteric exercises in decision theory.
The payoff matrix used in determining solutions by application of
the decision criteria, and even the decision criteria themselves, may
very well be used by managers implicitly if not explicitly. Furthermore the concepts, if not the precise methods, may be used by operations research technicians in certain kinds of problems. But the
direct, deliberate application of theory to decision making and planning is relatively rare.

The major advances in decision theory that have application to
the business scene are those based on mathematical techniques.
Pure mathematics and some fields of applied mathematics such as
physics utilize model building as a technique in determining the
relationship of variables. Model building is also applicable to the
solution of business problems. But to the difficulty of the mathe-

matical formulation of the model must be added the difficulty of identifying the variables that enter into the decision model.

This identification of variables is difficult not only because of the potentially vast number of variables that may exist but simply because it is not always possible to know their nature or even to be aware of their existence. This same problem plagues economic theory, where sufficient rigor to permit determinate solutions was not forthcoming until the development of partial equilibrium theory. General equilibrium theory acknowledged the interdependence of all the possible factors that might affect the solution to a problem or exploration of a phenomenon. Then the concept of *ceteris paribus,* or *other things being equal,* was advanced to reduce the variables to the point where they could be manipulated to give determinate solutions or reasonable explanations of the observed phenomena. This is called partial equilibrium theory by the economists; its application to economic theory has resulted in useful, predictable theories of economic behavior.

Management theory deals primarily with microeconomics (the theory of the firm) and with price theory, which explains the behavior of the individual firm in production and distribution. Macroeconomics, which deals with the behavior of business in general, labor, government, and world trade to explain national and international economics, is considered an external factor in management theory, albeit one that conditions internal policies and decisions.

Economic theory, through *ceteris paribus,* makes some assumptions about the business firm that are not realistic in terms of management theory. For example, economic theory considers the entire firm as one entrepreneur making decisions. It does not take into account the behavioral influences, the effect of suboptimization, and certain other considerations that may negate the maximization premise. Decision theory does consider the behavioral aspects, but only in the context of the decision maker's attitude toward taking chances. Economic theory does not recognize possible effects of the organization structure as it tends toward compromise in decisions.

Neither economic theory nor its stepchild, decision theory, at the present time adequately describes the operation of the business firm. They provide the rigor necessary for theory but not the reality. Unfortunately management theory, although it may come closer to reality, lacks the preciseness of economic or decision theory.

It is not the task of this book to present either esoteric excursions into current thought or detailed descriptive procedures for management. Therefore it does not seem appropriate to delve deeply into the mathematical or quantitative side of management theory since current development of this approach is oriented toward the single decision and not to the totality of the management process. This is not to say that the econometric mathematical approach is unimportant or even that it may not make a major contribution to management practice. But it is not within the scope of this book to develop decision theory adequately to integrate it within the larger framework of management theory and practice. Rather it is proposed to look more broadly at the methodology of decision theory within the more pragmatic framework of what is involved in decision making by the manager.

MATHEMATICAL APPROACH TO DECISION MAKING

Mathematically oriented techniques such as acceptance sampling, probability theory, and operations research have made major contributions to the practice of management, and the manager must certainly be aware of the potential application of mathematical techniques to his problems. An examination of operations research as a technique to sharpen decision making is a necessary prerequisite to understanding modern management.

Statistics through probability theory has made major contributions to decision making. Statistics from research in the physical sciences has established that the Poisson, or normal, distribution is applicable to the ordering of most variables. A further development is the theory of probability which permits the determination of the likelihood of a particular event's occurring. This development is invaluable to the management theorist, who can now utilize probability theory in constructing mathematical models to determine the probable effect of a particular combination of events.

OPERATIONS RESEARCH

Basically any decision requires the building of a model. It could be a scale model of the layout of a plant, or it could be an abstract program to be run on a computer. The model is used to simulate or in some way represent the events and variables that enter into a decision or a series of decisions. One technique increasingly used in industry as an aid to model building for decision making is operations research.

Operations research attempts to draw upon a number of academic disciplines for the solution of industrial problems. It has been defined as "the application of scientific methods, techniques, and tools to problems involving the operations of systems so as to provide those in control of the operations with optimum solutions to the problems" [2] and focusing "upon mathematical and statistical model building as techniques for representing the operations of an organization." [3]

When faced with making a decision, the manager is rarely explicit about quantifying facts or committing them to paper. He is more likely to draw upon a vast reservoir of experience against which he measures his problem. He extracts the similarities to other problems and notes, again implicitly, the differences. As he goes through this process, the manager is really building a model in the same way that the operations research specialist does, but this ordering is more in ordinal than cardinal terms. In other words, he is likely to sort out the variables and facts in such a way as to rank them in order of their importance to the decision.

The experienced manager will have trained himself over the years to consider the important variables affecting any decision and choice of alternatives open to the organization. This is not to say that this same experienced manager should not employ the model-building technique of operations research. On the contrary, operations research permits him to consider a much more extensive interrelationship of variables than is otherwise possible.

Models in operations research are normally programmed on a computer. Although a computer has infinite applications for data processing, it also has significant limitations. In particular, the computer must receive explicit and detailed instructions on exactly what it is expected to do. It has no power or ability to think through a problem on its own, although recent advances in computer and

[2] C. West Churchman, Russell L. Ackoff, and E. Leonard Arnoff, *Introduction to Operations Research* (New York: John Wiley & Sons, Inc., 1957), p. 829.
[3] Max D. Richards and William A. Nielander, *Readings in Management* (Cincinnati, Ohio: South-Western Publishing Company, 1969), p. 258.

programming technology have made it possible for a computer to "learn" from its own mistakes and correct its own program. In this sense the computer "reasons."

The program requires a model, which in turn requires management input as well as the technical input of operations researchers. Through experience and judgment the effective manager is in a position to know what variables should affect any decision and what choice of alternatives is open to the organization. But rarely does he understand model-building techniques to the extent that he himself could design a model and program it for computer application. The operations research technician, although well able to design a model and recognize what is involved in programming a computer, is normally unaware of managerial input required for the decision. This creates a difficult problem of communication, which may result in misunderstandings and abandonment of operations research techniques.

The busy manager who has given time and information to operations research technicians often expects miracles. Rarely is this input information monitored by the executive, and since the operations researcher is usually not qualified to screen it the input may be incomplete or inaccurate. Yet the model is no better than its input. Unsatisfactory information results in unsatisfactory decisions. If the executive, through his judgment and experience, concludes that the decision given by the model is unsound, he may lose faith in the entire technique. Worse still, if the executive fails to note that the decision is incorrect, the result may be chaotic and even cost the executive his job.

Unfortunately, management has a history of overdependence on particular techniques and has tended to overrate the managerial grid, market research, motivation research, PERT, and the rest. Similarly, managers have expected miracles of operations research but have been unwilling to expend the time and energy necessary to learn what is required to make this technique work.

THE MANAGER AND OPERATIONS RESEARCH

The operations researcher is a specialist in model building and computer programming. He is not a manager and cannot be expected to understand management's problems. He is a staff specialist whose job is to assist the manager through the construction of decision models. The responsibility for formulating problems and determining what factors affect their solutions clearly rests with the manager.

The role of the operations research group may well be extended into traditional areas of management prerogative for decision making when the decision models are relatively straightforward or adequate competence does not exist in the management ranks. This enlarges the scope of operations research considerably beyond the translation of management instructions into mathematical models and computer programs. At the same time it creates some special problems of liaison with management, operating management particularly, mainly because most operations researchers lack management experience.

The repetitive decision, such as determining economical purchasing quantities, falls well within the scope of definition and solution by the operations research group. Many companies have found that such programs sharply reduce the amount of management time required for the design of the decision model, and the ramifications of such a decision are more easily determined. Furthermore, the constantly recurring decision is of sufficient importance to merit the rather large expenditure required for model building and computer application.

There are many other major decisions—some affecting the very life of the organization—which can benefit by the preciseness of operations research. But all too often time itself is an important limiting factor. The operations research group may require a long time to build and test the decision model—too long for the comfort of the executive, who may have spent so much time programming his decision that he will not think the return worth the investment. This constitutes a real breakdown in communication that severely limits the use of the technique.

An interesting parallel can be drawn between the use of dictating equipment and operations research. The manager prefers a secretary of his own who is used to his particular eccentricities and who is able to compensate for any limitations he might have in dictating. There is little doubt that dictating equipment is more economical than a secretary. But the effective use of dictating equipment requires a period of training on the part of most executives. Given the choice, they will continue to dictate to secretaries rather than mechanical equipment, except perhaps for long reports or work taken home.

Similarly, the manager is often unwilling to invest the time required to understand operations research techniques and their applications to his own decision making. He is likely to prefer his own rule-of-thumb judgment measures, which he has found to be sufficiently effective in the past to permit him to make good decisions. Yet unless the manager is sufficiently versed in operations research techniques and computer applications, he cannot obtain the preciseness that might lead to better decisions.

MATHEMATICAL MODEL BUILDING

The mathematical model is an essential step in problem solving through operations research. The model attempts to represent the dimensions of the problem in mathematical terms. Building the model clearly demands special abilities of operations research technicians, although the manager must still provide the input required for the construction of the model.

The mathematical model must be discussed with management to insure that it is dealing with reality. As long as the manager understands how the model represents the real world, as long as he can evaluate it in light of his own experience and judgment, he need not be able to work through the mathematics.

Operations research techniques permit the solution of decision problems even when important information is not available in the records of the company. This is accomplished by what is known as the Monte Carlo Technique, which uses a table of random numbers as a substitute for the unavailable data.

Churchman et al. give an example of the application of operations research to a problem that does not lend itself to normal decision processes. The question is: How many trucks should a department store maintain for home delivery of packages? [4] The problem is to obtain the optimum number of delivery trucks so that there will not be idle time and cost for extra trucks or, alternatively, loss of

[4] *Op. cit.,* pp. 407–410.

customers through inadequate service. A trial-and-error method could be used by the executives of the department store to determine how many trucks are actually needed, but this might have the effect of either increasing the cost drastically or losing customers during the trial-and-error period. The Monte Carlo Technique permits the simulation of the trial-and-error solution.

The operations research technicians first determined the answers to a number of questions: (1) What is the average rate at which packages arrive at the loading point for delivery? (2) How representative is this average rate? This requires the determination of the standard deviation. (3) What is the average number of packages that can be delivered by a truck in one day? (4) How representative is this average delivery rate? This too involves the calculation of the standard deviation. (5) What is the cost per day of operating a truck? (6) What is the cost of the delay in package delivery?

Since it would be difficult to ascertain the actual costs per day of the delivery delay, the researchers decided to adhere to a policy of delivering all packages on the day they were available for delivery. Should the number of trucks be inadequate to handle the delivery load, there would be additional overtime costs. The problem in simulating a model was that although the average number of packages available and delivered and the standard deviation of this average were available, the *actual* deviation from this average on any particular day was not known. Without operations research, the manager could run a trial-and-error experiment to determine the actual variations, or he might consult the records on past performance.

To simulate the actual situation in a model three alternative conditions were imposed: (1) arbitrarily to include fewer trucks than were currently being operated by the department store, (2) to use the same number of trucks, and (3) to use a greater number of trucks. A variation in the number of packages to be delivered daily and capable of being delivered daily was found through reference to a table of random numbers. The overtime cost was established when the delivery capabilities were exceeded by the number of packages to be delivered. In addition, the cost of the purchase and maintenance of a truck was calculated. The interaction of these two costs as the number of trucks and packages were varied permitted the determination of the optimum number of trucks to be operated by the department store.

The operations research model must represent reality and must be able to predict the effect of changes in input information. This requires testing the adequacy of the model in terms of both input and output data. The model may be found to include a variable which does not affect the overall system and which, if utilized, would turn out nonsense results. Alternatively, the model may fail to include an important variable and hence not be representative of the system it is attempting to simulate. It is also possible that the model may express the relationship between pertinent independent variables incorrectly, which again would not make the model representative.

Another major consideration in testing a model is whether the solution yields better performance. This is accomplished by testing the model with past-performance input data to reconstruct what would have happened had the model been used in the past. These solutions and the resulting simulated performance are compared with the actual past solutions and performance to ascertain the validity and efficacy of the model. Of course if the past-performance data are inaccurate or inadequate, the judgment may be useless.

The optimum solution determined by the operations research technicians holds only if the general parameters of the problem remain essentially unchanged. In order to insure that the model is relevant to existing conditions, controls must be established to reveal whether there have been any changes in conditions and processes. Unless such controls are used, the model will give incorrect decisions.

The language and systems of operations research are little understood by the average manager or employee. The operations research technicians must translate the tested solutions into operating procedures that can be used by operating managers. This requires that operating managers have some understanding of how the solution was determined, at least in terms of the logic of the situation.

DECISION THEORY AND OPERATIONS RESEARCH IN REVIEW

The manager as a generalist cannot be proficient in every aspect and technique of management. Expanding horizons of knowledge make it impossible for any one man to be master of all disciplines, or for that matter of one discipline. This has created the need for highly trained and competent specialists to aid management in applying new technologies.

The methods and orderliness of economic theory, decision theory, and the more pragmatic operations research theory can be invaluable to the manager in ordering his thought processes and helping him to look more critically at his decision-making processes. To be effective, a manager should be aware of the limitations and strengths of these theories and should be able to call upon them to sharpen his managerial skills.

QUANTIFICATION PITFALLS

There can be an overdependence on quantified models whether they be simple or complex mathematically. Theoretically a model can encompass all possible exigencies and probable combinations of variables. But in practice, constraints of time, cost, and information do not permit such highly sophisticated models. Operations research can provide an optimum solution. The quantification of the input information will result in a numerical answer that may be compared with other numerical alternatives. But this optimum numerical answer must be tempered by the judgment of the experienced executive.

Let us consider the calculation of the economic order quantity (EOQ) for a particular part to be carried in inventory. This example lends itself well to operations research techniques. The model can be built either to indicate the exact EOQ or to determine the amount that should be ordered based upon the quantity discount. The model attempts to take into account all the major variables affecting the cost of carrying inventory, which would be measured against the cost of work stoppages caused by inadequate inventory. Such factors as quantity discount, delivery time, storage cost, and opportunity cost on investments would enter into the calculations. The solution would be expressed as the unit cost of carrying the inventory for various order quantities. A typical solution might be as follows:

Size of order	100	200	500	1,000	2,000
Unit cost	$2.00	$1.50	$1.47	$1.45	$1.46

The lowest unit cost of $1.45 requires an order of 1,000 pieces. Is the saving in cost sufficiently significant at five cents per piece, or approximately 3 percent of the purchase price, to warrant ordering 1,000 instead of 200? If the decision were being made mechanically, without any input from a responsible manager, 1,000 pieces would be purchased.

If no other factors were involved, the manager would undoubtedly decide that the savings are insignificant compared with the uncertainties involved in the larger inventory and that 200 pieces should be purchased rather than 1,000. However, such factors as potential changes in the annual usage of the item could sway the manager in deciding between larger or smaller quantities. (The operations research specialist would note that this model is not well constructed. If the cost differential of less than 5 percent was not significant, the model could be designed to choose automatically the smallest quantity within the 5 percent allowance. But this all the more reinforces the need for the manager to be involved in the design of decision models, since preliminary studies would have shown a unit cost curve, which would preclude the use of the lowest possible unit cost as a criterion for decision. The decision criterion would have been not the lowest unit cost but the smallest order quantity within the range of lowest unit costs.)

Since the major quantification pitfall for the manager is overdependence on mathematical techniques he does not understand, he must learn how a decision model is formulated. This is especially so because his logic and experience serve as the raw data for such models. If the manager understands what is involved in arriving at the operations research solution, he is in a much better position to bring exceptions to the attention of the technicians.

Operations research gives the manager precision and a range of alternatives and frees him from having to make decisions on constantly recurring problems. It must be kept in mind, however, built-in control factors are always required to guarantee that basic conditions have not changed. Such changes invalidate the model.

The computer can process operating data at high speed with relatively low cost to yield up-to-date, accurate information. No longer is it necessary for the manager to make guesses or to rely on estimates because information is unavailable or incomprehensible. Furthermore, he is no longer burdened with endless details of information. These can now be automatically culled by the computer and fed into a model constructed by operations research technicians.

Electronic data processing, decision theory, and operations research represent new frontiers for management. But their future success is entirely dependent upon management's acceptance and understanding. Ignorance and prejudice can greatly hinder advances and applications of these techniques within industry.

Such scientific techniques as operations research can make significant contributions to the practice of management. The horizon of the programmed decision is being extended further and further into the territory of the nonprogrammed decision. It is in this extension of model building and a total systems approach to decision making, planning, and control that quantitative techniques can simplify the tasks and extend the capabilities of management. The onus of responsibility here cannot be solely on management. There must be a marriage of the model-building skills of the operations research technicians and the managerial skills of the manager to develop these sophisticated tools for more effective decision making.

Selected Bibliography

This bibliography in no way claims to be exhaustive but is instead a short list of useful and important references which should prove of interest to the readers of this book.

General References

Dale, Ernest. *Management: Theory and Practice.* New York: McGraw-Hill Book Company, 1965.
Drucker, Peter F. *The Practice of Management.* New York: Harper & Row, Publishers, Inc., 1951.
Gross, Bertram M. *Organizations and Their Managing.* New York: The Free Press, 1968.
Hutchinson, John G. *Organizations: Theory and Classical Concepts.* New York: Holt, Rinehart and Winston, 1967.
Riesman, David, et al. *The Lonely Crowd.* Garden City, N.Y.: Doubleday Anchor, 1953.
Whyte, William H., Jr. *The Organization Man.* Garden City, N.Y.: Doubleday and Company, 1956.

Formulation of Objectives

Batten, J. D. *Beyond Management by Objectives.* AMA, 1967.
Hardwick, Clyde T. *Administrative Strategy and Decision Making.* Cincinnati, Ohio: South-Western Publishing Company, 1966.
Schleh, Edward C. *Management by Results.* New York: McGraw-Hill Book Company, 1961.

Planning

Ansoff, H. Igor. *Corporate Strategy: An Analytical Approach to Business Policy for Growth.* New York: McGraw-Hill Book Company, 1965.
Branch, Melville C. *The Corporate Planning Process.* AMA, 1962.
Drucker, Peter. *Managing for Results.* New York: Harper & Row, Publishers, Inc., 1964.

Johnson, Richard A., et al. *The Theory and Management of Systems,* 2d ed. New York: McGraw-Hill Book Company, 1966.
Steiner, George A., ed. *Managerial Long-Range Planning.* New York: McGraw-Hill Book Company, 1963.

Organization Structure

Brech, E. F. L. *Organization: The Framework of Management.* London: Longmans, Green, 1965.
Dale, Ernest. *Organization.* AMA, 1967.
Haire, Mason, ed. *Modern Organization Theory.* New York: John Wiley & Sons, Inc., 1959.
Holden, Paul E., et al. *Top Management Organization and Control;* a research study of the management policies and practices of 15 leading industrial corporations, conducted under the auspices of the Graduate School of Business, Stanford University. New York: McGraw-Hill Book Company, 1968.

Decision Making

Ackoff, Russell L., et al. *Scientific Method Optimizing Applied Research Decisions.* New York: John Wiley & Sons, Inc., 1962.
Barnard, Chester I. *The Functions of the Executive,* 30th Anniversary ed. Cambridge, Mass.: Harvard University Press, 1968.
Baumol, William J. *Economic Theory and Operations Analysis,* 2d ed. Englewood Cliffs, N.J.: Prentice-Hall, Inc., 1965.
Churchman, C. West, et al. *Introduction to Operations Research.* New York: John Wiley & Sons, Inc., 1957.
Emory, William, and Powell Niland. *Making Management Decisions.* Boston, Mass.: Houghton Mifflin Company, 1968.
Greenwood, William T. *Decision Theory and Information Systems.* Cincinnati, Ohio: South-Western Publishing Company, 1969.
Miller, David W., and Martin K. Starr. *Executive Decisions and Operations Research.* Englewood Cliffs, N.J.: Prentice-Hall, Inc., 1960.

Management Control

Forrester, Jay. *Industrial Dynamics.* Cambridge, Mass.: The M.I.T. Press, 1961.
Jerome, William Travers, III. *Executive Control—The Catalyst.* New York: John Wiley & Sons, Inc., 1961.
Le Breton, Preston P. *Administrative Intelligence—Information Systems.* Boston, Mass.: Houghton Mifflin Company, 1969.
Lewis, Robert W. *Planning, Managing, and Measuring the Business: A Case Study of Management Planning and Control at General Electric Company.* New York: Controllership Foundation, Inc., 1955.
Schell, Erwin W. *The Techniques of Executive Control,* 8th ed. New York: McGraw-Hill Paperbacks, 1963.

Index